What people are saying about …

Deep Night, Bright Morning

'Some people are so real and easy to talk to, exchanges with them are heart to heart and so you are not only connecting but you are changed by that connection, this is Anita. In these pages Anita will share her story, you will feel understood deeply, you will be touched by Jesus and inspired to pursue him and you will be changed. Anita is authentic; she truly lives the life she encourages us to find.'

Debby Wright, Senior Pastor of
Trent Vineyard, National Director of
Vineyard Churches UK and Ireland

'Anita's searing description of the grief, guilt and heartbreak she has endured confronts us with the horror of suffering, and yet this is a book that pulsates with life and hope. Her testimony will surely help those facing their own personal darkness to discover the light of Christ and inspire many to a life of adoring, trusting, radical discipleship. Anita writes beautifully—I was moved to tears at times.'

Vaughan Roberts, Rector of St
Ebbe's Church, Oxford

'I am so grateful Anita has been able to recommission this important and moving story for a new generation hungry to find the realness of God in the middle of the realness of life's struggle. Anita and Charlie remain so soft-hearted and deeply committed to being followers of Jesus over the long-haul, and their commitment to investing in young adults has been a real gift to the Church more widely over the years. To have such a story that disciples the reader in God's presence in the suffering and pain that inevitably comes with being human and walking life's road is vital. This is especially powerful for those who might have been taught more about God's wonderful plans and dreams for our lives, and less about the reality of disappointment and the resilience of faith in the midst of the dark that is also true. Thank you for how you live your life, Anita, and thank you for sharing some of it with us in this book.'

Miriam Swaffield, Global Student Mission Leader for Fusion Movement

'This is a book for our time, an awesome piece of work on how to survive the darkness that can afflict us; in the case of Anita Cleverly, whose many admirers will be thrilled at the reissue of this powerful book, under a new title, the darkness starts with the cot death of her son Samuel at the age of two and a half months. The tale is told with a brutal, and at times uncomfortable, honesty, which leaves nothing concealed. How can a good God allow such terrible suffering? Read this beautifully written book, including a majestic chapter on the Book of Job, and see how it is possible under God to find the way out of deep night into bright morning.'

Fr Nicholas King SJ

'Anita Cleverly experienced a loss that drove her to her knees—first in agony, then in prayer. And from that posture she rose to write this stirring call to radical discipleship that reaches the broken, lost and lonely. May these stories and reflections move you too from darkness to light, so you can help others find their own bright new mornings.'

Sheridan Voysey, Author of *The Making of Us* and *Resurrection Year*

'Anita writes with a burning honesty about the hardest experience of her life yet her book is filled with compassion, wisdom, grace and hope.'

Steven Croft, Bishop of Oxford

'Like its author this book exudes wisdom, grace, comfort and Jesus. Anita writes beautifully and with great depth.'

Simon Ponsonby, Pastor of Theology, St Aldates Church, Oxford

'This book is truly wonderful; beauty from ashes indeed. To anyone whose life has been touched by tragedy and loss, and who still walks with a limp as a direct consequence, it will become an immediate close friend and companion. It is brutally honest, and for this reason the author deserves huge respect. Her honesty compels us to be honest about our own situation. This most tender and elegantly written book will provide both hope and inspiration because of the abiding truth that nothing can ever separate us from the love of Christ.'

Eddie Lyle, President of Open Doors, UK and Ireland

'*Deep Night, Bright Morning* is the brightest of lights on the darkest of topics. Uniquely gifted in the depth of her wisdom and the beauty of her writing, Anita Cleverly weaves together Scripture, literature and her own story of suffering and triumph to offer a captivating vision of the comfort, meaning and hope found preeminently in Christ. In a rare union of tenderness and strength, this book sits with those suffering in their grief and then lovingly takes them by the hand and walks them out of the debilitation of pain and into God-given promises. In a generation when young people are increasingly disillusioned with religion, Anita paints a riveting picture of dynamic, holistic, life-giving faith. *Deep Night, Bright Morning* stirred my heart to dream of what the world could be if it were introduced to the God of all comfort and invited into authentic, prayerful, Christlike community.'

Vince Vitale, Americas Director,
Director of the Zacharias Institute

Deep Night, Bright Morning

Rediscovering the Power of Hope

Anita Cleverly

DAVID C COOK

transforming lives together

DEEP NIGHT, BRIGHT MORNING
Published by David C Cook
4050 Lee Vance Drive
Colorado Springs, CO 80918 U.S.A.

Integrity Music Limited, a Division of David C Cook
Brighton, East Sussex BN1 2RE, England

The graphic circle C logo is a registered trademark of David C Cook.

The website addresses recommended throughout this book are offered as a
resource to you. These websites are not intended in any way to be or imply an
endorsement on the part of David C Cook, nor do we vouch for their content.

Unless otherwise noted, all Scripture quotations are taken from the Holy
Bible, New International Version® Anglicized, NIV® Copyright © 1979, 1984,
2011 by Biblica, Inc.® Used by permission. All rights reserved worldwide.
Scripture quotations marked ESV are taken from the ESV® Bible (The Holy
Bible, English Standard Version®), copyright © 2001 by Crossway, a publishing
ministry of Good News Publishers. Used by permission. All rights reserved;
and THE MESSAGE are taken from THE MESSAGE. Copyright © by Eugene H.
Peterson 1993, 2002. Used by permission of Tyndale House Publishers, Inc.

Library of Congress Control Number 2019943466
ISBN 978-0-8307-7853-9
eISBN 978-0-8307-7854-6

The Team: Ian Matthews, Jennie Pollock, Jo Stockdale,
Amy Konyndyk, Susan Murdock
Cover Design: Nick Lee
Cover Photo: Getty Images

Printed in the United States of America
First Edition 2019

1 2 3 4 5 6 7 8 9 10

080519

Contents

Foreword

This is a book which conveys, with great beauty, tenderness and passion, the life of a pilgrim. It is deeply personal. It is all about Anita Cleverly's spiritual pilgrimage—and all about yours and mine too.

Paradoxically, because this story is so personal and so detailed, it has a much greater universal appeal. There is nothing vague or generalized or abstract here. This is a book about a burning love for God which illuminates a whole life, in every particular and every circumstance. It is heart-breaking at times, harrowing in its honesty, but touched with humour, joy, profound insights into biblical stories and unforgettable 'glimpses of heaven'. Read this, and re-read this, and you will go deeper and further in your own pilgrimage, whatever is happening in your life. You will come to know God in a new and wonderful way.

This is the adventure which began for Anita in 1973 and *Deep Night, Bright Morning* is the story of her life since that first awakening, her experience of the overflowing love of God for all eternity.

As it happens, I first met Anita a few months before this extraordinary time. I can say that she was always a beautiful person, in every sense of that word, with a wonderful readiness to laugh, a disarmingly direct manner, an ability to ask just the right question. She was a 'questing soul', someone who longed to begin a pilgrimage of faith but couldn't quite take the first step. I will never forget our first encounter, when she arrived at my rooms in Cambridge. Her first words were, 'Hello, I'm Anita. My sister Miranda told me I should meet you. What's all this God business then?'

I still laugh about this, not least in joyful recollection of her incredible journey of faith over the last forty-five years. What a privilege to know her! And to witness this abundant flowering of passionate belief and deep discipleship, the 'hundredfold' promised by Jesus himself to those whose hearts are fertile and who truly receive the word of God. As I look back over the years, I also laugh ruefully at Anita's attempt to influence her boyfriend, then later husband, Charlie to follow the same pathway of faith. She invited me to stay with them in Oxford and all my fine explanations, quotes from C. S. Lewis, and forceful pronouncements were unimpressive to Charlie, who was far too laid back to be bothered with theological discussions. He simply said, rather mildly, that he couldn't see 'why the Bible was relevant to the twentieth century'. This was an unpromising beginning for someone who would later become the rector of St Aldates, Oxford. I went to bed feeling an abject failure, still rehearsing the things I should have said but couldn't think of at the time. However, the Holy Spirit had a far more subtle strategy than student arguments and it wasn't long before Charlie experienced the fragrance of the love of Christ, through Anita and through every doorway and window into his soul.

Now, Charlie and Anita Cleverly, after so many years of ministry in London, Paris and Oxford, are shining lights, outstanding leaders and witnesses to the gospel, not least because they are still travelling, still searching, still yearning for more of the mystery of God's love and the richness of his mercy.

One of the most profound moments in my friendship with Anita and Charlie was the heart-rending privilege of meeting them off the plane, and staying with them the first few days, when they came back to Britain following the tragic loss of Samuel. This bereavement, this terrifying pilgrimage through the 'Valley of the Shadow of Death', lies at the heart of *Deep Night, Bright Morning*. A few years later, I was able to visit Samuel's grave in California by myself. I will never forget the sorrow and the presence of God in that place.

As you read this book, you will see how Anita allows a shattering human event to be the doorway to a radiant and healing experience of God, intensifying over many years. Her heart is broken, but it is filled with compassion and empathy. You will travel with her, into a passionate love for other nations, a prophetic concern for the 'global village', from Brazil to Uganda, France to China. You will find yourself challenged to care for single people, marginalised by the churches; you will experience the kingdom promise of new 'mothers and brothers, sisters and fathers'; you will find deep comfort in your own domestic struggles; and above all, you will find yourself called to fall more deeply in love with God, to surrender to the divine embrace and to transform the pilgrimage of your life into the most beautiful expression of a 'Sacred Romance.'

This is the story of Anita's own life and I am a witness to its power.

As I look back over my own life, I see many Christian friends whose painful spiritual journeys over many years have sometimes led them to lose their early passion. So often suffering, disillusionment, even success and 'the spirit of the age,' take their toll. These fine people still believe in God, they still serve him in so many ways, but the words of the angel to the church in Ephesus, in Revelation 2, ring out loud and clear: 'I know your deeds, your hard work and your perseverance … yet I hold this against you: You have forsaken your first love. Remember the height from which you have fallen! Repent and do the things you did at first'.

It is impossible to read Anita's story without being challenged in this way. I certainly was. Here is someone who, through suffering and adversity, ultimately found a deeper love. Her story is not over, and knowing her as I do, *Deep Night, Bright Morning* will not mark the end of an era but the beginning of another. For Anita is always in search of adventure—and there is, of course, no end to the heart's quest. There is no end to the love affair between God and the human race.

Murray Watts
Playwright and director of The Wayfarer Trust
Freswick Castle
Scotland

Acknowledgements

I dedicate this book to my husband, Charlie, who has been at my side throughout the long walk upward and onward since the day Samuel died, and my closest *companion in the suffering and patient endurance that are ours in Christ Jesus*, as John writes to the churches from Patmos.

And to our children, Samuel's siblings; Hannah, Alice, Jack and Jemimah, now with families of their own. May this book bring you comfort in times of deep night, and encouragement and hope as the dawn of a bright morning steals over the horizon.

It has been a joy to work with the team at David C Cook; my thanks to Jennie Pollock and Jack Campbell for their meticulous and eagle-eyed work, and seriously reassuring efficiency! Thank you to former VP Wendi Lord, who was not only encouraging but extremely affirming. And then thank you to Ian Matthews, Publishing Director here in the UK. Shortly after reading the 2005 publication of the book, Ian contacted me with great enthusiasm to say that he definitely wanted to republish. It had struck a chord with him for personal as well as professional reasons. From that moment on, working together has been a privilege and a pleasure, and Ian has been a tower of strength throughout the process, always understanding where I was going and why.

I thank Flo Judson, our friend and tireless PA, both for reading the manuscript through with the perspective of a millennial, and making many very helpful comments, but also for making multiple copies of it without demur. Thank you too to author Cheryl Hardacre, who generously gave hours of her time to pore over the manuscript and make insightful suggestions; and to Jacinta Reed, lecturer in creative writing, who did the same thing. All three of you made a lot of difference.

I thank prayer partners Chris and Noelle Gillies, Andrew Miller and John and Annie Hughes, who have been unstinting in their encouragement and relentlessly gracious in the face of endless 'book stuff'! Thank you too to friends and colleagues Simon Ponsonby and Mark Brickman, unfailingly supportive during the lengthy birth; and to Colette Lloyd and Jemma I'Ons for their contributions of the heart. And my thanks to the wonderful community of St Aldates—I have so often drawn strength to carry on in your midst, and you have taught me more about suffering and healing than I could ever have imagined.

Theology of place is something we often talk about, and surroundings play a big part for me where creativity is concerned, so my thanks to Richard and Katharine Hill, whose Welsh cottage, where I could write looking at the sea, was a locus of inspiration and peace during the process.

I thank co-pilgrims who have walked the hard road of losing a child, for the strength they lend because of who they are—Elliott Tepper, founder of the global redemptive work of Betel Ministries;

Paul and Charlotte Braithwaite, whose daughter Joanna, about whom I write, was a former PA, but much more than that, a beloved friend; John and Gretchen Steer, and Rebecca Paterson. And Stuart and Celia McAlpine; you effectively lost a child when we lost Samuel, and without you the trajectory of our onward journey would have been very different ... thank you both with all my heart.

Last, but not least, I thank God. You revealed yourself to me in Jesus Christ, and changed my life forever; and you are still patiently leading me to learn that though there will always be deep nights, there will also always be bright mornings.

Preface

The seed of this book was planted with the death of our son Samuel at the age of two-and-a-half months in 1982. About two years later, when the grief was subsiding, though not yet fully done, I felt the first stirrings of the desire to communicate the story, not for the sake of it, but because subsequent to Samuel's death I had met many parents grieving without hope, through the work of the SIDS Foundation.[1] Surely, I reasoned, we who had a hope in the face of death should share it with those who were walking in a terrible darkness.

Many years have passed, and as I write, Samuel's younger brother Jack is in his mid-thirties, an accomplished lawyer with a rewarding job and a wonderful girlfriend. We are now grandparents to eight delicious, delightful and intriguing grandchildren—who are they? Where will life take them? Who will they grow up to be? Just as a child in the womb develops in a mysterious and marvellous way, imperceptibly yet obviously, so this book has distinctly evolved from the days of those first stirrings. The trigger of it may have been Samuel, and much of what I write is seen through the lens of his brief life, but I am here to say, 'Yes! It is possible to reconcile life's inevitable trials and tragedies with a desire and determination to embrace the life God created us for, and flourish in it. It is possible to recover hope and be sustained by it.'

So I write for you whether you are an adult needing hope for yourself, a parent desperate to give your child hope, a young person longing for your mother or father to rediscover hope, or a student, an apprentice or a young professional searching for hope and meaning.

I write for you if you are unemployed for whatever reason, or if you are in a season of ill health; if you are alienated from those you love, or you feel like an outsider but long to belong. All these latter contexts carry their own additional darkness. Whoever you are, and whatever your age, you can, though you doubt it today, survive the darkness and despair of suffering or loss and tragedy, and emerge into the light stronger and deeper. You really can.

I lived in inner-city Paris for ten years from 1992 to 2002. My family's stamping ground was the 19th and 20th arrondissements, a multicultural part of the city, well off the beaten track of the tourist. Traditionally host to the latest wave of refugees from around the world, poverty of all kinds was painfully visible, not least the poverty of spirit. Every day we rubbed shoulders with the broken-hearted, those who mourned and those who were clothed in a spirit of despair. My sense of unease and helplessness in the face of the anguished multitudes of sheep without a shepherd led me to reflect about the themes of this book, feeling acutely inadequate in the face of such overwhelming human misery.

Widen the perspective from the local, and almost every day the intimacy of our global village brings us stories of loss and tragedy, sometimes even as they are happening, thanks to the power of technology and social media platforms. At the time of writing the world is reeling from the brutal assassination of fifty people in a New Zealand mosque by a white supremacist. At the same time, a cyclone has caused the death of an estimated 1,000 people in Zimbabwe, Malawi and Mozambique, some of the poorest countries of the world. But it's not only about numbers.

Every life lost in these two very terrible and different events was created by God for a purpose. It takes time for us to assimilate the magnitude of such catastrophes, both man-made and natural. Why so much suffering? The power of nature and the fragility of man are graphically illustrated by these things, yet we resent and deny the uncomfortable truth that many of them occur because of humanity's greed and carelessness in the case of natural disasters and because of our prejudice, racism and hatred in the case of man's cruelty to man. We prefer to blame God.

Every day, lives end prematurely, and thousands of children die in war and famine zones. Just in one otherwise ordinary week we may read of the accidental deaths of skiers and students, climbers and children. We live in days of confusion, individualism, terrorism and, if we are Christians, of persecution. In some parts of the world this persecution is ferocious, unspeakably cruel, and too frequently murderous. In the West it is for the moment subtle, targeting freedom of conscience and expression, and traditional beliefs and practices.

How can you and I find hope and the energy to arise in the face of all this, let alone of our personal loss?

What was it that enabled us to ride the storm of Samuel's death? How did we find the healing by degrees that gave us strength and energy to serve and love a local church community in the bland suburbs of Essex, and then in the frenetic, dirty and vibrant part of

Paris that was our home for ten years? And then to do it again in the challenging atmosphere of Oxford's ivory towers?

I want to answer that question initially through some words of C. S. Lewis in *The Silver Chair*:

> Crying is all right in its way while it lasts. But you have to stop sooner or later, and then you still have to decide what to do. When Jill stopped, she found she was dreadfully thirsty.... The birds had ceased singing and there was perfect silence except for one small, persistent sound, which seemed to come from a good distance away. She listened carefully, and felt almost sure it was the sound of running water.

She follows the sound until:

> [S]he came to an open glade and saw [a] stream, bright as glass, running across the turf a stone's throw away from her. But although the sight of the water made her feel ten times thirstier than before, she didn't rush forward and drink. She stood as still as if she'd been turned into stone. And she had a very good reason; just on this side of the stream lay the lion.

Paralysed by fear, Jill deliberates for a long moment, while the thirst intensifies until 'she almost felt she would not mind being eaten by the lion if only she could be sure of getting a mouthful of water first.'

'If you're thirsty, you may drink'…. The voice was not like a man's. It was deeper, wilder and stronger…. It did not make her any less frightened than she had been before, but it made her frightened in rather a different way.

'Are you not thirsty?' said the Lion.

'I'm dying of thirst,' said Jill.

'Then drink,' said the Lion.

'May I—could I—would you mind going away while I do?' said Jill…. 'Will you promise not to—do anything to me, if I do come?'

'I make no promise,' said the Lion.

Jill was so thirsty now that, without noticing it, she had come a step nearer.

'Do you eat girls?' she said.

'I have swallowed up girls and boys, women and men, kings and emperors, cities and realms,' said the Lion. It didn't say this as if it were boasting, nor as if it were sorry, nor as if it were angry. It just said it.

'I daren't come and drink,' said Jill.

'Then you will die of thirst,' said the Lion.

'Oh dear!' said Jill, coming another step nearer. 'I suppose I must go and look for another stream then.'

'There is no other stream,' said the Lion.[2]

It was by drinking from the 'only stream' when I was dying of thirst that I found out how to get up, and what to do next.

My hope is that this book will bring consolation to you if you are fighting for breath after tragedy; that it will explain things that have long been a source of pain for you, or that it will kickstart you into a diligent pursuit of God and the discovery—or recovery—of what you were made for. And I pray that if you have never tasted this water, 'the coldest, most refreshing water she had ever tasted,' that 'quenches your thirst at once,'[3] you might taste it here and be introduced to the wonders of knowing Jesus Christ, the one who paradoxically made himself nothing, and yet in whom all things hold together.[4]

Mine is the tale of an ordinary family, and yet any life that is touched by Jesus is transformed, like those of Peter, James and John who saw him transfigured. For a brief moment they saw into heaven and their lives were never the same again.

My prayer is that together our lives will also be touched by Jesus as we turn the pages, and that like the disciples we might catch a glimpse of heaven, and find that we shall never be quite the same again either.

Anita Cleverly
Oxford, March 2019

1

Unless a Seed Fall to the Ground
Diary of a Death

There is no mystery on earth
Exceeds the mighty miracle of birth
Not all the fearful mystery of death
Surpasses that first
breaking into light
And timid, fragile breath.

- John Kitching, quoted in Judith
Nicholls (ed.), *Otherworlds*

Death be not proud, though some
have called thee Mighty and
dreadful, for thou art not so.

- John Donne, *The Complete*
English Poems

Like a sharply focused photograph, I remember the room quite clearly. A crowd of well-dressed, smiling Americans were seated at round tables, enjoying a copious meal after an address from the Hispanic evangelist. I don't recall much of what he said, but I clearly remember his small, taut form and the energy that poured forth as he exhorted his listeners to pray for the souls in Silicon Valley and the Bay area, and earnestly lamented the decline of American society. I remember that he was dark and had a certain attractiveness and that he was accompanied by more than one very glamorous woman with big hair, brightly coloured nail polish on long nails, well-fitting suits and heels. Newly arrived and rather bemused, I remember too feeling unsettled in a context so different from my experience of church gatherings so far. Of course we were pretty tired, partly from jet-lag, partly from sheer excitement at having arrived for three months in the dream destination of California, but perhaps most of all because we had a new baby, only two-and-a-half months old, who had been restive since our arrival and had given us broken nights.

Now, as the meal drew to an end, the room was full of people milling around, and our host for the day was introducing us to a steadily growing number of people. It was exciting to have been brought to this meeting, and very thoughtful of the close and dear friends with whom we were spending these months to have released us by baby-sitting for our three children. Everything was new and fascinating in what I saw as a romantic wonderland, and the months stretched out ahead of us, full of promise and interesting meetings, events and trips. For a start the next day was my birthday and a champagne breakfast was planned. A champagne breakfast! Whoever heard of such an indulgence! Well, I was certainly up for it as a birthday treat.

We had come for an extended placement as part of my husband Charlie's training for ordination in the Church of England. We had somehow persuaded ourselves and our theological college that close observation of a Pentecostal church, where our friend was principal of the attached school, would be the best preparation for ministry in a British parish! More seriously it was an opportunity that presented itself to widen our vision and stretch our theological education. Added to this, it was a chance to spend time with close friends. Indeed, the goodness of God was boundless, and we were people with grateful hearts as we basked in this extraordinary treat that he had afforded us. Sometimes I could barely believe that we were on the road to becoming a pastoral couple; to fulfilling our dream of serving a local church.

Suddenly our host, who had briefly left our sides, pushed his way unnaturally quickly through the crowded room and said tersely, 'We've got to go. Now. I've had a call and something's wrong with Samuel. Come on.'

'What's wrong?' I said, following him out of the room with Charlie. 'What's wrong?' I repeated, more loudly and with less control.

'I don't know,' replied David. 'He didn't know.'

'What do you mean, he didn't know? How can you not know?'

And so the questions without answers succeeded each other until we were speeding along the motorway in silence, all three locked in our own thoughts, our host David staring ahead, his jaw set. Road signs, directions, advertising billboards loomed up and were gone, almost lulling me like music as the clammy hand of fear tightened its grasp. As we passed a sign reading 'Hospital: 300 metres', my stomach lurched and the first tears spilt over the edge. I turned to Charlie, silently pleading for help as my face crumpled, and he reached an arm round me, but I could see he was frightened too. Then the two of them began to pray. Raising their voices, they began to call on God: that he would drive out whatever was threatening Samuel, that he would heal and restore. Soon running out of words, they lifted their voices in heavenly languages. I remained mute, my whole body paralysed with a fear that was now uncontrollable, feeling myself to be in a reality outside time, in which the sole element was pain that might last for ever. Only it wasn't real.

The car turned into our road and in the distance we saw a figure standing outside the gate. As we drew closer we could see that it was our friend, his face ashen, his body rigid. 'Drive to the hospital,' he ordered tersely.

'What's happened, what's wrong, is he all right, will he be all right, how did it happen, he will be all right, won't he?' Our garbled questions matched the hope draining out of our bodies, our hearts, our minds.

'I don't know; I don't know,' repeated Stuart. 'He wasn't responding properly when I went to check him.'

San Jose, the capital of Silicon Valley, is a geometrically designed city, like so many in America. Left, right, right, left, right; we swung from street to street, almost rhythmically. There were no sweeping bends, none of the unpredictability of the English road system with its idiosyncratic and haphazard layout; just 90 degree turns, one upon another, and they seemed to go on for ever. I wondered if I would ever get there, if I would ever see Samuel again, ever hold him in my arms again. The city which this morning almost literally sparkled with light was this afternoon as grey and menacing as a mausoleum.

Turning yet another anonymous corner as David silently followed the clipped instructions, we came suddenly upon the huge, faceless institution, rising like a grey and gloomy giant out of nowhere.

Suddenly my best friend appeared, running towards us, her dark hair flying round her face. Getting out of the car, with a curious sense of slow motion and what felt like a Herculean effort, I fell into her arms. 'Ani,' she said, 'Samuel will be yours for all eternity.'

It was 23 January 1982.

The blow, when it came, hit me head on. Inside me the noise of its impact resounded as in an echo chamber. In an instant my life unravelled with the speed of lightning, and chaos replaced order. Focus gave way to blurred vision and the next moments—or were they hours?—seemed to take place in another dimension, at another remove, through a glass darkly. Although my hearing was unimpaired, I just couldn't reach people. Most terrible of all I couldn't reach Samuel. It's curious what tiny details make their way into the memory files at a time like this. The doctor was tall, young and had fair hair and he said, very gently, 'The child is not alive.'

I heard, but I didn't believe. A nurse led us, with our friends, into the innards of the great, grey hospital, and then to a room in the centre of which, on a full-sized hospital bed, lay the tiny, motionless body of our only son, Samuel, 'asked of God'. Of course, he wasn't really dead, because he couldn't be. Every fibre of my being rose up to refuse the sight before me. He would soon revive, we would take him home, and the doctor would help us.

'Sudden Infant Death Syndrome,' the doctor was saying, 'is a relatively common phenomenon; there is no real explanation for it, although progress is being made through research.'

I still wasn't registering. I knew he must be talking about someone else and that cot death, or crib death as it is known in the US, had nothing to do with us. It was strange, though, I admitted to myself in a fleeting moment of lucidity, that he should be talking about this here in this room, and now.

With infinite tenderness, and beginning his own journey through the valley of the shadow of death, Charlie bent over the bed and took Samuel's lifeless, already bluish and stiffening frame in his arms, seeming to impart new life, willing him to come back. As if at a signal, though none was given, the two men lifted their voices, just as he and David had done hours earlier, and commanded the spirit of death to let go, and the child to rise in the name of Jesus. Their prayers continued for several minutes, but Samuel didn't move. We stayed for some time, and I stared uncomprehendingly at my son, an unutterable grief expanding like a hot iron in my chest. Yet I made no move to hold him and, to this day, I don't know why. Perhaps I knew instinctively that he wasn't there anymore, and that, much as I loved this child and fiercely longed for him to return, the inert body before me was just that: a body, a tent.

'Now,' says Paul, 'we know that if the earthly tent we live in is destroyed, we have a building from God, an eternal house in heaven, not built by human hands'.[1] And a little earlier, 'The body that is sown is perishable, it is raised imperishable; it is sown in dishonour, it is raised in glory; it is sown in weakness, it is raised in power; it is sown a natural body, it is raised a spiritual body.'[2]

We had to leave him, hard as it was. I think I probably knew, with a mother's instinct, that he was gone, long before we got to the hospital, but now we had to go, and no mother wants to leave her child unprotected, however irrational her desire.

Still in my world of chaos, I hammered on heaven's door. 'How could you let this happen? You promised him to me....'

Two months earlier, two thousand miles away from that hospital room so imbued with death, we had been gathered excitedly in another hospital room, where two little girls had come to welcome their new brother. Two months earlier we had been overwhelmed with joy, excitement and gratitude as we welcomed Samuel into the world, when the summer was ended and the winds of November were howling, snatching up the leaves and plucking at the coats that people pulled tightly around them. Now Samuel was dead. One hospital room is much like another; it is a place of work, of deliverance to life, or from sickness and death, if possible. But it is not always possible, and hospitals are houses of death for many. All that distinguishes one hospital room from another is what triumphs or tragedies of humankind are being played out in them.

All of us weeping, all of us in the surreal world that accompanies death, we drove slowly home. For the moment not even intelligible questions could be formed, and my mind was a scramble, the very worst sort of computer crash, the work of years irretrievably lost in an instant. Worse than that was the pain, hard to locate and intensifying by the minute, spreading slowly all over my body. Samuel, asked for and granted, was today lying stiff under a sheet in an anonymous morgue in a hospital. Not really, of course. Soon I would wake up and this terrible nightmare would fade away, like the times when I would wake to Charlie's voice gently speaking my name as I rose out of a confused scenario in which he was leaving me. Just as those increasingly infrequent dreams related back to our student days in Oxford, so this event must simply reflect the earlier fear that I was not pregnant after all, and normality would soon return...

Back at the house a cup of tea was put into my hands and my little daughters were running into my arms and clambering onto

my lap, elbowing each other out of the way. Our friends' two small
children circled about us excitedly, and there seemed to be quite a lot
of people and movement in the house, and they all seemed quite real;
frighteningly real. Because if they were real and this was not after all a
dream, it meant that Samuel was really dead, was really not going to
breathe any more, and my arms, though now around my daughters,
would not hold him to me again. All these thoughts brought unbearable pain, as did catching sight of my friend's rounded belly, home
for the moment to their third child.

'Let's just gather together and honour the Lord and proclaim that
God is God, even in the face of death.' The voice that spoke was deep
and rich, had a strong Scottish accent and belonged to Gramps. Gramps
and Mabs, our friend's parents, had moved to the States in the early
1980s. Both were well known in the prayer world of the charismatic
renewal, to which we had been introduced and were now discovering.
They had embraced their son's friends with open arms and already been
wise counsellors to us who were so new to the things of God.

Gramps would often appear unannounced at breakfast time, his
arms laden with doughnuts, his face beaming, and stand beneficent
as the four children hurled themselves at him shrieking with delight.
In response to the patriarchal generosity represented by such simple
acts, a spontaneous well of love had sprung up in my heart for him
and his wife.

Now all of us were confronted with calamity, and we were suddenly in much more urgent need of their wise parenting. Somehow,
we were all collected together with them, including the children, in
the spacious sitting room. Bread and wine had appeared on the table
and the cacophony gave way to a respectful quiet. What followed

was one of the most significant moments in the whole process of living through the death of Samuel. Quietly, simply and with great authority, we were led through a celebration of communion. We partook, in all our disarray, of the body and the blood, and proclaimed that Christ is risen and that he lives today and that nothing can dim the power and the truth of this historical fact, not even such a catastrophically violent blow from the dark as the one from which we were all reeling, even as we shared the eucharistic meal.

> For I am convinced that neither death nor life, neither angels nor demons, neither the present nor the future, nor any powers, neither height nor depth, nor anything else in all creation, will be able to separate us from the love of God that is in Christ Jesus our Lord.[3]

Somehow, I got hold of this; somehow, the powerful, all-embracing words of the Bible rang wonderfully true, crazed as I was with pain and desperately yearning to hold my son and feel his heartbeat. Somehow, I was able to compute that, though 'things fall apart; the centre cannot hold,'[4] there was meaning and order to be retrieved, and that true reality lay not in the chaos of what had befallen us, but in the presence and parenting of God.

Samuel's funeral took place a few days later. We chose to have him buried in San Jose, in the children's area of the huge city cemetery. Perhaps, had we had more time and less pain, we might have made other choices; we surely would have had more thought for our own parents, their pain exacerbated by the distance between us all. Decisions made in desolation will often be regretted, yet we had to decide. A 'Catch-22' that maybe you are familiar with too. Nevertheless, we have since been able to make several visits to California, despite the enormous distance, and to sit around his grave with our daughters and the two children born to us later, and thank God for his goodness and for giving us such a treasure in heaven.

Being able to return to California relatively often has been important for those two little daughters as they have grown up. In the turmoil of events surrounding the immediate aftermath of Samuel's death, we made the decision not to bring them to the funeral; a decision we have bitterly regretted ever since, though it was made with the best of intentions. Our regret has grown rather than faded with the passing of the years, and we'll explore this further in chapter 11. It was our first real brush with death, and we didn't understand the importance of saying goodbye, until we did it ourselves that blustery January day.

Our surrogate father, Gramps, presided over and preached at the funeral, and it was a declaration of life over death. I, normally so timid about such things, but curiously liberated by the enormity of what was happening to me, lifted my voice and led the congregation in a song. It didn't seem to matter so much what people thought. 'I will enter his presence with thanksgiving in my heart', I sang.[5] How could I have given utterance to such words? Could it have been the courage and consolation of the Holy Spirit?

The funeral parlour director had greeted us kindly and with compassion on our arrival and led us in to see the tiny coffin. 'He's all ready,' he said. 'Cute as a bug's ear.' To this day, I've never understood that phrase, but I suppose it's a florid way of saying tidy and tiny. After the service the solemn cortège wound its way up to the children's section where the cemetery workers had dug a fresh grave and were waiting to fill it in. I remember a light drizzle falling and the little box being awkwardly lowered. I remember my long inward cry, echoing in the chamber of my spirit; '*Eloi, Eloi, lema sabachthani?*'; 'My God, my God, why have you forsaken me?'[6]

Now we had to live on, and learn to lament.

2

Double Blessing
Joy Comes in the Morning

*A woman produces an egg and receives
a man's seed into her womb and grows a
baby and brings another person into the
world. Utterly simple. Or so amazingly
complex that it cannot be understood. So
far beyond us that it is a mystery. And
yet it happens every minute of every day.
How can something be utterly simple and
amazingly complex at the same time?*

- Bernard MacLaverty, *Grace Notes*

*Those who sow with tears will
reap with songs of joy.
Those who go out weeping, carrying seed
to sow, will return with songs of joy.*

- Psalm 126:5–6

For some time after a death, every morning brings a painful rebirth into reality. Swimming into consciousness from powerfully realistic dreams in which Samuel was, for example, returned to us having been found lying swaddled in a graveyard, took a heavy toll on my emotional energy, already so decimated. I remember one morning being so convinced by my dream, so relieved and excited to see the pink cheeks and feel the warm breath against my breast, that it was hard for Charlie to break the truth to me again, and provoked an anguished bout of sobbing before the day had really begun.

When both members of a couple are in extreme pain and the need for relief is more acute than any other impulse, all defence systems are on red alert and any concern for the welfare of the other is at its lowest ebb. We soon began to grow irritable with each other and, although we would weep in one another's arms at night, we each sensed the other's inability to really nurture the void of the loss with comforting words or to bring solace to our souls. Not surprisingly, we became fractious and over-reacted to the slightest word or gesture that seemed less than gentle. When a wound is raw, the merest touch triggers a startled jerk away from the source of the touch, usually accompanied by a yelp of pain. In this uncomfortable way we spent many of those early days on the journey of bereavement, hobbling through the valley of the shadow of death. We felt a pitiful sight to the eyes of God into whose hands we had confidently placed our lives and futures several years earlier.

Needless to say, this fragility affected our physical relationship. To me, nothing seemed more inappropriate—even vulgar and distasteful—than the idea of making love, and I shied away from anything that might have been construed as an amorous approach, turning away and drawing my knees up to my chest with a despairing moan. Didn't I realise his need of comfort? And didn't he realise my paralysis and the impossibility of arousal in the face of this monster? Didn't he realise the storm cloud of thoughts that broke with the merest suggestion of sex? Making love might lead to conception, conception to pregnancy, and all those changes and tiredness and a huge belly and the pain ... and all, all for nothing, for Samuel was gone. Inside me, another wave of anguish would surge up.

Later, I would realise that Charlie's needs were equally authentic. Somehow, we muddled through. Sex is an area of potential conflict during a time of bereavement and has shipwrecked many couples. Understanding and patience from both parties are required, but at the time all we knew was that we were hurting each other with our unreasonable demands.

Apart from the Holy Spirit himself and the comforting presence of Jesus, there were three things that saved us from the potential destructiveness latent in any such life-changing event. In fact, I believe that these three things are always the agents that God seeks to employ for help and healing. They are the natural family, friends, and the body of Christ. In our case, having made the decision to stay in America, our own families could do little to help us. Only much later did the realisation of how painful this must have been for them come to me—they felt our pain but could not hold and console us. It's another regret that has grown sharper through the years, specially in relation to my mother.

So it was with our friends, and with the wider family of the church that we had come to America to observe, that we would initially experience some very deep healing. As things turned out, we were going to observe a lot more than we had expected of this church. We'll look more closely at the subjects of family, friends and church in later chapters.

A Refuge and a Fortress

In the middle of one night, tossing and tormented, not wanting to wake Charlie from what little sleep he had, and knowing he had no reserves for me, I crept into our friends' bedroom and under the blankets next to my pregnant friend. My body was aching for Samuel and for human touch and comfort. How shocking! Or was it? There are a thousand images of those days, like a photograph album that captures a life, and this is one of the clearest, quite in focus, a pure and precious moment of balm.

Although they too were living through shock and grief, coming to terms with having found Samuel blue in his bed on that dreadful day, and knowing their own third child to be bursting with health in his mother's womb, their faith didn't waver for an instant.

'Even youths grow tired and weary,' says Isaiah, one of the Bible's prophets, 'and young men stumble and fall; but those who hope in the Lord will renew their strength. They will soar on wings like eagles; they will run and not grow weary, they will walk and not be faint'.[1] These dear friends soared and ran and walked. They were a fountain of life to us, from that moment at the hospital 24/7 through the days and weeks until we waved a final and tearful goodbye as we boarded the plane to go home. And well beyond, of course—miles and seas are no obstacles to friendships forged like these.

The morning after Samuel died—Day 1 of our new reality—there was a knock at the door and Celia came into our room. 'Darlings,' she said, 'here's tea.' She gently put the tray down beside Charlie, came round the bed and sat down by me. 'Listen to this,' she said, 'Psalm 91.' She read it out and our eyes spilled over again. 'Whoever dwells in the shelter of the Most High will rest in the shadow of the Almighty. I will say of the Lord, "He is my refuge and my fortress, my God, in whom I trust"'.[2]

What? No terror at night, no arrow by day; no pestilence from the dark, no destroying plague in broad daylight; no harm befalling us, no disaster coming near us? What could this possibly mean in the light of our present circumstances? All these things had, rather, combined their forces to strike us with one gigantic blow, and we lay slain beneath them. So why did I feel a curious warmth stealing into my tired and aching, exhausted limbs? I couldn't deny that, despite the seeming contradictions, my heart was strangely comforted by these words.

Later, I would understand that, no matter what happens, if we do make the Most High our refuge, he will be just that, and though we walk through the valley of the shadow of death, we will fear no evil, for he is with us and his rod and staff comfort us.[3]

'Though he slay me, yet will I hope in him,' says Job.[4] Deep in the being of this blameless and upright man who has lost everything is a knowledge inscribed there by God, that defies his earthly circumstances by faith, and causes him to prophesy: 'I know that my redeemer lives, and that in the end he will stand on the earth. And after my skin has been destroyed, yet in my flesh I will see God'.[5]

Job, like Stephen and like Paul hundreds of years later, and like John the Divine in the book of Revelation, was seeing heaven opened.

And in a much lesser way (though a way that I believe to be available and accessible to all who cry out for it), as I huddled weakly in the refuge spoken of by the psalmist, I too gained a glimpse of heaven. I began to grasp that 'Christ has indeed been raised from the dead, the firstfruits of those who have fallen asleep'.[6] About eight years earlier in Cambridge I had assented to this intellectually: now I was faced with a chance to apply what I claimed to believe, and a decision made in safety needed to be ratified in danger. My faith certainly hung in the balance by moments. I do not at all write as one who has never wavered, nor doubted. But here the clouds parted to reveal a shaft of light, the sort that makes you take a sharp intake of breath as you walk by the sea under a setting sun, and something quickens your inmost being.

My friend had brought us this psalm with the quiet confidence of one who knows her Father in heaven. Through it I began too to understand that 'the perishable must clothe itself with the imperishable, and the mortal with immortality ... then the saying that is written will come true: "Death has been swallowed up in victory"'.[7]

What did all this mean? Inevitably these early days were an emotional helter-skelter, and some of them were passed in an access of weeping. But we talked and talked without stopping, questioning and railing at God, and these precious friends never once gave us the impression that they were bored or exhausted by our clinging needs; on the contrary, they lavished upon us their time, their imagination and their inexhaustible love.

They sent us out to the shopping mall to stroll around and buy clothes. A strange idea, you might think. Yet this was the time when we understood the therapeutic value of shopping, even though our purchasing was minimal. It was the drifting with a disengaged mind that soothed us, though it brought us face to face with an early hurdle in bereavement.

Everyone, but everyone, had a tiny baby in a smart American stroller. How was it that the mall was filled exclusively with young couples shining with health and energy? Was this an area with a particularly high birth rate? Was it perhaps a mall reserved for young families?

Such are the slightly deranged thoughts of the grieving mind, and they are a normal part of the process of adapting to a new reality. One's whole being is straining towards the unattainable, and there is an intensity of focus, a sort of visual concentration that automatically sifts out uninteresting material.

I was taken out to have my hair done and I had a frothy American perm. I remember the particular kindness of the woman who effected this rather dramatic transformation of my hair. Did she know?

The Saturday after Samuel died we all set off, with our four children, for a day out at Carmel. Carmel is a beautiful resort for the rich, with palm-lined avenues dividing gorgeous weatherboard properties. The shops are seductive and the restaurants irresistible, and at the time Clint Eastwood was the mayor, which rather added to the kudos. But we were there to walk the wide white shores for which the town is equally famed and, if truth be told, to pass some of this endless time which surprised us by continuing despite the death of our son. Contrasting with the natural beauty around us, the skies were leaden and a grey pall hung over the place. Acute pain had given way to a dull and heavy ache, and for all of us the day was desperately dreary, despite our best efforts to run with the children and exchange inconsequential remarks.

If Celia's gift was in a supernatural capacity to love and mother all at the same time, Stuart would draw us out with laughter. He has a wit second to none, and within days of Samuel's death we had broken a certain sound barrier, and felt our muscles uncoil as we all gave way to unrestrained mirth. At first we felt guilty: surely grieving must be a serious business and we should be circumspect in its presence? But we could sense the beneficial effect on our taut bodies. We talked about this together too and decided that laughing was doing us more good than harm, and that neither Samuel nor God would mind. On that day in Carmel, as the 'What if?' questions periodically and unpredictably made us wince, there was a hilarious exchange between Simon and a policeman who had halted our car. It made us all rock with laughter, then fall abruptly silent, wondering about the appropriateness of our reaction. I don't remember what the exchange was about, but I remember the laughter, then the sudden silence.

A month or so later, they sent us away for a weekend alone together, again at Carmel. We set off in a borrowed car, feeling at once elated and agonised. It was good for them and it was good for us. Here, in a little hotel, we made fragile steps towards recovering our intimacy; we were reassured by our love for one another, shaken as we were by the recent hurricane. We went to see the film *Chariots of Fire* and became intoxicated with the soaring music and the glory of Eric Liddell's integrity. To this day, the music of Vangelis is bound up for us with Samuel and it echoed in our minds as we walked the dunes and gazed out to sea, each absorbed in the business of trying to reconcile the undeniable majesty of God with the unacceptable loss of our son.

Difficult Milestones

March came, and with it the appointed day for our return to the UK. New mountains rose up before us out of the mist, and we clung to our friends as we parted, amid many tears and prayers in the impersonal atmosphere of the airport.

Many loving arms reached out for us as we returned to Bristol to pick up the threads of an English life that we had left so differently, so full of confidence and joy. The first hurdle, we knew, was to unlock our front door and climb the stairs to Samuel's bedroom, arrayed like a museum frozen in time, with his clothes, his toys, the pictures on the wall. Here was a welcome for someone who would never come. Here was a cupboard that needed clearing out when we had the strength. Our darling little daughters, by now accustomed to their parents' weeping, though certainly also troubled by it, and themselves struggling with this strange loss, patiently accompanied us in this painful rediscovery of a home.

Among my papers and documents was my Child Benefit book. One day, feeling stronger, I walked up the road to the Post Office to hand it in. Waves of defeat washed over me and each step became harder to take. 'How are you? We've had a wonderful time in America.' (Had we?) 'But a terrible thing happened.' I struggled to control my voice. I explained falteringly. The official, sympathetic voice reached my ears through the Perspex pane separating customer from state. My raw and heightened emotions detected the distant volcanic rumble in my troubled soul that heralded another bout of weeping as this relatively small but sharp consequence of death sliced into my delicate world with the precision and power of a butcher's knife. My stomach contracted as the familiar sinking feeling spread effortlessly through my body with the ease of a cloud obscuring the sunlight. My eyes prickled. I pushed the crumpled book under the glass, and turned, focusing on the door, through which I passed as the wave broke. Retracing my steps home, I railed at God: 'Why did you do this? Why did you take him away? Why didn't you protect him? Why? Why? Why? How could you? Are you God?'

In December 1981, three weeks after Samuel's birth, we had made a visit to a parish in Essex, with Samuel, where Charlie had been offered a job as a curate. Although anywhere within striking distance of the Dartford Tunnel would normally have been excluded from consideration, we had decided to pursue this avenue, albeit with some uncertainty, as a good friend whom we had made during the years at Trinity theological college in Bristol had contacted us and energetically persuaded us to do so. He had moved to the same parish a year earlier and was excited by the potential of this London overspill community, with its population of upwardly mobile and positive people. The thought of being able to work with friends mollified our prejudiced dislike of the geography.

Seven months later we sold our house in Bristol, packed up and drove back to Essex with our two little girls and Samuel's painful and tangible absence. The Bristol chapter was ended, a page had turned and the blank pages of our first job in the Church of England lay before us; a bleak and uninviting landscape on that day. But time was performing its silent, stealthy work of healing, not least in the intimacy of our marriage. As summer ended and the leaves turned again, I found I was pregnant for the fourth time, and together we found joy again in the midst of a strange concoction of conflicting emotions. An emotional rollercoaster ensued, as powerful memories of carrying Samuel blended with surges of hope and daring excitement about this new child.

'New house, new baby!' smiled the kindly people of our new parish, where the days began to pass by more quickly again, full of introductions, new routines and the milestone of primary school for Hannah. In November we celebrated Samuel's first birthday with a special tea for the girls. We put one candle on the cake and pored over all the photos we had of him. This was not a morbid occasion; far from it. The sitting room was festooned with cards from family and friends and from many members of our new church, who had tirelessly and selflessly laboured to make us feel welcomed and loved. They had embraced us in our loss and entered somehow into our suffering with us, thus drawing in some measure the sting of death. In the cosy warmth of our sitting room, the curtains drawn against the dark November evening and the wind whisking leaves along our suburban street, a small miracle took place. We found our hearts filling with gratitude and strangely warmed. Hope was stealing back and we spoke out our thanks to God, whom we had raged at so often since that black day in January, in a simple family prayer time. As Hannah and Alice uttered their sweet little thank-yous, an overpowering affection for them rose up inside me like a dam bursting, and I silently acknowledged the healer. It was a turning point on the road to wholeness.

The next hurdle was Christmas without Samuel, two stockings instead of three, but midwinter had passed by then and my belly was swelling with the new life that spoke to us all of a future and of hope. Days turned to weeks, weeks to months, and the days grew longer as the world turned towards another spring. Early one Sunday morning in April, the onset of contractions warned us of the imminent arrival of the baby, and we set off for the hospital. My thoughts and emotions were not surprisingly in chaos and turmoil. I was excited, but I was afraid. Hannah had been born by caesarean, Alice and Samuel with the help of forceps: all three births had been lengthy and painful. Would this be too? I felt faint at the prospect of all the pain: 'O Lord, please help me.'

The labour intensified, and my undivided concentration was needed for the huge upheaval that giving birth brings to the body. There was no mental space to think about Samuel or to be fearful for this new child; nor did I ponder on the sex of the infant so nearly with us. As the pain increased, so somehow did my ability to bear it, and to my incredulity my prayer seemed to be answered as the instruction to push came much sooner than during the previous births. After what then did seem a long time, I heard the words I hadn't dared to hope I would ever hear again: 'It's a boy!'

The words came swimming through the haze of exhaustion and the whirl of delivery room activity, and as if from somewhere far, far away. For a fleeting second, other words pronounced in another hospital superimposed themselves, fading to the echo … 'It's a boy! It's a boy!'

'Is it? Are you sure? Is it? Is it really? Oh, Charlie….' A dreamlike euphoria engulfed me, an intensity of joy and amazement that comes but infrequently in a lifetime. It was about four hours since we had arrived, and I had given birth without forceps. A tiny boy lay on my breast. And I lay on the hospital bed, laughing and crying, my eyes meeting Charlie's in our unspoken ecstasy. John Samuel, to be known as Jack, had arrived.

The congregation, voices lifted in worship, fell silent as their young curate strode up the aisle with a broad smile on his face. They held their breath as one, waiting for the news ... what would it be?

'It's a boy,' said Charlie, but he could say no more, for the people erupted with clapping, cheering and weeping with joy. This was the church as God intended, and this was a day of inexpressible joy.

It was to be many years before I really understood the depths of this day. I didn't really understand that all my days had been written in God's book of life before one of them came to be, or that God knows the whole course of our lives, both the deep joys and the tragic sorrows, because he is outside time; he is the very essence of eternity. In my understanding—and this is a profound conviction—every child, wanted or unwanted, planned or unplanned, is wanted and planned, known and called by God. Every child has a potentially assured future and path mapped out by heaven. But the very creation is groaning because it is in the grip of decay and destruction and many of the perfect plans of the Lord are aborted. Jack would be almost twenty by the time the mists cleared and I felt I received a little understanding about lives cut short, and about the deep purposes of God as generation succeeds generation.

3

Every Sparrow Falling, Every Grain of Sand

There's Only One of You

There's a divinity that shapes our ends,
Rough-hew them how we will.

- William Shakespeare, *Hamlet*

The key to understanding our value
is not just in seeing that we are
capable of transcending ourselves by
giving attention to other persons and
things in the process of learning to
love them; or of creating, as artists
do, beauty and order out of chaos.
It is the realisation that each one of
us is quite literally irreplaceable.

- Michael Mayne, *This Sunrise of Wonder*

The service was drawing to a close at St Aldates Church in Oxford. Twenty years had passed since that glorious day in April 1983. All through them, as we lived and moved and had our being, for the first ten in Essex and the other ten in Paris, I had wrestled with and reflected on the questions of life and purpose, of destiny and suffering that the loss of Samuel had awakened in me. But parish and family life was busy and full, with little time for ordering my thoughts or trying to assemble them in writing. You could hardly find two environments more dramatically different from one another than suburban Essex and central Paris! So my experiences in both places gradually shaped my thinking and informed my spiritual journey in very different but complementary ways. Returning home to England in 2002, Charlie took up the appointment of our dreams as he became Rector of this church, well and widely known for the generations of students who encounter Jesus there and spill out across the nations to serve him. Healing had come to me little by little, a day at a time, as I tried in my wrestling with the notion of suffering to understand why God allowed so much of it. My long, slow journey was not made easier by Charlie receiving a defining experience of healing that reassured him of God's love and purpose for him, and seemed to set him free in a way that made me jealous despite being glad for him—and if I'm honest, cross!

But back in England, the time had come to start writing …

On this particular Sunday morning of our early days in Oxford, the preacher was the Ugandan pastor and church statesman John Mulinde, a man who had become a close friend since we met him several years earlier in Paris. The day before, the church had been full of people attentively listening to John addressing the question and title of our weekend conference: 'Can a nation be changed?' He had talked of being set apart for God and what that means; of the power of Western world systems to control us; of holiness; of desperate prayer. This morning he was tired, not surprisingly, and finding it difficult to engage what by any standards can be a daunting audience. We conferred quietly and a little anxiously on the front row about how to facilitate a response to what he was saying. Closing his Bible, John bowed his head and invited the congregation to stand.

Suddenly, I knew what to say and, going to the microphone, I began to speak. 'Lots of you are tired of being lukewarm. You long to be all that God intends you to be, but are held back by a spiritual weariness and disillusionment; by the pace of life; by the ease with which you can and frequently do postpone your pursuit of God. Your spirit has been stirred, hearing what you know to be an authentic message coming from a life that matches the words. Ask God to help you start again, come back to a life of pursuit.' And I also knew in that instant that I was speaking to myself.

There was a rush of movement and people began to stream to the front of the church, many of them running and many of them young. Many fell to their knees, and tears began to flow. Some of us moved among them to offer prayer or simply bless the obvious engagement with God that was taking place. Where there had been dignified order five minutes earlier, there was now a noisy chaos with a hubbub of voices lifted to God. Half an hour later, as people were making their way home and the church was emptying, two young girls remained prostrate in front of the stage. Someone asked me whether I thought they were all right. 'They're all right!' I said, smiling. When I finally went to talk to one of them, she could barely speak and nodded her head in a drunken way in answer to my questions.

What was happening? Something that is not at all unique to one church in an English city, but common to churches in every denomination and I dare say in every nation, did we but know it. The presence of God is a holy thing and, as testified in the pages of the Bible and beyond through times of revival down through the centuries, his presence can affect us physically. Daniel and John fell on their faces as they saw the Lord and this young girl was experiencing the same thing … motionless and speechless in the presence of God.

Despite the global turmoil of this new century, you and I live in days of awakening around the world; awakening to our urgent need of prayer and of God's intervention to save. In many parts of the world, though sadly not yet in our own Western cultures, God is calling the younger generations in unprecedented numbers. Nation after nation is experiencing outbreaks of young people not only turning to God, but doing so in a radical way. That's to say, they are not interested in the form of religion, but in the power of the cross to save and deliver, and they are unafraid. They know they were born for something and instinctively they know that to discover that something they have to discover God.

I think of large youth movements, such as Soul Survivor, or Passion, gathering multitudes of teens and young adults who are hungry for God, and for whom Sunday is not enough. Words are not enough either, and in the summer of 2000, Message 2000 saw thousands of youngsters descending on the city to paint houses, weed gardens, clear rubbish, run summer camps for schoolchildren, go shopping for the elderly and infirm, talk with the homeless and the drug addicts, and invite anyone they could to the huge celebrations held every evening. It was a massive operation that took a year to plan, had the support and co-operation of the Manchester Constabulary, and cost thousands. But they were undaunted by the size of the vision because it was a vision from God, and this is a generation with a passion to see communities transformed and the church overflow her walls. A similar project took place in July 2004 in London, as have many others in the intervening years.

I think of The Call, a gathering of 600,000 young people in the Washington DC National Mall in 2000 to spend the day pleading with God for their nation. No big names, no personalities to attract people: the publicity focused on the reason for the event. One after another, young boys and girls spoke passionately of their yearning for America—a nation whose constitution declares, 'In God we Trust'— to return to God. Nearly twenty years on, the world, and certainly the church, is still waiting for this prayer to be answered. If anything there is more, not less, anger and division emanating from Washington DC. But what we are recording here is longing and perseverance, and the pursuit of God though he be silent and the times be dark.

Faces in the Crowd

Crowd events come and go. Nonetheless they achieve things that we cannot measure, because someone has taken seriously a demand or requirement of God. In some small way the outworking of history and of individual lives is different because of the obedience of this someone. You cannot have a crowd without individuals. Let's look at some of the faces in the crowd.

One of those present at The Call all those years ago was a girl called Michelle. To this day I could show you the exact spot in our Parish Centre where I first met her. She had come to Oxford for just one term, but as so often, God had other plans. Within two minutes of meeting her, I had a strong impression that I was talking to someone who would not be gone after a term. And so it turned out. She stayed on to join our intern programme for a year, went on to study theology at Wycliffe Hall, became one of our student pastors, and now works for Ravi Zacharias Ministries while based in her home town in the US.

I think of a young man who left Oxford shortly after our arrival to serve with a mission distributing medical supplies on the border of the Democratic Republic of the Congo (DRC) and northern Uganda. War was raging between the two nations and it drew close to the compound where he lived and worked as an administrator. Gun battles were an almost daily occurrence outside the gate and men were slaughtered with machetes within yards of the mission.

I think of another young man who gave up a life of potential comfort to serve in Burundi, also an area of conflict, tribal in this case. Only in one sense he has given nothing up, for he held fast to nothing; it is his joy to follow Jesus where he calls. He writes of his feelings following a severe accident that befell a cousin in the UK, causing him to fly home from Burundi to visit her:

> There are so many gifts that we take for granted and presume are rights. I want to shake the millions of people who are sacrificing everything to attain a certain standard of living, at the expense of having

a life. I want to reach out to the millions who cram their lives and schedules so full while they themselves remain so empty. I want to give blood which can bring life to someone else. Debs has had literally dozens of units of blood pumped into her—three times what is in her body, but she has kept on losing most of it. It makes me think of the ultimate sacrifice of the One who gave his blood for me—what incredible love! And in turn I want to lay down my life in His service, be it in Burundi or here.[1]

I think of Eric Liddell, the Scottish missionary who was also, and more famously, an Olympic athlete who gained a gold at the 1924 Games when he set a new world record for the 400 yards. Born in 1902 to missionary parents in Tientsin, northern China, Liddell's true notoriety sprang from his remarkable boldness in honouring God. He had qualified for the Olympics in the 100 yards, but on discovering that the heats were to be held on a Sunday, declined to participate and instead preached in a Parisian church. He agreed to run in the 400 yards, however, and despite not having trained for it, won the race four metres ahead of the next runner. This event was brilliantly captured in the 1981 film *Chariots of Fire*, in which Liddell says, 'God made me fast, and when I run, I feel his pleasure.' This is a pleasing expression of rejoicing in who you are, and not only pleasing but inspiring. David Puttnam, the producer of the film, is but one man who was affected: 'In many ways Liddell was the kind of person who, in my heart of hearts, I'd always dreamed of being ... few lives have more to teach us about the virtues of honour and probity.'[2]

Liddell returned to China to become a missionary in 1932, for all of his life was a race for the kingdom of God. There, growing political tensions caused him to send his pregnant wife and two daughters home, but Eric remained. He was interned in a Japanese camp in China in 1943 and died two years later of a tumour and typhoid.

The Cambridge genius mathematician and classicist Henry Martyn, who is pictured in the stained-glass window at the east end of St Aldates, forsook a distinguished career to become a missionary. He was moved by reading the journals of the puritan David Brainerd and stirred by hearing the great Charles Simeon recount stories of William Carey, the cobbler who established a strong gospel witness in Bengal between 1792 and 1802. Undeterred by opposition, Martyn was determined and, on arriving in Calcutta in 1806, he wrote in his journal, 'I almost think that to be prevented going among the heathen as a missionary would break my heart ... I feel pressed in spirit to do something for God ... I have hitherto lived to little purpose, more like a clod than a servant of God—now let me burn out for God.'

And this he did, dying at the age of 31, but not before he had employed his intellect to translate the New Testament into Persian, Arabic and Hindu, thus opening the way for thousands upon thousands to encounter the gospel.

I think too of the houses of prayer that are springing up across the nations. Church as we know it, gathering together for a few hours each week to celebrate our faith, is good, but not enough to satisfy an increasingly desperate hunger for God rising around the world, among the so-called generations X and Y in a particularly striking way. Mike Bickle, of the International House of Prayer in Kansas City, describes his own hunger:

> As I knelt to pray in my office, little did I expect to receive a new direction that would result in experiencing an entirely new dimension of spiritual desire.
>
> I began to pray because an unusual quiet yearning had filled my heart. It grew as my heart was stirred, and it became an intense longing, a thirst that felt impossible to quench…. 'Lord, seal me. Put fiery love in me.' As words of desire began to pour from my lips, the desire for God felt stronger and stronger, until it almost hurt. I began weeping, not from pain but from desire. But the longing for Christ only became more intense…. Before long the room was filled with his wonderful, divine presence, and my heart was spilling over.[3]

American pastor Lou Engle explains the birth of constant prayer in his church:

> Several years ago the Lord had been speaking to me concerning presenting before the Lord an offering of day and night worship and intercession. God had been calling me to a sense of longing for day and night intercession in Mott Auditorium, the building where our church gathers.

One day, up in my office, I was reading the testimony of Jim Goll who had taken an intercessory team to where the original Moravians were and where a 100-day prayer meeting of day and night intercession took place that launched a massive wave of missions. He said in this article that God was going to launch 120 of these houses of prayer in cities, and as I read that it just broke forth in my spirit and I began to weep and groan, 'Here, Lord, here. Mott Auditorium, 24-hour house of prayer.'

As I was groaning and weeping under the presence of the Lord, the phone rang, and there on the phone was a friend of mine. As I was weeping on the phone, I said, 'I'm just right now reading an article by this man named Jim Goll and this 24-hour house of prayer.'

He said, 'Lou, that's why I'm calling you right now. This very moment I was in a meeting and Jim Goll was preaching, and he just stopped in the middle of his message and said, "Lou Engle, Mott Auditorium, 24-hour house of prayer."' I was blown away. I knew God was shouting to me.

Two years later, we went on a 40-day fast, we built a room only for prayer and we launched the vision of a 24-hour house of prayer. That morning I went to pray and the Lord began to put this prayer in my heart: 'Raise up a Moravian lampstand, raise up a Moravian lampstand.'

The Lord spoke to my heart Matthew 5:15: 'Neither do people light a lamp and put it under a bowl. Instead they put it on its stand, and it gives light to everyone in the house.'

And I felt like the Lord was saying, 'I am going to raise up this lampstand. The 24-hour house of prayer is going to give light. It is going to be brought out of its hiddenness and I am going to put it on its stand in the nations of the earth. Day and night, intercession will arise all over the globe....'[4]

Breaking off abruptly in the middle of a message, as Jim Goll is recorded doing in this story, seems a curious thing to do. But there are many instances of those who are prophetically gifted behaving what to us seems unpredictably; we have only to think of Ezekiel (Ezek. 3–5) or Agabus (Acts 21:10). I clearly recall listening to Joy Dawson, a noted teacher on intercession, at a conference and being amazed and alarmed as she suddenly stopped speaking, knelt down on the platform and left us all hanging in an uncomfortable silence for several minutes, before explaining that she had needed to listen to the Lord there and then. It seems that such people are in dialogue with God even as they teach or preach, and subject to such interruptions.

I think of a prayer mountain a few miles outside Kampala. 'Africa Prayer Mountain for all nations', proclaims a large billboard as you crest the hill, leaving the Entebbe road and the glimmering shores of Lake Victoria far below. Here you walk into an open heaven. You may not see, as the prophet Isaiah did, the Lord seated on a throne, high and exalted, but you will know that he is there and you will feel an almost tangible sense of his presence. Day in and day out, the hundred acres of the hill are inhabited by men and women, young and old, walking, weeping, pleading, prostrate as they pray, often with loud shouts and groaning for the nations of the world. Everywhere there are tents where those who come for extended periods of prayer and fasting spend the few hours necessary for sleep.

I think of the 24/7 prayer movement that has generated continuous prayer since 1999:

> In 1722 a rag-tag band of several hundred young people gathered on the estate of a wealthy count by the name of Zinzendorf. Five years later, God showed up and they began to pray. They prayed in strange and creative ways, but they prayed. They prayed 24/7. Their prayer led to compassion for the poor and those who had never heard of Jesus. Their prayer meeting went on for 125 years without ceasing—the longest prayer meeting in history.
>
> God has decided to do again what he did among the Moravians almost 300 years ago. A 24/7 prayer meeting has started again, but now it has circled the globe overnight. We should not be surprised God chose an unlikely candidate to lead the 24/7 prayer movement. Pete Greig struggled to hear God's voice and wasn't very good at praying, but he was determined to chase the Spirit wherever that took him.... He reminds us that prayer doesn't belong

to the stodgy or the religious. Nor can prayer be
controlled by religious types who think they have
a corner on the right words to use, and the correct
way to stand. *Red Moon Rising* … stirs faith in us
to believe that when we talk to God he responds.[5]

Pete Greig describes the impact of visiting Herrnhut, the village
established by the ragtag band: 'We moved a mile or so down the road …
to Berthelsdorf. Here … the community had gathered on 13 August
1727. As they … committed themselves afresh to unity, the Holy Spirit
had moved so powerfully that some of the congregation, it is said, stag-
gered from the building hardly able to stand.' For the Moravians, this
moment was, 'the culmination of a process of renewal (three months
previously they had drawn up a "covenant for Christian living", something like a monastic rule of life).… I knelt in a pew and said a little
prayer, deeply conscious of the fact that an event in this building almost
exactly 272 years earlier was somehow still impacting my life at the dawn
of the third millennium.' It was a life-changing day. 'In many ways I
left the apartment that morning as a tourist and returned as a pilgrim.'[6]
Likewise, I think I could say that in a sense I left the UK in January 1982
as a tourist, and returned in March as a pilgrim.

A Spiritual Battle

As such stories show, what we are seeing today is not a new phenomenon. Every historical revival has been preceded by intense and
sustained prayer, from the eighteenth-century revival in America
spearheaded by Jonathan Edwards to the Hebridean revival in the

mid-twentieth century. What many think to be new is the scale of what is happening. This is partly due to the way ever more sophisticated technology facilitates the dissemination of information at speed.

But perhaps it's more than that: the heart of man, where God has 'set eternity',[7] knows that sophistication and intellect do not necessarily lead to altruism and philanthropy, nor up to the throne room of God. Rather they can lead him up the blind alley of calling himself God. He knows that war, civil and international; slavery; hunger; sickness and murder ravage the face of the earth not less but more than in all the centuries of his history. And he knows that we are no nearer our goal of peace on earth than we have ever been.

Today's young adults, children of the internet, global travellers who have more in common with the culture of their generation than that of their nation, are profoundly aware of the evil that is polluting the face of the globe like thick, suffocating smoke. This is exactly the image that was used by John Mulinde in a prophetic word that he offered when he first began to come to Europe during the 1990s:

> I saw the map of the continent of Europe, and as I looked there came out of this map a big pillar of smoke. It was a tall, thick and dark pillar of heavy black fumes as from a factory chimney. The fumes rose up very slowly and gradually began spreading out.
>
> From the pillar came a thin mist, and it began spreading out almost imperceptibly, but within a short time it had formed a dark film over the entire continent. As the mist grew thicker, the features

below it blurred and became difficult to distinguish under the black fumes.[8]

Few would venture to disagree that this is a pertinent image for the Europe of today. The war that is greater in scope and goal and savagery than any currently scarring nations is the war between good and evil, between the Creator and his opponent, the one who fell like lightning from heaven[9] and who has sought from that moment to seduce mankind from the safety of relationship with his Maker. This is the war towards the resolution of which history is slowly making its way. This is the war for which God is training up saints and soldiers, prophets and priests, and it is a war greater than any earthly war.

Many would agree that thousands of young men and women are arising to take hold of who they are created to be, more aware of the true state of the world than any previous generation. God is calling them and they hear his call. It's why they cannot abide hypocrisy in any shape or form; why they can smell the stench of dishonesty and double standards a mile off; why they are impatient when they find authenticity or integrity lacking; why they couldn't care less about style or form, but care passionately about content. They have long relinquished the desire to impress with appearance or money, to manipulate or to seek the power of control. It's why so many churches are emptying. They understand much better than many of their parents the true state of corruption in the nations. They understand too that neither politics nor humanism is going to unlock the door to peace in the nations.

War means casualties, and where a war between tribes or nations is concerned we understand this without any difficulty. We are also coming painfully to understand the concept of war as expressed through terrorism, hearing too often of a suicide bomber snatching away a handful or dozens of lives in just an instant, or of a gunman ending them in minutes. Soldiers die, and we study their faces as they appear briefly in our newspapers or online, curious about the years, the experiences, the joys and sorrows looking out at us through their eyes. Far away in safety from the battle front, politicians justify the need for men, and increasingly women too, to be there.

We understand much less well the notion of casualties in the other, bigger, universal war, the spiritual war. We do not make connections easily. In our day hundreds of lives are being snatched away, snuffed out or incapacitated, and we are not noticing. And if we do notice and lament, we do not understand that there is a master plan behind the loss. When God raised up Moses as a deliverer for the captive people of Israel, all hell broke loose in the form of an edict from the king of Egypt instructing the Hebrew midwives to kill baby boys on delivery. When the Magi ingenuously enquired of Herod, 'Where is the one who has been born King of the Jews?'[10] they did not realise that their question would lead to Herod signing the death warrant of scores of baby boys from newborns to two-year-olds. So during the absence of the infant Jesus in Egypt, the bitter sound of mothers wailing for their children resounded in the town and surroundings of Bethlehem. The plans and purposes of God were not thwarted, cannot be thwarted, but there were casualties, there was loss of the most painful kind. And so it is for us all in our tiny personal worlds.

This is how I came to understand the personal loss of our firstborn son. Before he was born, in a time of great anxiety over my pregnancy, I asked for prayer at a church service, and the person who prayed did so in a prophetic way, implying that the child I was carrying was marked out by God for a future. At the same time a GP had diagnosed an abnormal pregnancy and advised what was effectively a termination. So it would be possible to think that his life was already contested at this stage. Not, of course, by the GP, who was simply doing his job as best he could, but by forces of another order. Only the wisdom of our elderly GP when we returned home prevented Samuel's death occurring even earlier than it happened. 'Hmmm, I think we'll do a scan first,' he said thoughtfully. The scan revealed a healthy twelve-week foetus, and so this particular and unique story began; and you too have your particular and unique story.

Today we have passed laws, beginning in 1967, to legalise the killing of millions of unborn infants. Let's name it for what it is, though it make us squirm. And we have done it in the name of human rights. Every potential mother has so much legal control over her own body that she may choose to end the life of a child she has conceived through the freedom to have intercourse. Clearly the most obvious caveat to this is in the case of a rape. While rape is one of the worst travesties of human relations, any infant that may be created in the process is not to blame, and so clearly being put to death should not be his lot. Heather Gemmen's powerful testimony in her book *Startling Beauty*, where she tells of her lovely daughter who was conceived in a terrifying and traumatic rape, reminds us how little we can see of our children's future and how vital it is that we do right by them however they are conceived. Thousands of children are conceived in far from ideal circumstances, yet their lives are not taken from them. Where do we draw the line? I know three people who were conceived through rape, and none of them wishes that they had never seen the light of day, although all, like Job, have suffered severe trials and the pain of loneliness. Job, to whom a whole book of forty-two chapters in the Bible is devoted, was just an upright man who respected God and resisted evil. Many tragedies befall him, yet he steadfastly refuses to blame God, even when his wife exhorts him to do so.

Lives are not being picked off by abortion alone. Many sell their souls for drugs, for sex, for alcohol, for a multitude of bondages. They have been told that God is dead, but they know they need him. Douglas Coupland confesses this need at the close of his book *Life after God*:

> Now here is my secret ... I tell it to you with an openness of heart that I doubt I shall ever achieve again, so I pray that you are in a quiet room as you hear these words. My secret is that I need God— that I am sick and can no longer make it alone. I need God to help me give, because I no longer seem to be capable of giving; to help me be kind, as I no longer seem capable of kindness; to help me love, as I seem beyond being able to love.[11]

What a cry! Who will answer? The voice of God calls us to recognise and embrace who we have been created to be and become; he calls us to be followers of Jesus, and he calls us in our turn to call others to him, or back to him. Will we answer? God calls us to love and communicate his word. The word of which Jesus says: 'Heaven and earth will pass away, but my words will never pass away'.[12] The word of which, centuries earlier, Isaiah writes: 'My word ... shall accomplish that which I purpose, and shall succeed in the thing for which I sent it'.[13]

God calls to us, to you and to me, to be the kind of people who diminish the shame of the church and the mockery of God. He calls us to become the kind of reformers who seek to eradicate world poverty and hunger and who call the nations to respect the planet (which we were commanded to care for long before the creation of church or missions) through their engagement with ecological issues. He calls us to knock on heaven's door with our prayers and plead for God-focused worship to resound across the earth, wooing humankind to their father's embrace. He calls us to love people into his company. His prophets speak of this.

A Plan and a Purpose

Prophets are often strange people, none more so perhaps than some of those who straddle the pages of the Old Testament. I have often wondered what the church today would make of Ezekiel. He spoke of fantastical visions, and was apparently instructed by God to prophesy the coming siege of Jerusalem by making a model of the city, placing an iron pan between the model and himself to symbolise a wall, then lying down first on one side, then the other, tied with ropes to symbolise immobility until the days allotted to the visual aid were completed.[14] All this was to warn of the following: 'Son of man, I am about to cut off the supply of food in Jerusalem. The people will eat rationed food in anxiety and drink rationed water in despair, for food and water will be scarce. They will be appalled at the sight of each other and will waste away because of their sin'.[15] Such an event would make it to the pages of our national newspapers for sure; we love the quirky and the bizarre.

So the biblical prophets are strange, and their prophecies need cautious consideration and wisdom as we try to understand them. The same caution and wisdom should be applied to today's prophets; they can carry an authentic message, but they can also carry a false message, as some have done in prophesying imminent revival which never materialises. God spoke through the mouth of Jeremiah, with a warning against false prophets,[16] and careful discernment is needed in pondering prophetic words. Paul instructs the Thessalonians: 'Do not treat prophecies with contempt but test them all; hold on to what is good'.[17] And we do well to remember that the principal meaning of prophecy is forthtelling the word of God, not foretelling the future. It is primarily for comforting, encouraging and exhorting people.

I once heard a prophecy of the foretelling (and therefore questionable) kind, about God calling the young generation of the time to be a great army of the Lord, who would be unafraid of living for Christ. It spoke of it being easier to die for Christ than to live for him, but that where a life is extinguished in the battle, ten more would rise to replace him or her.

I first heard this 'word' as I drove through the rolling Oxfordshire countryside, lit by a Keatsian autumn sun. As is often my experience, the beauty of creation provoked an outpouring of thanks to God for his kindness in bringing us home after our ten years in Paris. Straining to catch the words of the message, I repeatedly replayed it to make sure I was hearing correctly. The speaker was saying that he had 'heard' these things about a courageous generation in October 1981. A month before Samuel's birth. Just the mention of a date so special to me was, understandably, enough to trigger deep-seated emotion. I felt the presence of God close in the car, and a sudden burst of grief poured out in my tears.

Looking back, I think all sorts of things about this so-called prophecy were wrong, from the motivation onwards. Pretty much anything that we venture to pass on as being something we think God has said to us will at the very most be good in parts, like the proverbial curate's egg. I am certainly not suggesting that it had any kind of authority, but in line with Paul's teaching, I tested it to discern what was good. What it did for me was to reignite my desire and energy to pray for my children and their generation.

If, like me, you are a parent, you may need to recognise that God may speak louder and more clearly to your children than to you. We shouldn't suggest otherwise to them, but encourage them if they think they hear from him. This means accepting that sometimes they will be wiser than us: they can see further, their fingers are more accurately on the spiritual pulse of the church, even of the nation. It means acknowledging that truths that have taken us years to appropriate may have been grasped with alacrity and spiritual acumen by our children.

If you are a Millennial, or a member of Gen X or Y, God is calling you too, and looking for an answer. He calls you not to give up the quest to discover who you were made to be and what you were made to do. No one would contest that this is a fearsome challenge in a postmodern age increasingly hostile to Christianity. God is surely calling you, and us your parents, to stand up and be counted, and to lobby and fight for righteousness.

So we are made to measure, made for a purpose, and becoming who we are made to be is a journey that can make us flourish. It's a given that this journey will include sorrow and suffering as well as success and joy, but whether you stand on a mountain top or struggle through a valley today, God is with you, and he knows the way that you take. He is your refuge and your fortress. These truths about God slowly burned their way into my spirit and onto my heart in the very depths of loss—like spiritual tattoos. If you, dear reader, are in a season of loss or suffering, please take heart; God has a purpose for you that can't be thwarted. 'I know that you can do all things; no purpose of yours can be thwarted'.[18] Thus speaks Job, who could be forgiven for feeling very differently from this … and perhaps you do too. We'll take a closer look at Job in chapter 14, but the key to his statement lies in his obdurate clinging to God through the very worst of times. If disillusionment or despair have loosened your grip, reach out for his hand again, even as you read. If as you read you are mentally excluding yourself from the people, ideas and visions we've been talking of, please know that your heavenly Father doesn't exclude you; Jesus calls to you, and says 'You belong'; 'Come to me, all you who are weary and burdened….'[19]

Because the concept of eternity is written into the heart of man, or to put it another way part of his DNA, we are hardwired to make an impression, have a story and find meaning and significance. In our postmodern, post-war world, where public meaning has been drained of any sense of purpose as we have left the metanarrative of God behind, many create their own meaning. Yet even those who reject God sometimes acknowledge the intimation of eternity. Jean-Paul Sartre, the French existentialist philosopher, said; 'I don't see myself as so much dust that has appeared in the world, but as a being that was expected, prefigured, called forth.'[20] That we have a calling and purpose is inescapable; whether we find it and live it out, be it for two decades or for ten, is a different matter entirely.

Supremely in all history, the person and life of Jesus speak of purpose. 'When the fullness of time had come, God sent forth his Son ... born under the law, to redeem those born under the law, so that we might receive adoption as sons'.[21]

The Christmas story is more than a story. It is God speaking into and shaping history to fashion the salvation of mankind: the perfect rescue for the dearest of all his creation who had spurned his love and cherished pride in their heart. Seven hundred years earlier the prophets had spoken of this. They told of his birth from a virgin, of where he would be born, of how he would die, and that he would be raised from the dead. Creation spoke of it, as a bright star led the wise men to the stable. And the worldwide Roman census that Caesar Augustus had decreed gave the backdrop to the Bethlehem stable stage. Jesus resisted every pressure to deviate him from his purpose, whether pressure from crowds to meet their needs or to make him king, from Peter wanting to keep him safe,[22] or from his own fears as he prayed and sweated in the garden of Gethsemane.[23]

The exquisite history of Jesus Christ quintessentially captures the notion of calling and purpose, and you too have a calling and purpose. You too were made to measure, and made to be bound up in God's story.

4

The Hearts of the Fathers
Called to Love All Generations

For Michael Mayne, it is not enough that his grandchildren will be able to say that he was fond of reading, enjoyed the theatre, visited art galleries, went to concerts, was sensitive to the natural world etc; and that these pleasures enhanced his faith and became part of his ministry. He needs to tell them what books, what songs, which moment when the butterfly settled on the flower or the evening blackbird was heard. He also needs to put together for himself, as well as for future generations, an inventory of his joy, a list of what exalted his spirit, or what opened his eyes, or what produced in him contentment (or unrest), and what made him what he was.

- Ronald Blythe in the Foreword to Michael Mayne, *This Sunrise of Wonder*

This problem of society's contempt for the old is going to occupy us at some length ... even today there are few parents who recognise their own ignorance and their mistakes with their children and who do not always claim to know better than their children what is good for them.

- Paul Tournier, *Learning to Grow Old*

I held the sobbing girl gently, feeling the anguish she was expressing. Unable to stop the flow of tears, her eyes had become red from rubbing, but the normal teenage preoccupation with appearance didn't matter right now. Several moments later she was just about ready to explain what was wrong.

'It's my father. He's so distant with me. He never seems to listen to me. He always brushes me off. And I love him so much ...' More tears.

We are living in an era of pronounced alienation between the generations. No man is able to be a father as God is a father, for every successive generation fathers out of its own pain and inadequacy. We should be careful not to apportion blame to our own fathers for the pain in the pit of our stomachs, for they too had their pain to carry. It seems inconceivable that the mother of a baby should feel indifferent to the child's fate. Yet the Bible asks the question, 'Can a mother forget the baby at her breast and have no compassion on the child she has borne?' and answers, 'Though she may forget, I will not forget you!'[1] History as recorded through our newspapers testifies to the truth that blood relationship is insufficient to ensure love, protection and faithfulness. Far too often we open the newspapers only to read of terrible family conflicts that have ended in tragedy. The great majority of women who suffer rape suffer it at the hands of someone they know.

Yet whatever our biological provenance, I believe each of us can find spiritual mothers and fathers in the family of God who can add to the good parenting we experienced, or fill the ache of what was missing for us. Mike Bickle, in his book *The Pleasures of Loving God*, writes about Simeon and Anna, from the presentation of Jesus in the temple found in Luke's gospel.

Simeon and Anna are wonderful testimonies of the significant things that can happen when senior saints in the body of Christ enter into the ministry of prayer and fasting. I believe that this type of ministry will occur again among young people, but there will always be a strong, dynamic contingent of elders who are praying and fasting across the world. The young people will be bonded to them as to mothers and fathers in the spirit. Adolescents will look into the eyes of their elders in the Lord and will wonder why they feel such a strong spiritual connection between them. Young people will look up to you, senior citizen, and say 'I don't know why, but I really like you.' You may smile knowingly because you were the one who birthed these young people into the kingdom of God.[2]

Bickle's words express well that praying for the next generation does not concern only families related by blood. What about the unmarried? Where do they fit into the picture? What about those who are not able to have natural children? I believe that the call to become mothers and fathers extends beyond the biological. God is far more interested in our maturity than in our particular status and circumstances, as far as what happens to the next generation is concerned. He needs every soldier who will sign up.

I have experienced myself the truth of what Bickle says. There are elderly saints in the family of God who elicit a response from the depth of my being that can often cause tears to flow. One such was Campbell McAlpine, one of the fathers of renewal during the 1960s.

He became very personally a father at the time of Samuel's death, which no doubt accounts partly for the strength of feeling.

Another is a woman who was my spiritual director for some years and became a dear friend. Words fail me in trying to express the love I feel for both her and her husband. And a third is John Wimber, although I knew him in a much more superficial way, meeting him at conferences from time to time, and occasionally having the opportunity to pick his brains, such as when he visited us in Paris in 1995. Nonetheless I found a strength of feeling towards him that I can only account for as the bonding of the Spirit described by Bickle.

Many experienced a strong attachment to Wimber, but curiously his relationship with his own father was tragically lacking. 'John grew up knowing almost nothing about the Wimbers. What he did know about his father didn't cause him to want to know any more.'[3] This only further confirms the notion that spiritual parenting can go well beyond natural.

Many men carry a deep longing to be a father in the mould of the heavenly Father, but are crippled by their own experiences as a son. Fathers can be withdrawn, emotionally repressed, drunken, violent or absent, among other things. So to know the Father's love is a foundational need for every human being, and it is God's desire that we should know it. To be a father in the Lord is a calling for every man who knows Christ. Paul, who was not a father of flesh, was an eminent example of a father of the Spirit, referring to Titus as 'my true son in our common faith', to Timothy as 'my true son', and to the Galatians as 'my dear children, for whom I am again in the pains of childbirth until Christ is formed in you'.[4] And though he predominantly addresses the Corinthians as brothers, he reverts to the parent image at moments of passion as opposed to moments of persuasion. 'We have spoken freely to you, Corinthians, and opened wide our hearts to you.... As a fair exchange—I speak as to my children—open wide your hearts also'.[5]

The same call pertains to being a mother. Again, my life has been shaped to a certain extent by women who have modelled godliness in one way or another, women as different from one another as Campbell McAlpine was different from John Wimber. These women awakened in me a desire to emulate them, to pursue wisdom and integrity as they had done, and to grow old gracefully as they have done or are doing. They have discovered the Father's love, and lost the never-ending need to live by earning the approval of others.

Other women who were not mothers of the flesh also become role models for younger women. I think of such as Corrie ten Boom, the Dutchwoman who saw her sister die in a prisoner of war camp during the Second World War and years later famously expressed forgiveness to her German captors. A beautiful gospel truth is that biological status as a mother or father is almost inconsequential in the kingdom of God, whereas the wholehearted pursuit of God defines true biblical parenting. The brokenness of so many who are natural mothers and fathers, damaged by their own parents, and damaging their children in turn, is in itself a clear call to every one of us to take up our mantle of mother or father to the generation that follows us.

Generational Conflict

Today, we are all familiar to a greater or lesser extent with the different generations and what makes them tick. Baby Boomers, Generations

X and Y, Millennials and now Generation Z each respond very differently to a wide range of things, from technology to disposable income to relationships. A growing number of social commentators and marketing experts seek to divide society along generational lines and to target different generational groups. This in turn reflects evolving legislation that, while purportedly acting to protect children and young people, in fact can sometimes distance them subtly from their parents. A good example of this is the 1994 UN Convention on the Rights of the Child. Originally drafted as a Declaration in 1924, this international agreement was certainly beneficent. Almost a century and several iterations later, in a very different cultural climate, the document is vulnerable to subjective interpretation, and can lead to state support for an under-eighteen-year-old wielding more influence than his or her parents. This can lead in turn to parents being disempowered, and although in rare cases protection from parents is vital, for the vast majority good relationships with their children are a life priority.

In addition, we are witnessing the appearance of an alarming imbalance in generational statistics. As President Bush was inaugurated for his second term of office at the beginning of 2005, he promised to restore the crumbling pension scheme of his country. Why was it crumbling? Because improved health care and working conditions meant that whereas in 1960 there had been 16.5 million people aged sixty-five and over (nine percent of the population), by 2005 there were 36.3 million (over twelve percent) and rising.[6] Obviously no law could ever suffice as the sole agent of solving this problem. Something needs to happen in the soul of a nation if we are not to see increasing numbers of the elderly physically and financially isolated.

Parallel with the increase in longevity has come a diminishing of the respect traditionally accorded to the elders in many cultures. This is reflected in many spheres; for example, the market place. A woman who has chosen to be home-based during the child-rearing years may experience difficulty in re-entering the workplace, particularly if she is over fifty. Very different, though just as disturbing, is the disappearance of respect in the street. My elderly parents lived on a quiet estate for some years, but were increasingly upset and intimidated by sporadic bouts of verbal aggression from children as young as ten who roamed through their street at all times of the day and night. A clergy friend was loudly sworn at in response to an offer of help—because he was wearing a dog collar. In this latter case, some responsibility should probably be owned by the church, for the plethora of abuse scandals emanating from within the church in recent decades has given rise to an instinctive distrust of her people.

Another contributing factor to the distancing between generations is the dramatic acceleration of technology that has opened previously unparalleled access to information and travel. Today we live in a postmodern, post-truth culture; there are no absolutes, and everything is relative. Knowledge and money are power, and combine to further dispel any remaining sense of dependency on elders that was at one time the norm.

In his book *Devil's Advocate*, John Humphrys addresses this disappearing sense of mutual responsibility. He argues that, in the brief span of some fifty years, Britain has turned from courage and self-sacrifice to compensation and self-indulgence. He illustrates this by contrasting the noble response to and rescue operation for the Aberfan Colliery disaster of 1966, with the very different aftermath of the 1989 Hillsborough disaster. In Humphrys' account of this later tragedy we read almost as much about rescuers claiming compensation and counselling for the trauma occasioned by their involvement as we do about the trauma suffered by bereaved families or injured individuals.[7] Few would dispute that today we are a people who are consumed by our own welfare, success and comfort, or that we have become what Humphrys calls a victim culture. Sadly, these attitudes are all too prevalent in the church, and perhaps this is one reason why she is a ready target of the media, and therefore widely scorned or considered irrelevant.

It is not only respect for elders that needs to be retrieved; those of us who are older must stop tut-tutting at what we see and hear, and ask instead how we should interpret and respond to the seeming disappearance of all restraint and modesty.

One way is to understand the generation born roughly between 1965 and 1980, dubbed Generation X by Douglas Coupland. In his 1991 novel so titled, an argument between the narrator, Andy, and his Boomer boss, Martin, encapsulates the Xers' rejection of the Boomers because of the pain caused by perceived abandon: having in his youth espoused the Woodstock generation's desire to recover a spiritual dimension, Martin has sold out and become a middle manager in an advertising agency, where he is now devoted to promoting hamburgers.

> Hey, Martin … Put yourself in my shoes. Do you *really* think we enjoy having to work in that toxic waste dump in there … and then have to watch you chat with your yuppie buddies about your gut

liposuction all day while you secrete artificially sweetened royal jelly here in Xanadu? ... Or for that matter do you really think we en*joy* hearing about your brand-new million-dollar *home* when ... we're pushing *thir*ty? A home you won in a genetic lottery, I might add, sheerly by dint of your having been born at the right time in history? You'd last about ten minutes if you were my age these days, Martin. And I have to endure pinheads like you rusting above me for the rest of my life, always grabbing the best piece of cake first and then putting a barbed-wire fence around the rest. You really make me sick.[8]

The church is haemorrhaging Gen Xers and Millennials, and we can see why if we care to look. Yet they are increasingly those who are shaping the form and direction of British society in these early decades of the new millennium. Little wonder then that the prevailing wind is blowing away from rather than towards God, in ethical, legal or moral matters.

Well over eight million abortions have been performed in Britain since David Steel's Abortion Law of 1967. Today we are on the verge of following Holland and Belgium in legalising euthanasia. Where society is struggling to cater for increasing numbers of people completing ten decades, little imagination is necessary to envisage where this might lead. Legislation is quietly advancing to make marriage no more than one of a number of documents signifying an agreement to live together. Many European nations have legalised same-sex marriage, and many parts of the church have followed suit. Divorce has become easier, and traditional forms of family and relationships are fading into a smorgasbord of options.

Centuries ago, King Alfred drafted British law beside an open Bible, and until 1917 British Lord Chancellors had expressly stated that Christianity was part and parcel of English Common Law. Since then we have all but eradicated any trace of biblical content from our statute books.

All these things constitute a challenge and a clarion call to the church, and to those who follow Christ, clearly to model a tri-generational, indeed increasingly a quadri-generational, community. We're called to heal generational rifts, to love and care for the elderly, to listen to and learn from the young; to respect the wisdom of the elders but not to despise the young. The Bible tells us that before darkness becomes so great on the earth that it leads to the dreadful day of the Lord, the hearts of the fathers will be turned to their children, and the hearts of the children to their fathers.[9] The darkness on earth is continually intensified by war. Currently wars of different types rage in many nations—in Iraq, South Sudan, Yemen, Syria, Afghanistan, Mexico, the Central African Republic, the DRC, Ukraine, Somalia, Mexico. Let's pause and pray for a minute as we read this fearful list....

A surfeit of killing numbs the senses of the living. We think death cannot come near us but it does ... in New York, in Madrid, in London, in Paris, in Brussels, in Munich. To process these things, we have to rediscover our mortality here in the West; we have to find spiritual anchors and something bigger than our little lives.

What better place than in a multigenerational community where truths are handed down from generation to generation, lending security in an age of change? The Bible is a manifesto for intergenerational community, recounting failure as well as success.

Not only is generational unity written into the commandments, since the first commandment about human relationships is to honour our parents, but it is woven throughout the Scriptures. Moses instructs the Israelites:

> These commandments that I give you today are to be upon your hearts. Impress them on your children. Talk about them when you sit at home and when you walk along the road, when you lie down and when you get up. Tie them as symbols on your hands and bind them on your foreheads. Write them on the doorframes of your houses and on your gates.[10]

What goes around comes around, as they say, and while we find comic the idea of putting things on our foreheads, we still wear wristbands or badges to signal various allegiances. The well-known WWJD[11] bands drew criticism from some, yet they arise from the same principle: a desire to remain mindful of something. Make Poverty History's white wristbands carry the same message: Don't forget.

Many years ago we borrowed a caravan for our family holiday. With growing excitement and a certain unease between the parents, created by the responsibility of looking after something as large as a caravan, we drove sedately all the way to Cornwall. To our great consternation the entrance to the caravan site was a narrow gateway with large granite gateposts looking like some escaped menhirs from Stonehenge. Mounting excitement was replaced by tension in the front of the car, exacerbated by the now fractious and tired children in the back. We inched towards the ghastly gap, which seemed to narrow before our eyes, and words were reduced to sharp 'Shut-ups', and 'CAREFUL' … all to no avail as an ugly rasping sound, caused by the caravan coming into contact with the gatepost, struck our disbelieving ears. Our hearts sank and our tempers boiled over. By the time the caravan was in place, all six of us were in far from what is often called a holiday mood. Opening the door of the caravan for the first time, we were greeted by a display of stickers: Bible verse stickers! 'Set a guard over my mouth, Lord',[12] pleaded one. 'Be kind and compassionate to one another, forgiving each other, just as in Christ God forgave you',[13] exhorted another.

Hmmm! We weren't very impressed and we did not appreciate the décor, but wait a minute … it did remind us of something; and it did defuse what could have continued degenerating, given the fatigue and the frayed tempers we were all displaying.

Over 400 years after Moses, David proclaims the same message as Moses:

> I'll let you in on the sweet old truths, stories we heard from our fathers, counsel we learned at our mother's knee. We're not keeping this to ourselves, we're passing it along to the next generation—God's fame and fortune, the marvellous things he has done. He planted a witness in Jacob, set his word firmly in Israel, then commanded our parents to teach it to

> their children so the next generation would know,
> and all the generations to come—know the truth and
> tell the stories so their children can trust in God.[14]

Elsewhere he says, 'Future generations will be told about the Lord. They will proclaim his righteousness ... to a people yet unborn'.[15]

This was a theme dear to David, who had suffered a generational breakdown between his predecessor, Saul, and himself, caused by Saul's jealousy of David's friendship with Jonathan, and of David's abilities and prowess in war. Jealousy is perhaps the greatest threat to intergenerational peace and harmony, for the success of a younger person can provoke the irrational feeling that being older we must be wiser or know better. But wisdom comes from the knowledge of God. It is not simply to be kind that Paul tells Timothy not to let people look down on him because he is young.[16] It is because he knows that Timothy has great wisdom and leadership gifts, nurtured by Paul himself. He encourages Timothy to use the gifts of preaching and teaching that he has. The text clearly states that these gifts were given through a prophetic message when the elders prayed for him.[17] This speaks of encouragement and releasing from the generation of his father. However, there is another reason that Timothy has much wisdom at a young age. Writing that he misses him, Paul mentions Timothy's faith: 'And what a rich faith it is, handed down from your grandmother Lois to your mother Eunice and now to you.'[18]

Clearly David's priority of passing on the faith succeeded with his son Solomon, who emphatically delivers the same message in his writings. According to the prologue of Proverbs:

> These are the wise sayings of Solomon … written
> down so we'll know how to live well and right … a
> manual for living, for learning what's right and just
> and fair; to teach the inexperienced the ropes and
> give our young people a grasp on reality.[19]

There are frequent references to 'my son(s)' which emphasise instructing the young so that they know how to become wise and avoid pitfalls, but although it is a practical guide to living, reverence for God and reliance on him are clearly the baseline that makes this possible.

In a multicultural, multifaith culture, the stories of God's dealings with man are no longer standard fare for a child's education; we can't even assume that the name of Jesus is familiar. On the other hand, an example of what is rapidly becoming standard fare is a homework exercise for eleven-year-olds that requires them to go out and practise buying condoms from the chemist.[20] Bothered? You should be.

So more than ever the church must be a source of learning and wisdom, and a shelter for the lonely and the disorientated. As the family slowly breaks down, there is an ever greater call for spiritual mothers and fathers to parent a lost generation.

> The increasing breakdown of the marriage-based
> family is leaving an ever-widening wake of human
> suffering and social chaos. Drug abuse is now
> out of control. The media glorify sexual license,
> violence and obscene and blasphemous language.

Degrading pornography has become a major industry, promiscuity is actively promoted and sexually-transmitted-diseases are racing out of control. Vandalism has become a national disease ... and there is widespread fear because of growing violence and lawlessness on our streets.... Human relationships are increasingly presented as temporary, valueless and dispensable, vast numbers of children have been deprived of family life, and especially of their fathers.... We have robbed our children of their innocence.... We have poisoned their minds by what they see, by what they read and what they hear.... We have allowed them to be abused, corrupted and exploited....[21]

Statistics tell their own story: there are 75,420 children in care of some kind in England:

47,530 children were identified as having a primary need caused by 'abuse or neglect'—the most common reason identified. 11,270 were in need due to 'family dysfunction' and 5,980 were due to the 'family being in acute stress'. 4,860 were identified as in need due to 'absent parenting', almost all of whom are unaccompanied asylum-seeking children.[22]

The Parliamentary Office of Science and Technology estimates that 'between 189,000 and 208,000 children in England live with an alcohol-dependent adult.'[23] A support and advocacy group for families raising children with Foetal Alcohol Spectrum Disorders states that 'Research suggests that at least 1% of the population is affected by FASD, meaning that 7,000 babies are born every year in the UK with this debilitating condition.… More than 70% of children with FASD have progressed through the care service'.[24]

Police recordings of sex offenses committed against children 'more than doubled between 2013 and 2017, increasing from 24,085 to 53,496'.[25] *The Guardian* reported on hidden homelessness in 2017 and stated that 'one in five young people in the UK have sofa-surfed in the past year and almost half of them have done so for more than a month'.[26] One in eight five-to-nineteen-year-olds 'had at least one mental disorder when assessed in 2017',[27] and *The Independent* reported that 'the number of teenage suicides in England and Wales increased by 67 per cent between 2010 and 2017'.[28]

These statistics are inevitably limited in how accurate a picture they can provide, but they show something of the challenges that affect the nation before children have even left school.

That's just the beginning; that's just the children. But statistics soon numb our faculties. As with the colossal numbers lost in natural disasters, we wonder helplessly what we can do.

Spiritual Fathers and Mothers

Well, God is seeking parents who are like him. You may not be a biological parent, but you can be a parent; this isn't my idea. It comes from the Bible:

'Sing, barren woman, you who never bore a child;
burst into song, shout for joy, you who were never
in labour; because more are the children of the
desolate woman than of her who has a husband,'
says the Lord.[29]

God is calling us to be fathers and mothers to the next generation. While some will grow up in homes that welcome Jesus, many
will not, and they need spiritual parenting. They desperately need as
role models those who live out of knowing who they are in God, in
other words people who gain the mind of Christ, and become 'fully
mature adults, fully developed within and without, fully alive like
Christ. No prolonged infancies among us please ... God wants us to
grow up, to know the whole truth and tell it in love—like Christ in
everything'.[30]

Every generation has its Simeons and Annas who are soaked
in the presence of God, who know his love for them. What better
aspiration could we have than to be like the barren woman in Isaiah,
to whom God himself grants fruitfulness; and like Simeon who was
righteous and devout, and who had the Holy Spirit on him? Do
you long to be at ease with every generation? Does your heart yearn
for parents or for children? Pursue God with all your being, and
search out the people of God. Whatever your situation and status as
you read this, it is your destiny to be connected with grandparents,
parents and children, whichever of the three you are, and to give and
receive healing as you form the community of God's people where
you live.

My Big Fat Greek Wedding and *Monsoon Wedding* are two films that remind us in the individualised West that this dream can be realised. Both are full of movement, colour and laughter, and portray the whole gamut of emotions belonging to the complex web of family relationships. I am privileged to be reminded of the glory of family every Sunday morning at St Aldates. As we begin the service, there is a wonderful time of holy chaos, as swarms of little children crowd onto the stage with all their helpers and teachers and the whole church sings a couple of worship songs. I confess I'm often laughing at the antics of the children rather than worshipping! Some stare into space, some scowl, some wriggle, some come dressed as a superhero or a fairy … and some sing: but if I were an angel, leaning over heaven's balustrade, I would be looking at the bride of Christ dressed to make his heart beat fast with passionate love as he sees one generation tell another.

5

Simeons and Samuels, Hannahs and Annas

Invited to Pray

*To pray is to descend with the
mind into the heart, and there to
stand before the face of the Lord,
ever-present, all-seeing, within you.*

- Henri Nouwen, *The Way of the Heart*

*I have never found anyone who
prayed as well as those who had
never been taught how. Those
who have no master in man
have one in the Holy Spirit.*

- Stuart McAlpine, *Just Asking*

Early in 2019, a little Japanese boy aged seven breathed his last after a prolonged period of undiagnosed illness. A few days before he died, one of his mother's friends wrote to us:

> For quite some time this little boy has had gastro-intestinal problems that has resulted in him not being able to eat any food. He has been admitted to the hospital several times and the doctors have not been able to figure out what is wrong. For several months now he has needed to be fed through a tube and they were planning for a bone marrow transplant but that has not materialised. We've just found out that his lungs are filled with fluids and he has been intubated. As far as we can tell, the doctors are no closer to finding out how to treat the problem. His parents are not Christians. His mum is open but his dad is not so.

Every week brings us news of children or young people losing their lives through accident, illness or violence. However, such terrible events are in one sense the tip of the iceberg. Across the nation, untold numbers of parents, many of them Christians, are also silently suffering at the disappearance of their children. These children are not physically dead, but they are dead to spiritual realities and every choice they make takes them further from the light. The less light they have, the more they risk making poor decisions as a result of impaired vision. To see young people find the way that God has prepared for them we need to understand what it means to be provoked to prayer, and respond by taking up the challenge and learning to pray with desperation and urgency.

Some of the stories that come to us through the media become famous worldwide, such as that in 2015 of the little four-year-old Alan Kurdi, whose body washed up on a Turkish beach, lost as his parents tried to flee Syria. These stories can sound a faint alarm signal in us, but they are more likely to go viral and trend than tear at our heart strings and trigger a reflex to pray. It's all too big and too far away. The sad truth is that we rarely engage in persistent prayer for those we don't know. We are more likely to be numbed. But occasionally danger comes closer.

We experienced something of the utter terror that grips one's being at the possibility that a child is missing and in danger during our time in Paris. One day I came home to our flat to be greeted by one daughter blurting out that she didn't know where one of her sisters was. The school had phoned to enquire about her absence, since the next day her A-Level art exhibition was due to be examined, but it was not even hung. Fearing the wrath of her parents (but also succumbing to the crushing sense of failure), our daughter had taken off. As the realisation dawned that I had no idea where she was, a sickening contraction seized my stomach, the same physical reaction as to the events of Samuel's death years earlier. Control had been snatched from my hands. A blinding panic invaded my senses as my vivid imagination went into overdrive. There was nothing I could do to retrieve my child. Or was there?

Coincidentally, or perhaps by a larger design, our friend John Mulinde was making one of his visits to Paris. He had been due to address the elders of the church that evening, but came instead to our house to pray with and for us since Charlie, distraught, had telephoned to cancel the meeting.

'There is only one thing you can do in a situation like this, and that is to pray,' he said in his quiet but authoritative voice. We had heard from John how the Ugandan Christians had learned to pray in situations of desperation under the reigns of Idi Amin and Milton Obote. We had heard him tell of babies bayoneted at road checkpoints and of family members disappearing; we had heard how, confronted by an anarchy and violence beyond our comprehension, they had turned to prayer. And we had heard of God's answers to their cries and of miraculous interventions that turned the nation around. We sensed that there was a power and authority in the prayers flowing out of John and his friend Enos.

We had listened to many teachings on prayer and read many books on the subject, but we learned more than all we thought we'd learned until then in that one afternoon, as we experienced being at the mercy of God, and far removed from an academic exercise. We begged and pleaded with God that he would bring our daughter home to us. We didn't think about the composition of our prayers; eloquence was the last thing on our minds. We and our other children knelt on the floor and wept uncontrollably, uttering our desperation, while the steady voices of John and Enos called out to the God they knew and trusted and had seen respond in far more tragic situations in their own country.

Suddenly the phone rang. On the other end of the line was a woman we barely knew; the sister of a friend from church. Something, she said, had made her feel she must let us know that our daughter was safe with her. Something … and the rest is history. This is one of the most arresting answers to prayer that we have ever experienced. But prayer is not simply a matter of us being given what we ask for. God calls you and me to desperate prayer, and in his wisdom he sometimes allows us to realise our dependence on him by not relieving our circumstances as quickly as we would like. We learn things about ourselves as we wait. Through this experience of the brief loss of our daughter, our eyes were opened to the inner unhappiness of her Parisian school life that we had not really sought to address; and it brought sorrow and repentance. She needed to be found, but we needed to be forgiven.

God allows our lives to take certain turns because his heart is longing for intimacy with us, and he cannot force us to give it. One of the best expressions of this truth was penned by C. S. Lewis in the timeless classic *The Screwtape Letters*. Here the senior demon, Screwtape, explains God's mysterious ways to his nephew:

> You must have often wondered why the Enemy does not make more use of His power to be sensibly present to human souls in any degree He chooses and at any moment. But you now see that the Irresistible and the Indisputable are the two weapons which the very nature of His scheme forbids Him to use. Merely to over-ride a human will (as His felt presence in any but the faintest and most mitigated degree would certainly do) would be for Him useless. He cannot ravish. He can only woo. For His ignoble idea is to eat the cake and have it; the creatures are to be one with Him, but yet themselves;

merely to cancel them, or assimilate them, will not serve…. Sooner or later He withdraws, if not in fact, at least from their conscious experience, all … supports and incentives. He leaves the creature to stand up on its own legs—to carry out from the will alone duties which have lost all relish…. He cannot 'tempt' to virtue as we do to vice. He wants them to learn to walk, and must therefore take away His hand…. Our cause is never more in danger than when a human, no longer desiring, but still intending, to do our Enemy's will, looks round upon a universe from which every trace of Him seems to have vanished, and asks why he has been forsaken, and still obeys.[1]

One of the things that discourages us in our prayer is God's apparent deafness and silence; why, if we choose to pray with perseverance and discipline, do we not see what we are seeking sooner? The answer is that God provokes us to prayer by withholding the answer, not only for the development of our character but also because the answer must fit into his timing. This is because the answer is always much bigger than we realise. When God calls our children to follow him, it will not be for themselves alone, and not simply to give them a place in heaven, but for the village they live in, or the college at which they are a student, or the workplace they will one day be in. Some of them will become leaders in the city and some leaders in the nation. Some will be prophets, some will be priests and many will be worshippers who lead the people of God into his presence.

'The eyes of the Lord range throughout the earth to strengthen those whose hearts are fully committed to him'.[2] God is always searching out those who will be steadfast in prayer for others, and who trust him in the dark. When we feel we have reached our pain threshold it's very tempting to detach from wayward sons and daughters, committing them to the mercies of God. While that is admirable, it is not enough. God is looking for a people who will engage doggedly with him even when pain has numbed desire. He is looking for a people who will press in on behalf of prodigals even though they feel utterly forsaken; who will plead with him, and who won't rest until they see the fruit of their prayers. 'I will not let you go unless you bless me,' said Jacob at a time of crisis and need.[3] I think God is calling many of us who have laid down our arms out of pain and exhaustion to pick them up again and resume our partnership of prayer with him. If this is you, struggling with loss of hope and expectation, why not take a moment now to set the book aside and make a simple confession, and ask God for his help in recovering hope and finding new strength to pray?

Setting Our Feet on the Rock

Of the four intercessors who name this chapter, I've chosen to look more closely at Hannah, whose prayer, when it was answered, would contribute to a change of course in the history of the nation of Israel. When we meet her, though, she knew nothing of this, but only the suffering of barrenness and the ignominy it brought. In Old Testament times, barrenness was considered to be a judgement from God that brought shame, and Peninnah, Hannah's rival, cruelly taunted her because of it. The story in 1 Samuel 1 relates that it was God who had closed her womb, and brought this shameful sterility upon her. The received idea that this indicated divine disfavour and therefore legitimised social reproach and mockery drove Hannah to desperate prayer for deliverance. She was literally provoked to prayer, as many of us should be, but somehow there is often a veil over our understanding, and we relinquish our determination to press on. We fall prey to the idea that this is what we deserve, and the pain of waiting slowly robs us of hope; energy drains from our spirit and our call to God grows fainter and fainter.

All of us at one time or another will need an inner strength to tackle the suffering we encounter. I don't know any parent who has been spared pain in relation to a child or children. What can we learn from the example of Hannah to set our feet on a rock when the storm rages?

First of all I believe she had a longing, and this longing was so strong that at a certain moment something inside her snapped. The text says, 'Once when they had finished eating and drinking …'[4] What happened at that meal? Was Peninnah indulging in her sport of mocking Hannah? Was Hannah devouring with her eyes Peninnah's offspring, seated around the table, noisily laughing and talking to one another? Was she observing the powerful affection between father and children? Was the painful reality that none of these lively children were the fruit of her intimacy with Elkanah burning into her more than usual? Was she reflecting on how another year had passed and here they were at Shiloh again with everyone asking for news, and she had none? Perhaps it was a mixture of all these things, but whatever it was, the key is that the longing had more power than the despair. What longings do you have, buried beneath your present circumstances?

I remember the intense longing for a son that grew in me all those years ago. It was not like Hannah's in that it was not birthed out of barrenness. But I think it came from God. At the time I had no idea that, twenty years later, I would have developed a passion for prayer and an intense longing that every generation would know God and recognise the lordship of Jesus. I had no idea how intensely I would long and pray for this in my own children.

Equally I had no idea of all that lay before us in the political and technological arenas, and of how these things would affect the next generation. Likewise, Hannah had no idea that her son would be God's instrument to identify and anoint David king and thus affect the history of her nation. She had no idea that her son would be the one to reconnect the nation with God. Despite the religious festivals, the book of Samuel records that in those days the word of the Lord was rare; there were not many visions.[5]

Secondly, Hannah was authentic. She didn't conceal her bitterness from God. She didn't apparently feel the need to clothe herself in a religious garment before approaching God. I remember a friend, many years ago, describing her feeling of unworthiness in the presence of God in the following terms: 'I skulked around the kitchen, hoping I wouldn't bump into God.' We are so often like this. The idea of earning a hearing is so deep within us. But not Hannah. In bitterness of soul she wept much and prayed to the Lord. She was not only weeping but, the text tells us twice, not eating. Was she fasting? I don't think she had planned a fast to coincide with this spiritual pilgrimage. Not only does the text not use the word fasting, but the festival they were attending was in all probability the Feast of Tabernacles, commemorating God's care for his people during the desert journey to the Promised Land, and celebrating with joy and feasting God's blessing on the year's crops. The emphasis on fruitfulness would have made the whole event even more poignantly painful for Hannah. Because it was a feast, not a fast, it is unlikely that Hannah determined to act in a way which would have drawn attention to her plight. Clearly, Peninnah upset her so much on these occasions that she was reduced to tears and lost her appetite. She lost her appetite because the subject of her torment, her childlessness, mattered to her so deeply. Her whole being cried out to God, so in a sense she *was* fasting, because her hunger for God outweighed her physical hunger.

I believe that God is calling his church, especially in the indulgent, overfed Western world, back to the spiritual discipline of fasting; back to the possibility that time in his presence to nourish our soul far outweighs the short-lived pleasure of satisfying our flesh.

Thirdly, Hannah connected emotionally. She did not try to present a clearly thought-out idea to God. She did not have a project, she just had pain and longing, and she probably couldn't have explained it if she had been asked. The text suggests that she wasn't very collected or prepared, other than in the ongoing story of her heart, and I think God is waiting for us to cross the religious boundary and pour out our hearts to him in a similar way today.

The book of Romans says that the Holy Spirit helps us in our weakness, that we do not know what we ought to pray for, but that the Spirit himself intercedes for us with groans that words cannot express.[6] Likewise the author of Hebrews tells us that during the days of Jesus' life on earth, he offered up prayers and petitions with loud cries and tears to the One who could save him from death, and he was heard because of his reverent submission.[7] These two texts show us several things. First, that being emotionally in command of ourselves is not the key to being heard by God. Second, that to abandon ourselves to God in our grief or desperation or ignorance simply gives the Holy Spirit room to help us. Third, that to pray silently or quietly is not necessarily an indication of submission. All these things add up to what the Bible calls being filled with the Spirit. Hannah was connected with God; she knew she was making contact and Eli's blessing confirmed it. E. M. Bounds writes:

> We pray not by the truth the Holy Spirit reveals to us, but we pray by the actual presence of the Holy Spirit. He puts the desire in our hearts; kindles that desire by His own flame. We simply give lip and voice and heart to His unutterable groanings.[8]

Fourthly, part of the strength of the longing within Hannah was that it freed her from the tyranny of social conventions. She would have known that it was not unusual for drunken people to enter the temple, but she was not put off by the possibility of being misunderstood. As indeed she turned out to be. Apparently she was not embarrassed by Eli's interjection, but answered calmly. Her reply, that she had not been drinking but that she was pouring out her soul to God and praying out of her great anguish and grief—in other words, that she was engaging with God about a personal situation— clearly had the authority to reassure Eli, who gave her his blessing. I have pondered those words of Eli's over and over again: 'Go in peace, and may the God of Israel grant you what you have asked of him'.[9] I am sure that as he spoke them, Hannah knew that a heavenly transaction had taken place. Eli, after all, represented God, and in the days of the Old Testament priesthood, he carried the Lord's presence as mediator of his grace. I am sure that Hannah returned home from Shiloh with a sense of peace and release to resume what had hitherto been rather fraught intimate relations with Elkanah.

How do we find this sense of peace and certainty today, now that we have personal access to God through the crucifixion of Jesus on our behalf and no longer need a mediator? I think it comes from knowing that we too have left behind social conventions and allowed the real burden of our being to be expressed in the raw. We may not hear words of blessing such as those pronounced by Eli, but we may have an epiphany as words from the Bible suddenly spring to life with meaning.

I remember this happening to me with the words that Elizabeth spoke prophetically to Mary at that wonderful meeting of the two expectant mothers, one well along in years (which might mean anything upwards of twenty-five) and the other barely a teenager: 'Blessed is she who has believed that the Lord would fulfil his promises to her'.[10] Like most, I have struggled with confidence from time to time, and I drew renewed strength from this verse transformed into neon lighting. I know the confidence issue is a big one for so many—if this speaks to you, especially if trauma or tragedy have robbed you of hope, be alert to biblical neon lights....

Fifthly, Hannah was rash. In her desperation, she made a vow. She promised that if God gave her a son she would give him back to God for his whole life. She made a vow on behalf of this child that he would be set apart for God all the days of his life. Did she realise the implications of her prayer, one of which would be that she would not see much of him once he was about three years old? In the form of prayer we use for a Dedication Service at St Aldates, there is a question to the parents: 'If God were to call [child's name] to a life of great service or sacrifice, would you gladly consent and give your blessing?'

God is looking for parents to be willing to dedicate their children to him in this way. And there are many who might hear his call to rededicate their prodigal children all over again, in the secret place of prayer. If we are reckless in trusting him with the things that matter most to us, we will be strengthened and see answers as glorious as the birth of Samuel.

Sixthly, Hannah had a secret history with God. Though everybody in her entourage obviously knew her situation and her sorrow, they were unaware of the inside story between Hannah and her God. I don't think her outburst in the temple was an isolated incident between them; I think it gives us a privileged glimpse of a well-developed relationship. After all, her suffering had a long history. I don't think she suddenly thought of the idea of vowing to give the fruit of her womb back to God; I think this was a well-rehearsed prayer.

Too often our friendship with God is aired on a Sunday, or when storm clouds are gathering, but God searches for constant rather than intermittent connection, for friendship such as he enjoyed with Moses or Abraham. The intimacy of such relationships enables the deep level of persistent, desperate prayer in times of heartache that we have seen in the story of Hannah. Today, God is still stirring up his people to rediscover this same intimacy that is birthed in our secret history. In the corporate consciousness of the church, there's a hunger for depth, and contemplative, monastic and mystic ways are being uncovered and rediscovered. Everywhere, guided retreat and Ignatian spirituality are becoming available to discover and experience. I believe these things are meeting a deep need and hunger for God.

Another significant encounter with God through prayer took place during the time when the seeds of our move to Paris were being planted. Very early in 1989, a friend had invited me to spend a weekend in Paris with her to celebrate both our birthdays. She had found a cheap deal and, having never been on a plane, decided this was the moment. I agreed, on condition that we visit a church in the east of the city that we had heard of through friends. To this day, the impact of the smells, the noise, the bustle, the colour and the sheer buzz as we emerged from the metro at the bottom of the *Rue de Belleville* remains as vivid as it was then. I took a deep breath, and exclaimed excitedly to my friend, but inside I was saying, 'Oh God, I know that I know that I know that I want to live here among these people of many nations; I know that we must come and live here.' My ribcage felt as if it would explode, so intense was the certainty that I was standing in the very arrondissement that would be my future home. Simultaneously, my friend burst out, 'How disgusting! What a horrible, dirty place … look at all the dog dirt!'

Some weeks later, driving to Chelmsford to go shopping, I came to a tree-lined part of the road that always reminded me of a French *route nationale*, and suddenly heard the words, 'You will certainly go and live in France.' It is the only occasion when I think I have heard an audible voice from God, and that incident fortified me for the interval of three years that was to elapse before we did move to Paris.

A secret history builds confidence for the storms, the desperate times and the times of waiting.

Finally, Hannah co-operated in the natural realm. In other words, she and Elkanah made love. Perhaps a new confidence took the tension out of their intimacy and all the fears previously associated with what God intends to be pleasurable and fun. This is the paradox of intensity in our dealings with God. If we allow our suffering and trials to provoke us to prayer and perseverance rather than despair, we will grow in confidence that he is for us not against us, and that we are encountering not silence but the timing and purposes of God. All the principles outlined in this book apply to every longing generated by all kinds of sterility. We may long for marriage, or for a child, or for a fruitful ministry, or for healing, or for a host of other things. We may long for reconciliation with someone, or that we might overcome a violent temper or a paralysing timidity. In each case the Father makes his wooing call that we would not give up, but grow up by choosing to persevere.

If we are thinking of urgent prayer for the next generation, provoked in our spirits by an understanding of the enemy's plan to neutralise if not destroy them, how can we co-operate in the natural realm? Rob Parsons, in his excellent book *Bringing Home the Prodigals*, challenges the church to acknowledge that there are as many prodigals inside the church as outside. His thesis is that often we have cared more about the length of their skirts, the colour of their hair or their attendance at the youth group than about their passion for the poor or their search for integrity and authenticity.

The summer after we returned to England, a friend whom we loved very much died. His funeral was one of the most moving I have ever attended. It was very informal, washed in tears, and all his children, children-in-law and grandchildren took part, even if one or two of the little ones were too overcome once on the stage in front of all those people to do what was planned. My mind went back to the uncompromising stance of liberty that these parents had granted their teenagers years earlier. Not liberty in moral or ethical areas, but freedom, for example, to dress how they pleased, as teenagers will, however crazy they looked. They had refused to constrict their children in order to win approval from others for themselves, and I remember admiring them for it. Now, in these children at their father's funeral, I saw young men and women openly living for God. Death had brought them grief, but not confusion or defeat.

Our call is to follow our children's lead in the pursuit of content rather than style, in their rejection of superficiality and search for authenticity. It is to encourage them to explore what they feel they are called to, not to manoeuvre them towards the life we wished we had lived now that we can see a bit more clearly. It is to express approval in word and gesture at every opportunity, to show them respect and to listen to them carefully. It is to give them as much freedom as we can. And this principle of withholding criticism (spoken or not … criticism has a strong smell!) and extending freedom, whoever we may be praying for, holds good. If we do these things we will know how to pray for them, and the future stored up for them in heaven will be unlocked as we allow desperation to provoke us to persevering on their behalf.

6

Slowing Down and Sweetening Up
Invited to Friendship

*It redoubleth joys, and
cutteth griefs in halves.*

- Francis Bacon, *Essays*

*I don't think that it is always
necessary to talk about the deepest
and most private dimension of who
we are, but I think we are called
to talk to each other out of it, and
just as importantly to listen to each
other out of it, to live out of our
depths as well as our shallows.*

- Michael Mayne, *This Sunrise of Wonder*

Tears streaming down my face, I painstakingly tapped out my message: 'Not coping, please pray. A'. I pressed 'send' and watched the little envelope rapidly zigzagging away to the corner of my mobile phone. Two minutes later, back came the reply: 'Am praying, will ring later, love you. J'.

That day was a Sunday, and my struggles to acclimatise to a new role in a huge church were proving overwhelming. Suddenly the thought of being on view again while my emotions were in such turmoil was all too much and, dissolving in tears, I had told Charlie that I wasn't going to church; and none too gently at that. Now, in addition to sobs wracking my body, I was feeling guilty and a failure for giving in and giving up, albeit temporarily. But as the little beep announced the arrival of a message, the knot in my stomach miraculously dissolved and relief from pain stole into my weary being.

Friendship is a divine institution, and it is God's intention that each of us has a number of people whom we count as intimate friends. Indeed the root meaning of the word intimacy has to do with deep and close friendship rather than having a sexual connotation as it tends to today. Friendship used to evolve naturally through the community-based society, but the technological revolution of the latter part of the twentieth century has hastened the dissolution of community, which in turn has brought great loneliness. Henri Nouwen captures this well in his book *Seeds of Hope*:

> What most strikes me, being back in the United
> States, is the full force of the restlessness, the lone-
> liness and the tension that holds so many people.
> The conversations I had today were about spiritual

survival. So many of my friends feel overwhelmed by
the many demands made on them ... To celebrate
life together, to be together in community, to simply
enjoy the beauty of creation, the love of people and
the goodness of God—those seem faraway ideals.[1]

I remember being told just prior to going to live in Paris in 1992
that seventy-five percent of the Parisian population lived alone, a fact
mirrored in the make-up of the church we had gone there to serve.
Many things testify to the loneliness of our culture, from the despair
that sometimes leads to suicide, to the avalanche of lonely-hearts
adverts to be found in any newspaper, periodical or magazine. Often,
a person will want to escape loneliness by finding an intimate partner,
which is why so many such advertisements announce a very desirable
person seeking a very exciting person, sometimes very explicitly. Yet
what so often underlies the search is the longing for friendship.

In times of trial, when life seems a wilderness and a struggle, the
comfort and encouragement of a friend who believes that Jesus loves
us and is with us can be the difference between pressing on to take
hold of that for which Christ Jesus took hold of me[2] or giving into
temptations that come from our exhaustion or self-pity. These can
lead us to comforting ourselves with food, alcohol, drugs or sex. A
more serious source of comfort that is contemporary is the increasingly wide practice of self-harm. For some, the external pain is more
bearable, indeed preferable, to the pain inside, and for others the
sight of blood is evidence of life and creates a feeling of reality. In
a survey of students who self-harmed, over half said it was 'important to see blood when they self-harmed, with the most common

explanation being that it helps relieve tension and induces calmness. Other explanations were that it 'makes me feel real' and shows that 'I did it right/deep enough'.[3]

Any of these false comforters can lead to slavery. And slavery, as Paul notes in Romans 7, is notoriously difficult to escape from. He describes something we are all so familiar with: being motivated to do right and finding ourselves doing the exact opposite: wrong.

Studies show that the average number of people we can relate to in a meaningful way is six to twelve intimates, twenty-four to thirty maintained friendships and up to 200 acquaintances. Today we all have far in excess of 200 acquaintances. But we often don't have many real friends. We know we can't manage the number of people we 'know', and develop different ways of handling what is in some senses an insoluble problem. We may live on adrenalin or substances, or we may neglect and eventually lose former friendships. Yet we are designed to walk through life hand in hand with our family and friends. Friends restore perspective, reassure us that we are going in the right direction, and hold us in the dark nights of our life.

Such was my experience all those years ago when Samuel died, and all colour and hope drained out of my being. Any tragedy is a bleak moment, a moment of choice, and a moment when those observing might hold their breath: this could go either way. Our friends were there for us. They were there with tears, with laughter, with tea, with wine, with their bodies to hug us and transfer warmth where there was creeping coldness. They were there with the organising of our days, with suggestions of things to do, with the gift of sending us away for those days in Carmel and looking after the girls. In short, they were there in thought, word and deed.

Biblical Friendships

The Bible has plenty to say about friendship, and a touching example of this sort of close friendship is found in the relationship between David and Jonathan. When Saul realises that the young David is far more popular than him, a jealous fury is aroused in him, and from being pleased with David, and liking him very much,[4] his jealousy provokes him to make attempts on David's life. Although Jonathan is Saul's son, his loyalties lie with David. They have entered into a covenant relationship; in other words, a friendship that nothing can destroy, based on love and mutual respect. Jonathan helps David escape from Saul, and though they can no longer enjoy each other's company, their friendship endures.

> Jonathan said to David, 'Go in peace, for we have sworn friendship with each other in the name of the Lord, saying, "The Lord is witness between you and me, and between your descendants and my descendants forever."'[5]

I think God loves lifelong friendships; he offers us this covenantal—or unbreakable—model of friendship for our welfare. But to enjoy such friendship demands our investment and nurture. And this isn't just for ourselves; close friendships are attractive to others who observe them, and can prompt the desire to find such friendships for themselves. Equally, to see a close friendship being lived out can remind us of one we may have lost through neglect or misunderstanding and ignite a determination to rectify matters.

At the same time it's important to recognise that some friendships are seasonal. Circumstances often bring one very near to people, but later they change and a relationship that was once very close may gradually fade. Many relationships are simply hung up in a Christmas card once a year, and that's the way it has to be, purely because of limited capacity. There is no fault attached. But for each of us, a few friendships survive these circumstantial changes, and indeed are strengthened by them.

Intimate friends are the ones you can say anything to. The ones to whom you can confess your failures and your fears, your hopes and your dreams. True friends are also those who have the right to confront you: 'Wounds from a friend can be trusted, but an enemy multiplies kisses'.[6]

Recently we travelled up north to visit some friends we have known for at least twenty years. It had been very difficult to arrange the trip for all sorts of reasons, but it was good to have finally made it. Soon after arriving, though, we found ourselves in what could have been a difficult conversation, revolving around the question of whether we were really committed to them, since they felt they were always having to take the initiative. Explanations and assurances followed, and we had three wonderful days together, catching up at a deep level after a long absence. We came away strengthened in our friendship and grateful to have a relationship with no no-go areas.

In her book *Between Friends*, Mary Pytches speaks about this level of transparency being crucial for any lifelong friendship, illustrating her point with stories of a deep friendship that has included many years of ministry together.[7] This might be an intimidating notion for lots of us, because we have absorbed, as if by osmosis, the cultural norm of non-interference and relativism ('you do your thing, I'll do mine'). This means that the stuff of real relationships—what the Bible calls speaking the truth in love,[8] or being honest—is rare.

Another reason for the scarcity of inspiring models of friendship is the absence of natural community in the soil of which friendship can easily flourish. We are a commuting people, and increasingly this begins with our secondary school years, so that we grow up with little expectation of forging close friendships with those in our neighbourhood by the time we embark on tertiary education or go out into the workplace. In turn this leads to ineptitude in the social skills necessary for the cultivating of friendships. I have long lost count of the number of social encounters during which we have not been asked one single question!

The opportunity to share our experiences and debrief from our work remains a vital need for every one of us, so if a vacuum is created through lack of community we will instinctively search it out elsewhere, often through social media or via online platforms, neither of which will necessarily deliver what we long for.

Coupled with the gradual disappearance of the organic generational community, a vastly increased understanding of the human psyche has given rise to several helpful disciplines that palliate the pain of loneliness. Counselling, mentoring, spiritual direction and therapy have all risen up to meet the deep and universal need to be heard and understood that friendship offers. For many of us it can be hard to find the right person to listen to our woes about our parents, our boss or our spouse, someone who will talk us down from our cliffs, restore our perspective, and offer both a challenge ('Are you over-reacting?') and wisdom. It can be hard to find someone who we can trust to keep our confessions in confidence.

Thank God for these disciplines, but let's not substitute them for friendship; rather may they co-exist with our friendships.

Almost every week of our ten years in Paris, we met with our co-pastors, a German-Swiss and French-Swiss couple. Despite the considerable cultural differences, we lived a true friendship, laughing together, crying together, questioning one another and comforting one another. It wasn't always easy, and there were misunderstandings from time to time. But all of us were committed to one another and loved one another (as we still do!) and would take the time and the pain necessary to unravel things and restore peace. Indeed we knew that in some senses our lives depended on it, for we were out of our comfort zones, with tasks that we often felt were beyond us. Perhaps it is the very availability of so many false comforts that lure us away from the effort of friendship building—for more than a decade already it has been true in the UK that 'a line of cocaine can cost as little as a cappuccino'. Little wonder then that the 'cost of a cappuccino' could seem more appealing than the cost and complexity of making a friend.

The Bible furnishes many examples of close friendship. It calls Abraham God's friend[9] and recounts God confiding his plans to Abraham: 'Shall I hide from Abraham what I am about to do?'[10] The marks of friendship here are trust, confidence and revelation; being certain of loyalty if we open our hearts is one of the highest forms of friendship, and something that encourages us (imparts courage) and builds us up (edifies us). True friendship can survive disagreement, as the Sodom and Gomorrah incident that follows this choice to confide in Abraham illustrates. God does not hide from Abraham that he is on the verge of destroying these two cities because of their wickedness. Abraham engages God in a lively debate about the conditions under which the cities might escape destruction. As the story goes on to illustrate, our friends will not always do what we want them to, supremely so if the friend in question is God. Despite the fate of Sodom and Gomorrah, Abraham clearly remained God's friend, and there are several references to him as such throughout the Bible.[11] And why would he not? God had shown him such kindness and mercy. He had shared his secret plans with him, engaged with him as a friend, rescued his family, and much more besides.[12]

Likewise, Moses is portrayed as a friend of God. Exodus 33 describes Moses going to the Tent of Meeting to speak with God. One can well imagine Moses' fluctuating emotions as he led the recalcitrant Israelites round and round the wilderness, and we know from other passages that he railed at God for ever giving him such a depressing job. But here we see the presence of God, manifested in the pillar of cloud, staying at the entrance to the tent while Moses is inside and the encounter is described as follows: 'The Lord would speak to Moses face to face, as one speaks to a friend.'[13]

There is something about eye contact. The Bible tells us that the eye is the lamp of the body, and that if our eyes are good, our whole body will be full of light, but that if our eyes are bad, our whole body will be full of darkness.[14] A straight and steady gaze inspires confidence and suggests an openness and honesty, whereas we speak of a shifty look or stare which makes us suspicious. To avoid eye contact is a common sign of something being amiss or painful. If darkness has entered our life at the hands of another, as in the case of a person who has suffered abuse, it can be signalled through our eyes.

Early on in our time in Paris, I was called out of a service to see if I could help a young girl who had been brought to church by her mother. Following a drastic attempt on her own life after experiencing abuse, she had been sectioned, but was allowed to leave the psychiatric ward which had become her home for a few hours at the weekend. Not only was Sandra avoiding eye contact, but her very eyes were invisible, covered by locks of unkempt dark hair tumbling around her face. It was the beginning of a long story and an enduring friendship. One of the signs to us all that Sandra was on the road to recovery was that she began to make eye contact again for the first time in years. In allowing us to see into her eyes, she opened herself up to a level of intimacy of which she had been so fearful when we first met. Because of the terrible abuse she had suffered, she had been adamant that she would never ever marry or have children; but time, professional and pastoral accompaniment, and above all love slowly healed her self-rejection and pain, and today Sandra is a married mother of children.

The intimacy of friendship implies knowledge; familiarity with the way a person reflects and reacts, reasons and relates. Such friends to God were the prophets of the Old Testament, men and women who were familiar with God's law and character, but also with God's pain and suffering, as he watched his chosen people repeatedly turn away from his laws and betray him. These were people who could warn of God's coming judgement, but also tell of his mercy, confident in their knowledge and understanding of his nature. Amos even makes a point of this intimacy when he says: 'Surely the Sovereign Lord does nothing without revealing his plan to his servants the prophets.'[15]

Despite this, the sad story of the Old Testament is that the exhortations and warnings of the prophets went unheeded, and we are reminded of this as we hear Jesus, hundreds of years later, lamenting over it in the temple: 'Jerusalem, Jerusalem, you who kill the prophets and stone those sent to you, how often I have longed to gather your children together, as a hen gathers her chicks under her wings, and you were not willing.'[16]

Jesus supremely modelled friendship with his disciples. Indeed the very fact that he limited himself to twelve disciples reflects the truth that intimacy is only possible with a small number of people.

During the discussion between Jesus and the disciples at the Last Supper, Jesus makes an interesting remark about friendship: 'I no longer call you servants, because a servant doesn't know his master's business. Instead, I have called you friends, for everything that I learned from my Father I have made known to you.'[17]

So friendship is about an inner circle, about inside knowledge. Here it's also about revelation; about growing in the knowledge of God. In the intimacy of a shared meal, Jesus is conveying information essential for knowing what to do when he's gone. But the content of the discussion also reveals that through the Holy Spirit, friendship with Jesus is to be the norm for every person who comes to believe in him. The Holy Spirit is the Spirit of truth, the presence of Jesus in spirit form, who will be available to every believer once the bodily Jesus has ascended to heaven following the resurrection.

Just prior to this remark about friendship being to do with opening one's heart, Jesus has identified himself in another way as their friend: 'My command is this: love each other as I have loved you. Greater love has no one than this: to lay down one's life for one's friends. You are my friends if you do what I command.'[18]

So friendship with God has to do with knowing him, obeying him and being willing to follow him anywhere, whatever the risks and cost; and by implication friendship with man also involves sacrifice.

Mike Bickle writes:

> A deeply satisfied soul, a personal sense of meaning
> and significance and a rich treasure store of divine plea-
> sure can only come through the intimate knowledge
> of God himself.... Do you desire divine satisfaction
> beyond your greatest imaginations? Then focus on
> two things: first focus on the intimate knowledge of
> God's beauty, or what God looks like (in terms of
> knowing his personality). Second focus on the knowl-
> edge of what it means to be created in his image, in
> other words what we look like to God in Christ....
> Imagine, the beauty Jesus possesses is the very beauty
> he imparts to his bride in the gift of righteousness.[19]

Our ability to demonstrate real friendship on earth is related to the
quality and depth of our relationship and friendship with our heavenly
Father. How well do we know him? How well do we know his Word?
How well do we know how he thinks? What his plans and purposes are?
What he thinks about men and women? What he thinks about creation?
What the meaning of stewardship is? What the Bible tells us about
death? About heaven? The questions are endless, for God is infinite, his
judgements are unsearchable, and his paths beyond tracing out.[20]

Not long ago, I sensed a renewed challenge from God: How well
do you know my Word? How familiar are you, after nearly thirty
years of being my disciple, with the Bible? How confident are you in
handling it? How quickly can you find a story, a proverb, a saying,
a prophecy that comes to mind? Since that time I have redoubled

my efforts to become intimate with the Bible. Not with my favourite passages, but with the whole counsel of God. The more I read, study and meditate, the more I am intrigued by the unfathomable yet approachable God whom I love, who made himself accessible through his long, lingering love letter, and the greater grows my hunger to be more familiar every year with this living book, unique in being three-dimensional. In my best moments I long so much to know God better. I believe that to have a secret history with God is the surest route to wisdom and maturity, and the best qualification for being a good friend to those God has given me to love.

Passion and love are caught more than taught and you get them from being around such people. Much of my passion for God, to know and meditate on God's Word, has come through my long years of association with many men and women I have greatly admired because of their own friendship with God.

There are too many to name, but as a young woman, I was drawn by the perfume of many of these people. Not Gucci, Guerlain, Givenchy or Chanel, but Jesus. I couldn't get enough of their company and took every opportunity to listen to them, ask questions and soak up their wisdom; wisdom I knew found its source in the intimacy they enjoyed with God.

'We are to God the pleasing aroma of Christ,'[21] says Paul. Even if we are broken. 'We were under great pressure, far beyond our ability to endure, so that we despaired of life itself. Indeed, we felt we had received the sentence of death.'[22] If you identify with this, know that God is still with you as he was with Paul; your brokenness doesn't disqualify you from serving him. Rather, God will deliver you and delight in you, as he did Paul.

'What a friend we have in Jesus' goes the old hymn. And he is the greatest of all friends. The ups and downs, the joys and sorrows of my life and its most intimate moments are all recorded in dozens of journals stretching back over all the years since I met Jesus. It's one way of opening my life to him. I once told my son they would make really interesting reading for him and our other children one day: but not, I added hastily, before I turn up my toes!

I've been talking about friendship between people and friendship with God. While marriage is temporal, friendship is eternal, making it a true and vital treasure. Why not take this opportunity to do a kind of audit of your friendships? Are there those who really may be seasonal friends, but you keep feeling you should initiate contact after a long gap? Does it sometimes feel more like a duty than a joy? Or have you swept what might be an offence or a misunderstanding under the carpet because it feels too complicated to address the unspoken tension? Maybe you need to write to someone, or call or message them (a card is way better than an electronic message for my money, but up to you of course!). I think you have friends who love you and your company, and God is calling you to be the friend he has made you to be. Please remember that whatever grief has come to you, and whatever trials have befallen you, you are lovable. Yes, you are; so can I persuade you to refresh your friendships as needed and above all to ratchet up your friendship with God? Get into his word and get his word into you. Oh, and go and buy that journal!

A Church for All Nations

Invited to Join the Global Church

Let him who cannot be alone beware of community....
Let him who is not in community beware of being
alone.... Each by itself has profound perils and
pitfalls. One who wants fellowship without solitude
plunges into the void of words and feelings, and the
one who seeks solitude without fellowship perishes in
the abyss of vanity, self-infatuation and despair.

- Dietrich Bonhoeffer, *Life Together*

The Hebrew word hesed expresses two things:
fidelity and tenderness. In our civilisation we can
be tender but unfaithful, and faithful without
tenderness. The love of God is both tenderness and
fidelity. Our world is waiting for communities
of tenderness and fidelity. They are coming.

- Jean Vanier, *Community and Growth*

I remember receiving a card out of the blue from Jiang Hong many months after our return from France, and the surge of affection as I read her news. Jiang Hong first came to our attention when we prayed for her at the end of a service in the Eglise Réformée de France church, the *Temple de Belleville,* where we lived and worked for ten years in inner-city Paris. It was our custom then, as it still is now, to offer prayer after the service nearly every week. There wasn't much room to move if a lot of people took us up on our offer, so one could sometimes meet people rather up close and personal! This was how I came face to face with a tear-stained Jiang Hong. She had come to say, 'Yes, I want to commit myself to whatever God wants for me, wherever he will lead me.' Like so many we met in those heady days, she was sensitive to God's call on her life.

We came to know Jiang Hong well, and she opened the door to an exciting friendship with the Chinese church that met in our premises every Sunday afternoon, since she was the only language link between them and us. Despite her origins, she remained a faithful member of the 'church for all nations', as we nicknamed the *Temple de Belleville,* throughout our time in Paris. Like so many, she was an illustration of the nations flocking to the cities, and one of the things we loved so deeply about Belleville was the family of at least thirty-five nations that we represented together. By the time we left, there were a dozen mixed-race marriages, most of whom had presented the church with a child, thus creating an even more exotic colour scheme for this family that we were so proud to belong to. The church is a people and a body to which it is part of our life's purpose to belong, and the perfect forum for creating friendships. That it is our calling as followers of Christ to mix with all nations is clear from the book of Revelation:

> After this I looked, and there before me was a great
> multitude that no one could count, from every
> nation, tribe, people and language, standing before
> the throne and before the Lamb.[1]

The apostle John is describing his vision, given to him on the island of Patmos where he was exiled towards the end of his life. The vision came to him on the Lord's Day while he was in the Spirit. What does this mean? It means that he was in prayer and that he had connected with heaven. Like Stephen and Paul before him and like multitudes down the centuries after him, heaven was open to him and he was instructed to record his vision initially for seven churches in Asia Minor, and thus for posterity.[2]

The church is a unique body of people in many respects. It is, as has been said, the only club that exists for the benefit of its non-members. It is the only forum on earth where bonds of love and friendship can successfully unite individuals who are diverse in every respect other than their common commitment to and love of Jesus Christ. It is the Holy Grail that the human spirit searches for in terms of proving the unparalleled nature of love as incarnated by Jesus. There is no other place on Earth that exhibits the fruit of reconciliation so conclusively, or the nature of true brotherhood and community so powerfully.

History records hundreds of illustrations of this from the founding of the early church in the book of Acts to the birth of the Pentecostal church at the dawn of the twentieth century. One of the most exhilarating examples of co-operation and mutual submission is the coming together of the Fijian church leaders in recognition of their need of one another in the wake of the 2000 uprising. Laying aside their differences, they came together in prayer and saw extraordinary answers: an abating of violence, their prime minister openly confessing his faith and reliance on God, and many coming to Christ.[3]

In contrast, what do we see as we look around the world? A never-ending sequence of tribal hostilities, often resulting in open conflict, if not outright war, is played out before us. Tribes are not necessarily familial or even national: they can be religious, political, ideological, elitist, sectarian or ethical.

Patrick Dixon, in his book *Futurewise*, throws out a challenge to be prepared for what the future will bring us, in a world

> which is being transformed before our eyes from an emerging industrial revolution and a technological post-war society into something altogether new and different. This millennium will witness the greatest challenges to human survival in human history, and many of them will face us in the early years of its first century. It will also provide us with science and technology beyond our greatest imaginings, and the greatest shift in values for over fifty years.[4]

He identifies six faces of the future, one of which is tribalism. There have been countless negative expressions of tribalism, many within our lifetime: we saw ethnic cleansing during the Second World War, and decades later in Bosnia, Kosovo, Rwanda and Uganda; then in the opening years of the new millennium, we watched helplessly as the Janjaweed forces in the Darfur region of the Sudan ruthlessly committed genocide. Our sensibilities have continued to be steadily anaesthetised by mass killings of different kinds and dimensions all around the world, including gun massacres in the US.

Territory and racism lie at the root of tribalism, demonstrating the profoundly acquisitive and prejudiced nature of humankind.

Dixon argues, however, that tribalism is 'an immensely positive force':

> Tribalism is the basis of all family, team and belong-
> ing. Tribalism provides a sense of identity. Tribalism
> helps us understand who we are, where we've come
> from and where we're headed.... Without tribes
> there is no geography in our relationships because
> there are no groups, just atomised collections of
> isolated individuals relating equally to everyone.
> Therefore if you want to understand the forces on
> someone's life, their motivation, the basis of their
> values and decisions, you need first to understand
> the person's own tribal culture.[5]

So tribalism carries both negative and positive forces. Competition and conflict have been rooted in the human psyche since the time of Cain and Abel, yet as Dixon says tribalism helps us understand one another. How can we reconcile these two attributes?

Jesus' amazing counter-cultural statement: 'If anyone would come after me, let him deny himself and take up his cross daily and follow me. For whoever would save his life will lose it, but whoever loses his life for my sake will save it,'[6] is a key. If we learn to do this we will find that instead of experiencing envy and hostility towards those of other tribes, we are gradually able to come to understand them. We will no longer feel threatened by them.

It's by choosing to follow the one who loved all people impartially and equally, and still does today, that we can reconcile tribalism's harms with its benefits.

In John's revelation of heaven we read that he saw 'a great multitude that no one could count, from every nation, tribe, people and language …'[7] No matter what our tribal origins, when we choose to follow Jesus we are welcomed into a new tribe. Now we are members of Christ's family, which gives us a new identity, and creates our primary tribal loyalty.

Now together with other tribes, and in the context of the other tribes to which we belong—the workplace, the multinational corporation, the ethnic group, the blood family and so on—we can become 'the aroma of the knowledge of him everywhere'.[8]

Living in a global village has meant that the nations have come to the nations—in many nations, cities and churches have become multi-ethnic, and this in turn has created the opportunity to discover the works of God in the nations at first hand from immigrants, and also to enjoy the spiritual blessings of international cross-fertilisation. At the same time, those whose work takes them to other nations bring home stories of what they have seen God doing. These stories can revive our faith and encourage us when we are flagging or weighed down by our personal and local cares and concerns.

In 1999 we travelled to Brazil to visit Shalom, the group of churches planted and developed over some thirty years by our friends

Harry and Elaine Scates. We first met Harry in 1997 when he was on an expedition to Europe as a Brazilian missionary (he had taken Brazilian nationality). He came with a Brazilian organisation called Go To The Nations! Some hundred Brazilians, ranging from a teen-age girl to a politician in his fifties, gathered in Manchester, in the UK, from where they set off in small groups to spend a week or so in different European capitals, one of which was Paris. During the planning stages of all this, I had felt stirred to undertake the admin-istration of the Parisian visitation, perhaps sensing an important cross-fertilisation to be imminent.

And so it was that I went to greet this collection of total strang-ers at the Gare du Nord. Each day of their visit we listened to tales of God's Spirit poured out in Brazil; tales of churches growing, of many giving their lives to Christ, of children being filled with a spirit of prayer, and testimonies of how individual lives were completely turned around and transformed from despair to hope. One of these was Jose Maria, an adoptive spiritual son to Harry, just as Timothy and Titus were to Paul, now planting a church in France. This real illustration brought the stories to life, encouraging our faith as we listened.

Two years later we were seeing the Shalom churches for our-selves. Travelling up to Uberlândia in the heart of Brazil where Harry and Elaine live, we stopped for a night at the town of Ribeira da Prata where we attended the Shalom Sunday evening service. I'll never forget it. The worship was exuberant, excited and high vol-ume; there were costumed dancers who created an amazing visual show of movement and colour; but the high point for me was the moment when they called for a time of praying for the nations. In a crowd movement that would have greatly alarmed any average English churchgoer, we were swept to the stage area, invited to pray for whatever nation we wanted to. Each nation was represented by its national flag, flags being a standard part of the equipment for many Brazilian churches!

We made straight for the French flag and began to pour out our hearts to the Lord for the nation he had called us to so clearly in 1992. I found myself weeping almost immediately, able to release lots of the pain I had accumulated through the inevitable highs and lows of life, framed for me by building church in a foreign country. The Brazilians are a noisy crowd—they have been described by some as the world's troubadours, and they are certainly dynamically creative in the realm of the arts—and with them I felt quite uninhibited in expressing my longings for the church in Belleville, in Paris, in France. But the real snapshot in my memory album was when they wrapped us in the huge flag, and *they* began to weep over us and for us.

The rest of our trip continued to unfold the riches of the Brazilian church. We were there to teach a marriage seminar, but I remain convinced that we learned far more than we taught. We drank in their amazing hospitality, as they often gathered after church for a long, late and uproarious evening meal, or took us to experience the unforgettable *churrascaria* restaurant at which an array of different meats were offered and then cooked on mobile grills around the table. We loved their wonderfully eventful services, with every generation seemingly happily integrated; we were moved by the passionate prayer uttered with tears by young children; and we were impressed by their work among the poor through the orphanage established and run by the church.

The list was endless and we returned invigorated to Paris, where we soon purchased a set of international flags, which were cleverly installed by Jean-Claude, our quixotic handyman (whose principal work was leading the youth department of the Paris YWAM[9]) for whom no task suggested by Charlie was beyond his ability or inventiveness. He was a true illustration of the dictum that where there's a will there's a way! The church in all nations was making us a church for all nations.

Elsewhere I have described the uplifting experience of walking on Prayer Mountain near Kampala. In our days of companionship with John Mulinde, we accompanied him to an annual prayer conference, AfriCamp, part of which took place on Prayer Mountain. The contributors spoke more loudly than we are used to, but they also spoke with authority and grace, somehow releasing courage in the listener despite the culturally alien yet somehow exciting presentation. With the typical reserve of the British, I may have been alarmed or exhausted by the experience of praying at such a volume that I couldn't hear myself, let alone the others in my group; or repulsed by the body odours of those pressed up against me in the crowd; yet I couldn't help being energised and inspired, and to this day I think it was an important contribution to my prayer life.

In yet another expression of the global body of Christ, one of my most colourful memories is of a celebration following a marriage conference we had taught in the north of Togo in West Africa. As dawn stole across the sky, and we heard the familiar creaking of the well as it was cranked into action outside our window, we heard the bleating of a goat as it was led protesting to the slaughter and knew we were hearing the last cries of our lunch! Hours later the celebration was under way and began with a renewal of vows ceremony for the participating couples. How moving it was to watch the primary-educated men with their mostly analphabetic wives share a common covenant with us from whom they were so different. Next, Joseph, who with his wife oversaw the Community Health Programme, took the stage in order to hand out twenty condoms to each couple, cheerfully emphasising that they were for single use. All this to the accompaniment of riotous laughter and cheering. Catching each other's eyes, Charlie and I mutually acknowledged a fascinating moment as this indigenous programme sought to improve the health and quality of life for couples, many of whom struggled to care for large families. To us it spoke of mercy and the kingdom of God. Then it was time to celebrate with a feast of goat stew, cooked to a turn by the female kitchen crew in a corner of the compound.

Towards the end of our time in Paris, the relationship with the Chinese church that had begun with the arrival of Jiang Hong had developed to the point of a visit to their home provinces being earnestly requested by the leaders of the church. The church was affiliated to a denomination with churches in many parts of the world, but principally in China and in Hong Kong where the headquarters are situated. So a trip was arranged, and Jiang Hong, Jean-Claude and Benedicte, the much-loved church secretary, who had been involved with Open Doors for many years, set off. Back they came, armed with photos and stories, and poured inspiration and faith into the family at home.

As a church family we were affected and inspired by different aspects of the global church of Jesus in each country: the faith and development of the Togolese church, the extraordinary corporate prayer life of the Ugandans, and the courage and bravery of the Chinese.

More recently, we have been privileged to meet and listen to Brother Yun, nicknamed The Heavenly Man. This nickname forms the title of the book that describes Yun's pilgrimage through persecution and torture following his conversion to Christ. Yun is a courageous and outspoken evangelist, who continues to bring many to faith, and as such became the nemesis of the authorities. The name Heavenly Man stemmed from an incident in 1984 when Brother Yun refused to reveal his real identity to the authorities knowing it would compromise and endanger his fellow Christians. In response to threats and beatings from the Public Security Bureau to disclose his name and address, he shouted, 'I am a heavenly man! My home is in heaven!' Hearing this, his friends, the local believers, were able to flee and escape arrest.[10]

Yun was captivating; he seemed to overflow with love, and I found myself struggling to comprehend the ability to undergo so much suffering and yet be so full of praise for God. In no way do I have any tribal affinity with such a godly man, with the crucial exception of our common faith in Jesus, his so much stronger than mine, and seemingly etched in the lines of his compelling face. One of God's purposes in calling us to belong to the international church is of course to challenge us where we are lazy or apathetic, undisciplined or self-centred. Men and women from around the world who have followed Jesus' injunction to take up their cross and lose their lives will confront us with areas of our lives where we are indulging ourselves or compromising our faith. They will bring sharply into focus the real work of God in and with his church and they will stimulate and goad us to return to our first love, to remember our first flush of love for Christ.

It is your calling and mine to belong to the church for all nations and the church in all nations. I think God wants us to know that he is inexorably fulfilling his plans and purposes throughout the earth, and wants us to continually broaden our comprehension of how he is doing it. We will discover this by reading, listening to and meeting our brothers and sisters from other nations and cultures. We won't discover it by reading media reports of the church in decline …

New Models of Church

At this point it's important to acknowledge that here in the West, many Millennials and Gen Y-ers are leaving church in its traditional forms. Online communities such as Nomad[11] are being birthed as (mostly) younger people throw off the shackles of formality and also, it must be admitted, empire building, frustrated by organised religion. This reflects the internet world of social media and purchasing that we all now inhabit whether we want to or not, but it also reflects a complete rejection of anything that appears power-based, or that is exposed as abusive in any way.

Set against such a background we should not be surprised that gathering God's people in a building at a prescribed time to be led through a scripted programme by an approved authority figure often no longer seems relevant, and will not satisfy everyone. Particularly those who were born into the world of technology.

Generation Z (born in or since 1995) are different again. Millennials were considered the first 'global' generation with the development of the internet, but the global nature of Gen Z's thinking, interactions and relatability (yes ... a new word!) has quickly exceeded theirs. Thanks to apps like Snapchat and Vine they process things faster than previous generations. They have short attention spans, are adept multitaskers, and are entrepreneurial, many aspiring to start their own businesses. While Millennials remember playing solitaire, coming home to dial-up internet and using AOL, Gen Z was born into a world overrun with technology, and what were taken as amazing and inspiring inventions not long ago are now a given for teens. They expect loyalty and efficiency from businesses, brands and retailers: 'If they don't feel appreciated, they will move on. It's not about them being loyal to the business.'[12] They are big on individuality and uniqueness, arguably—and ironically!—as a result of the celebrities and media they follow, and already 91 percent of them have a digital footprint.

If church is to be attractive, those who serve her communities need to be aware of the impact rapidly expanding and developing technology makes on those whose lives are often defined by it. We shouldn't be surprised or dismayed that new forms of church community, made possible by these advances, should spring up.

Whether the body of Christ takes the form of an online community, a group of people gathering in a home, a pub or a café, or a larger community meeting in a traditional church building or a rented venue, these well-worn words remain profoundly true: it's not about the style, it's about the content. It's about devotion to Jesus Christ.

There is nothing like the local church when it's working right. Its beauty is indescribable. Its power is breathtaking. Its potential is unlimited. It comforts the grieving and heals the broken in the context of community. It builds bridges to seekers and offers truth to the confused. It provides resources for those in need and opens its arms to the forgotten, the downtrodden, the disillusioned. It breaks the chains of addictions, frees the oppressed, and offers belonging to the marginalized of this world. Whatever the capacity for human suffering, the church has a greater capacity for healing and wholeness.

Still to this day, the potential of the local church is almost more than I can grasp. No other organization on earth is like the church. Nothing even comes close.[13]

8

All You Need Is Love
The Greatest Invitation

Love seeketh not itself to please,
Nor for itself hath any care;
But for another gives its ease,
And builds a heaven in Hell's despair.

- William Blake, *Songs of Innocence*

I desired often to know what was our Lord's
meaning … and I was answered in inward
understanding, saying, 'Would you know your
Lord's meaning in this? Learn it well. Love was
his meaning. Who showed it to you? Love. What
did he show you? Why did he show you? For love.
Hold fast to this and you shall learn and know
more about love, but you will never need to know
or understand about anything else for ever.'

- Julian of Norwich, *Revelations of Divine Love*

As a child I used to dream that one day I would hold audiences captive by playing a piano while dancing on the keys and singing! I think this vision may have been triggered by seeing Picasso's 'Circus Acrobat'. I longed with all my being to be a performer, an artist with gifts that merited being displayed. By the time I was wading in the shallows of adulthood, I knew this vision was eluding me, and somewhere in the recesses of my subconscious I knew that it would always elude me. Reality was never going to meet the fantasy. At the same time, life's path had led me among artists of every description. My boyfriend's family and many of their entourage were wonderfully bohemian, many were actors and artists, and he himself was an amateur but talented actor. Oxford days were spent in a dizzy whirl among writers and poets, actors and producers. I was hungry to learn and yearned to be on a par with any one of them, throwing myself into any opportunity that presented itself.

Then I split up with the boyfriend, moved to another city and encountered God (a story I come to at the end of this book). Once again, I found myself in an artistic milieu, invited to participate in open-air sketches on a beach mission. Once again, my appetite was whetted, my ambitions were fanned into flame and my hopes reawakened.

But one day, alone in my room, I came face to face with my limitations, and confronted them. By now, daily dialogue with my heavenly Father was the norm and I poured out my heart and my tears as I acknowledged that no one was ever going to exclaim about my talent or write about my amazing gifts! Of course I came to understand that peace doesn't come from the affirmation of others, and that gifts and talents come in a thousand forms, but at the time it was painful as

I struggled to come to terms with the fate of being born without the aptitudes and talents I so longed to have. It was an important reality checkpoint. I wrote a long letter about all this, to someone who had become a close friend during my months of searching to make sense of God, and who had answered many of my questions about faith, Jesus and the Christian hope. In it I poured out my sense of inadequacy and my feelings of insecurity.

Not long afterwards he wrote back; a twelve-page letter that I still have. It contained such wisdom, encouragement and consolation, and made such a significant contribution to my being able to press on and escape from the binding feelings of hopelessness and failure, that it must necessarily become a treasure.

This is some of what he wrote:

> This is what God says to those caught on that particular fork: 'I will bend it into my cross and you shall carry it and learn from me. You will be weighed in the scales of the world and found wanting, but your achievement will last when all this world and its scales have vanished into oblivion, for your work will be the work of love. You will not work with the shape of things that perish, but with the shape of people, destined for eternity. My greatest achievement is not the making of this world, though all men, including many who do not obey me, praise me for this; my greatest achievement is in the shaping of your soul. Work then with me to shape the souls of others,

and from this very day your achievement will be
recorded in the book of life.'

Famously above everything else, Paul says:

> If I speak in the tongues of men or of angels, but
> do not have love, I am only a resounding gong or a
> clanging cymbal. If I have the gift of prophecy and
> can fathom all mysteries and all knowledge, and if
> I have a faith that can move mountains, but do not
> have love, I am nothing. If I give all I possess to the
> poor, and give over my body to hardship that I may
> boast, but do not have love, I gain nothing.[1]

It is not our doctrine that will draw men to God, nor our style of
worship, nor even our response to the poor. Behind all these lies a key
without which they are but a resounding gong or a clanging cymbal.

John says that the proof of loving God is that we love one
another: indeed he emphasises that to be in any way deficient in
love towards our fellow man annuls any claim we might make to be
a lover of God, because God is love. And Jesus said that it's by the
love we show one another that all men would know that we are his
disciples. I once challenged a fellow teacher with this truth, because
each day in the staffroom she would give vent to her resentment
and criticism of other members of staff who were not present. My
audacity unleashed a torrent of anger, and I shudder to think what
came over me. No doubt she thought I was a little upstart; and I was.
I was in my probationary year of teaching and, although I was filled

with the fire of the newly converted (and no doubt a good dose of self-righteousness), my cause was not helped by the fact that I still smoked, and used to cadge a cigarette off this very woman most days, having stopped buying them as a strategy for giving up!

Men, women and children are thirsty for love because they are created to give and receive love. 'The hunger for love is much more difficult to remove than the hunger for bread,' said Mother Teresa, who was perhaps uniquely qualified to make such a statement. She also said that the success of loving lies not in its fruit but in the loving itself.

Of course a person may be a loving artist of one kind or another, and the friend who wrote me that saving letter is a case in point as a gifted writer. All the same, many are the artists who have trodden a tortured path where love and its expression are concerned. So often the success granted to the gifted is the very thing that frustrates their search for love. Boris Becker, the famous tennis star of the '80s and '90s, said, 'I had everything, from flights on Concorde to the best hotels. Everything but love. And I was very lonely.' And others, from a singer like Freddie Mercury to a painter like van Gogh, have admitted to this same desperate lack, whether in words or in tragic deeds.

In the universal quest for love, artists take their place alongside every working person in every sphere of life, be they plumber, professor, police officer or physician. Where then is love to be found? I think it is found in the disposition of a man or woman who has discovered something of the real presence of God; not God as a benefactor, but God as a Father, God as perfect lover of their soul. Such were many of the mystics, who lingered over their communion with God. Thérèse de Lisieux, Julian of Norwich, St John of the Cross, and much more recently, Henri Nouwen, Jean Vanier, Thomas Merton ... they all knew about this.

> I was at the most dangerous time of life for young girls, but God did for me what Ezekiel recounts: Passing by me, Jesus saw that I was ripe for love. He plighted his troth to me and I became his. He threw his cloak about me, washed me with water and anointed me with oil, clothed me with fine linen and silk and decked me with bracelets and priceless gems. He fed me on wheat and honey and oil and I had matchless beauty and He made me a queen. Jesus did all that for me. Jesus did all that for me.[2]

Something so intimate could never be born of head knowledge. Lest we should think this to be an exclusively female response to God, listen to Brother Lawrence, the seventeenth-century monastery chef:

> The King, full of mercy and goodness, very far from chastising me, embraces me with love, makes me eat at His table, serves me with His own hands, gives me the key of His treasures. He converses and delights Himself with me incessantly.[3]

And to Jim Elliot, the missionary martyr of the 1950s:

> Oh the fullness, pleasure, sheer excitement of knowing God on Earth! I care not if I never raise my voice

again for Him, if only I may love Him, please Him. Mayhap, in mercy, He shall give me a host of children that I may lead through the vast star fields to explore His delicacies whose fingers' ends set them to burning. But if not, if only I may see Him, smell His garments, and smile into my Lover's eyes, ah, then, not stars, nor children, shall matter—only Himself.[4]

Count Ludwig van Zinzendorf, born in 1700, has been called by historians the rich young ruler who said yes. He was born into one of the great families in Europe and destined for the Emperor's court, but he gave it all up and instead spent his great fortune on carrying the gospel to the ends of the earth through the Moravian church for whom he was a leader and provider. Why? Because he met the risen Christ:

> While completing his tour of the great European cities, Zinzendorf visited an art museum in Dusseldorf. There he happened upon Domenico Feti's Ecce Homo, Behold the Man, a striking portrait of Jesus crowned with thorns. The inscription read, 'I have done this for you. What have you done for me?' The Count was stunned. 'I have loved him for so long,' mused the young nobleman, 'but I have not really done anything for him.' Standing before the portrait, Zinzendorf made a commitment that would become the compelling focus for the rest of his life. 'From now on I will do whatever he leads me to do,' he vowed.[5]

He taught unity and lived it, loving and befriending Lutherans, Moravians, Pietists, Puritans, Anabaptists and Catholics. He would never judge a man by his doctrinal or denominational affiliation, but by the content of his heart.

Such individuals have a magnetic attraction that draws one as a lamp draws a moth. While a moth is often literally consumed in the flame, we will find the sharp edges of our characters undeniably honed in the company of such saints, for there is something of the presence of God in them that compels us at once to seek them out and subdue our passions. People like this have yielded to the hunger for God that is written into the human soul, but that for many is suppressed or suffocated. They have sought intimacy with God and paid a price for it. They have chosen the knowledge of God over knowledge of the world.

And they leave a legendary legacy. Part of Zinzendorf's legacy is Pete Greig, the 'bewildered founder' of the 24/7 Prayer Movement, as he calls himself, and arguably one of the most influential spiritual leaders of our times. So too was Paula Bonhoeffer, a disciple of Zinzendorf, and her son Dietrich who used his 'texts' (daily devotionals) throughout his life.

Like Thomas à Kempis, and like the apostle Paul, such people have understood that the highest of ambitions is to live in the imitation of Christ. Today there is a recovery of the yearning for God's presence and company as it is expressed in Psalm 63: 'You, God, are my God, earnestly I seek you; I thirst for you, my whole being longs for you, in a dry and parched land where there is no water.'[6]

It is this yearning that is at the root of all revivals. It's a yearning illuminated by the revelation and confession of our shortcomings in the light of the glory of God. It could be cautiously likened to the disciples' experience at the transfiguration.[7] A recent, though flawed, example of revival-like phenomena was the Toronto Blessing of 1994. I believe it sprang from a genuine hunger for God, but it seemed to lack the dimension of repentance[8] that is a hallmark of any true revival, instead becoming more focused on personal blessing than the desire to see 'Thy kingdom come on earth as it is in heaven.' In this it reflected the individualism of the postmodern world. Less widely publicised was a similar season centred on the Burgundian town of Macon, also in 1994. In both these and other examples, normal religious procedure and ritual were found wanting, business-as-usual spirituality overtaken by an outpouring of response to God. Fascinatingly, again in 1994, our own church, St Aldates, travelled through a revival-like season which did include significant expressions of repentance, and many tears.

However, all these examples, and indeed every historical revival, have involved a combination of the true and the false, and given rise to heated debate. The tares have grown with the wheat, feathers have been ruffled and the guardians of doctrine have snatched up their concordances and their commentaries. Many foolish controversies have arisen and many have been distracted by absurd and ill-advised arguments. It seems that the presence of God is often accompanied by a certain chaos, but this is only to be expected if we consider that every folly, greed and selfishness is laid bare in the burning light of his gaze. But the mess of so-called revivals also reflects the ease with which we can get caught up in the desire to make things happen which will reflect well on us. I have watched streamed prophetic prayer gatherings at which imminent revival was repeatedly prophesied; these are the false prophesies referred to in Jeremiah.[9] There are voices raised at the moment calling for the UK to repent of turning away from God, and to halt the humanist direction of travel in our legislation. But we can't make large-scale repentance happen; only God can orchestrate such a thing by his Spirit. You and I can only ask him to birth repentance within ourselves.

Love Builds Up

I remember years ago visiting St Aldates, long before we ever dreamt of coming to work there, and hearing the late Michael Green preach a passionate gospel message. The church was excitingly crowded, and in the middle of his sermon a young man shouted out a challenge: 'How do you know that leading someone to Christ is the greatest of all experiences, it can't be better than sex?' (For Michael had indeed had the temerity to make such a claim, typically daring and dangerous, not to mention potentially self-disclosing.) There was an electric silence as the assembled company waited to see how Michael would extricate himself. And this he did, with boldness and confidence! If we choose relationship over religion, and we can say with confidence, 'I know Jesus,' we will not be threatened by challenges that spring from cultural norms, in the mouths or pens of those who know nothing of this sweet communion.

The point of this cameo is that the shout of the young man, appearing at first like a witty challenge, was really a heart cry. For so many the yearning for intimacy and tenderness, expressed through sexual experience, has not been met. The inner void remains, growing more painful with every disappointment, but so does the heart cry; and the call to those of us who have really found mercy and met Jesus is to love those like that young man.

As with Mother Teresa, a love affair with God must necessarily issue forth in works of love, for all that we receive we want only to give away. And to fall in love with God will lead us to turn our Western value system upside down and be drawn to the poor.

Heidi and Rolland Baker are unusual missionaries: they have degrees in systematic theology and have worked for years in Mozambique with illiterate pastors who raise people from the dead but don't speak in tongues![10] Heidi is also an unusual and discomforting conference speaker: she will often fall to her knees on a platform, hold long silences, and speak from her kneeling position, overwhelmed by the presence of God. If all our checking systems slam into place as we read of this curiosity, how much more will we question if we see it? I know, because I've done just this. Yet in fact we are displaying nothing other than the reaction of the Pharisees every time Jesus showed his power, either through healing or through breaking religious laws or tradition. Real love is at once threatening and overwhelming, but it is what we are called to if we are going to live the life God intends for us, and it will certainly earn us foes as well as friends, criticism as well as praise. Why are we so surprised? After all, Jesus said:

> Count yourselves blessed every time people put
> you down or throw you out or speak lies about you
> to discredit me. What it means is that the truth is
> too close for comfort and they are uncomfortable.
> You can be glad when that happens—give a cheer,

even!—for though they don't like it, *I* do! And all
heaven applauds. And know that you are in good
company. My prophets and witnesses have always
gotten into this kind of trouble.[11]

All of this challenges our Western mindset and outlook. We are
taught to acquire, to collect, to take and to multiply, whether the
object be education, possessions, money or knowledge. One of the
most magnetic truths about Jesus is his reversal of all this. If you
want to come with me, he says, you'll be on the road, or lodging
with my friends, for I own no home.[12] Later, an anonymous person
identified only as a 'rich young ruler' asks him, 'How do you get
eternal life?' Well, replies Jesus, you need to sell all your possessions
and give the proceeds to the poor, then your wealth will be in heaven.
'Ouch!' said the young man, and went away.[13] And we say 'Ouch!'
too … Yet paradoxically, the ruler went away sad. He was rich but his
wealth couldn't give him joy or meaning. Perhaps this explains why
we so often read of wealthy people in great pain.

Knowledge, said Paul, puffs up, but love builds up.[14] This from a
man who had an impeccable educational pedigree as far as the Jewish
authorities were concerned.[15] But he had discovered something that
went beyond the normal heights of achievement. He had been
caught up to paradise, and heard inexpressible things that a man is
not permitted to tell—in the sense that he cannot tell, because no
human language is adequate to tell such things—and it had changed
his life.[16] It had made him ready to bear anything in order to communicate Christ and see the yearnings of people like that young man
in St Aldates met.

Paul endured beatings, imprisonment, riots, hard work, sleepless nights and hunger. He endured dishonour, bad report, being considered a fraud and misunderstanding.[17] Why? Why would a man who had so much to gain be prepared to stake his reputation on preaching Jesus Christ? How could a man of his stature, humanly speaking, write to the Philippian church that he would prefer to die and be with Christ, and that if he did it would be much better than being in prison, as he currently is? He is there for no crime other than having had the audacity to be very outspoken about Jesus in front of the Roman authorities. The attraction of being dead rather than imprisoned certainly wasn't because conditions in the prison were unbearable. The end of the book of Acts tells us he was allowed to live by himself with a soldier to guard him, that he welcomed all who came to see him and that the leaders of the Jews came in large numbers to a pre-arranged meeting with him.[18] No. Paul had seen heaven open and it had changed the course of his life; he now lived only to talk about Jesus and be an agent of his power; and Paul's presence and exhortations in the canon of Scripture are a call to us to be imitators of him. In a sense we all need a Damascus road experience because capturing the heart of Jesus is a matter of revelation not reason, as the stories of Nicodemus, Gamaliel, Paul and Peter, to name but a few, testify.

My father took a decision with my mother, when I was about fifteen, to go and serve a school in Uganda. For four years my siblings and I spent our holidays there. Although the majority of our time was spent in the company of the expatriate community, a love for the place and the people somehow lodged in my being and deepened the calling to love all people equally. Many years later, I would come to understand those years as part of God's design for my life.

The first real opportunity I had to live out this conviction came during our years in Paris, living in the cosmopolitan 19th arrondissement, which seethed with humanity from all the corners of the globe. Walking down the *Rue de Belleville*, the main arterial road leading to the centre of the city, was like taking a stroll through the nations. People originating from China, Cambodia, Vietnam, Afghanistan, the Ivory Coast, Burkina Faso, the DRC, Mali, Togo, Benin, Algeria, Morocco and Tunisia mingled with members of the significant Jewish community (after the United States, Paris boasts the largest Jewish community outside Israel), and the numerous West Indians who come to Paris from the francophone islands that form part of the French colonies. Europe was there too, Polish and Russian alongside Portuguese and British. Even the Americans came to Belleville!

And the poor walked the streets, and begged as they do in every city of every nation. Marina lived in the old and dilapidated block of flats next to our ugly 1960s block. Behind the crumbling façade of No. 1 lay a rather beautiful if unkempt garden, where its inhabitants hung their washing and enjoyed communal barbecues in the summer months. Here Marina often roamed, shrieking in her deep and hoarse voice.

I began by approaching her in the street, only to be rebuffed as she turned away. It was my first lesson in understanding that the poor are seldom grateful for one's interventions. But I persisted through the years, inviting her into my kitchen for a coffee one day, taking clothes to her (which she declined since she was shortly going to collect her own from another planet!), visiting the dingy, dirty and chaotic apartment that she shared with her sister and teenage niece, and engaging in what approximated to a conversation as often as I could. Marina's mind had long been shot by a combination of abuse, traumatic experiences and electrotherapy, the latter during a period of psychiatric treatment. One day she disappeared, and I never saw her again or discovered what happened.

Loving the poor is really hard. You can't do it with a return in mind. We can't do it with building our church in mind. At least not in the way we often interpret what that means. I think though that every loving approach to the broken, whatever the visible outcome or fruit, may be counted in heaven as building the church, despite us not seeing another bottom on another seat on Sunday.

In Belleville it was impossible to shut your eyes to the poor. They lay beneath our windows at night; they knocked at our door with amazing stories of just needing a hundred francs to feed their little children until their money came through; they roamed the streets, challenging our lifestyle by their very presence; they came into our church with their dogs and their incontinence and their overpowering odours; and they daily threw down the challenge: Do you know what love means? They taught us that love is not an equation. I love, therefore I am loved. No. I love, therefore I am reviled and ridiculed; I am taken for a ride. The poor can be wily as well as winsome.

One Sunday, when Charlie was away, I was called to the back of the church to talk to a young man who said he longed to find God again and change the existence life had dealt him through circumstance and foolish decisions. He had decided to come to the church regularly, and had dug out his Bible from among his possessions. However, first he needed to go to Grenoble to his dying mother, so could we help him with the fare? Together with one of the elders we talked for some time, seeking to discern whether this was genuine or not. He repeatedly and earnestly promised he would repay the loan.

Finally persuaded, I accompanied him up the road to the cashpoint outside our bank and withdrew the 300 francs needed. It was as I put the money into his hand that I realised in an instant that I would never see either him or it again and began to berate myself internally for my stupidity. The poor can be brilliant thespians.

Opposite our house in Oxford, a world away from the noise and confusion of Belleville, is a fitness centre, and opposite our kitchen window, some three or four metres away, is the outlet of the extraction fan that heats and air conditions the centre. Here the homeless gather in winter to keep warm, and sometimes sleep. God, it seems, did not consider our move a reason to become immune to the call to love the poor! We live in the ongoing discomfort of that challenge.

To love the poor is not the extent of our mandate. We are called to love the rich, the arrogant, the hard-hearted, the powerful and the intellectual. We're called to pour out of ourselves a continuous overflow of God's love. So it stands to reason that only those who have an inflow of that same love could possibly pour it out. If an individual can be full of love, so can a church. What is the church but the assembly of all those who have had the amazing privilege of encountering Jesus and submitting their lives to him, nailing their colours to the mast and deciding to be his disciple?

Where those who are called to lead—in other words to serve—the church have understood this upside-down nature of love, you will find expressions of community that take your breath away; not only because there is a captivating beauty about the gathered people but because there is a perfume arising from them. The first time Charlie and I encountered this was shortly after discovering Jesus as a reality, during a spell at St Michael-le-Belfry in York, under the leadership of David Watson, one of the giants of the evangelical church in the heyday of renewal. For the first time we saw colour, movement, noise, tears, laughter, healing, faith, energy, dancing, vision, preaching, worship and prayer all bound up and expressed in the life of a community drawn from all walks of life and from every generation.

The second time was in very different circumstances. We were washing around in the aftermath of the emotional vortex that caught us like a tornado after the death of Samuel. Every day there was a knock at the door, which revealed upon opening it a pie, a casserole or a dish in the lovingly extended arms of someone belonging to the church of which we were temporarily members for our three months in California. Another lesson: you don't have to know everyone in the church for the whole thing to work and be a source of love. They brought us more than pies in those weeks.

We may talk a great deal about things like purpose and gifting, and get distracted into believing that it's all about us and our career; these things are important, but they are just the structure in which what we are born for is shaped; your gifts and career are the water filling the stone jar, and you are the wine into which Jesus transforms it.[19]

Many years ago, my father-in-law gave us a picture he had made. It is of a simple phrase immortalised by Augustine, framed and beautifully decorated: *ama et fac quod vis*. 'Love and do as you please'. Augustine understood that to love means to love God, for if we don't, we cannot truly love. It is only by truly loving God that we can truly love others, and thus be safely free to do as we please.

So I say to you wherever you find yourself today as you consider the question of destiny: *ama et fac quod vis*!

A Reformation of Manners

Called to Social Justice

I believe that we are not real social workers. We may be doing social work in the eyes of the people. But we are really contemplatives in the heart of the world. For we are touching the Body of Christ twenty-four hours.... There is so much suffering, so much hatred, so much misery, and we with our prayer, with our sacrifice, are beginning at home. Love begins at home, and it is not how much we do, but how much love we put in the action that we do.... How much we do to Him in the person that we are serving.

- Mother Teresa, *Nobel Lecture*

For I was hungry and you gave me something to eat, I was thirsty and you gave me something to drink, I was a stranger and you invited me in, I needed clothes and you clothed me, I was sick and you looked after me, I was in prison and you came to visit me.

- Matthew 25:35–36

One of the best loved chapters in the Bible is Isaiah 58. It is loved in spite of, or perhaps because of, the fact that it is a goad to the church. 'My people seem keen to know my ways, and seek me out as if they were those who understood how to act righteously, and hadn't turned their backs on my commands,' says God, through the lips of Isaiah; lips which, we might remember, have been touched with a live coal from the altar of the temple which Isaiah saw in a vision when he heard the call to serve God as a prophet. So we can trust that his words are reliable.

Often when our motives or behaviour are questioned, our reflex is to become defensive and assume that the questioner is missing some information or hasn't understood. Here the Israelites are offended because after all they are fulfilling all the religious requirements, even fasting. And goodness knows that fasting is demanding enough and a sure proof of godliness…. No, apparently not. Abstaining from food can appear spiritual but be selfishly motivated. Apparently, we need to loose the chains of injustice, set the oppressed free, release people from anything that restricts their movement, share our food with the hungry, give shelter to the homeless, provide clothes for those who are in rags, look after our own family, pass righteous laws that are fair and equitable, and do away with gossip and backbiting. Oh, and we should observe the Sabbath and make provision for rest and worship in our schedule. This is what God understands by fasting. Then and then only will the Lord answer when we call. Then and then only will we feel God's guiding hand, and live in peace.

There have always been men and women who have spent themselves fighting for justice and equality. Perhaps most universally famous is William Wilberforce who devoted himself to abolishing slavery in the nineteenth century. Yet we know that the passing of a law, though it may bring brief respite, cannot eradicate deceit and greed from the heart of man, nor his lust for power. Today there are more victims of slavery than in all the years prior to Wilberforce's Slavery Abolition Act of 1833: those who work in the sweatshops for the insatiable demands of the fashion industry; those who are captured to swell fighting armies and those who are trafficked for prostitution. The majority of these are women and children.

In Paris I would often take the Metro at our local station, *Pyrenees*, and get off three stops up at *Telegraphe* to visit my friend Christine at the church she and her husband, David, had planted some ten years earlier. The innards of any city are both surprisingly beautiful and dirty, dark and dangerous. In eastern Paris, doors could open to reveal breathtakingly beautiful gardens festooned with oriental trees, exotic plants and dazzling flowers, but they could also reveal misery. Walking up the alley to the church, I passed some large rooms. The windows of one of these were blacked out and through the small gap afforded by the door often being left ajar, presumably for air, I could see the curious combination of materials in every colour of the rainbow brilliantly draping the space, and the drab little figures that punctuated the colour as they hunched over their sewing machines. There were other sweatshops nearer our home, just yards from the Belleville church.

Slavery has many guises. Young girls seeking adventure and travel become au pairs, expecting an agreeable if hardworking experience. Instead many find themselves enslaved or forced to become sex workers. More distressing still is the trafficking of children for prostitution. How have we become so used to these facts that they no longer send shock waves through us when we read and hear stories about it?

Here's a typical such story: In January 2005 the national news carried the story of a sixteen-year-old from Lithuania who entrusted herself to an organisation that promised a job and freedom in the UK. Instead she found herself working in a brothel in Hounslow. Once she was no longer contactable, her mobile phone having run out of money, her family's suspicions were aroused and they contacted the British police, who tracked her down and organised her return home. She was a lucky one. Or was she? What sort of scars were left after even a short period of serving men with her body? Older men, whose dreams have faded or been broken and who carry unbearable sorrow or revenge in their souls, are often those who buy sex. Will she ever be able to trust a man enough to set up a permanent partnership with him? So often one abuse leads to another and the wounded seek healing where it cannot be found.

There are thousands of stories of missing children and young women and men, and only very few of them have this kind of happy ending, though many agencies such as the International Justice Mission, A21 and Stop the Traffik[1] make significant inroads into the human trafficking trade.

Another form of slavery thrives on war. Far beyond the frontiers of Europe, boys as young as ten or twelve are regularly kidnapped by the Janjaweed soldiers in the Darfur area of the Sudan or by the Lord's Resistance Army (LRA) in the north of Uganda. In both cases these children are taken as troops to boost the numbers of fighting forces; in both cases they are made to fight their own people.

The collective Western conscience is vaguely disturbed by all these things, but not enough to prioritise in such a way that they are definitively ended. After all, most of it happens a long way away.

In 2003 we met the Bishop of Kitgum in northern Uganda, close to the area where the LRA operates. A couple of months later Margaret, his wife, wrote to me:

> Two weeks ago, over ten people were killed in a camp near my village and about a month ago over 190 people were killed in Lira. Just about a week ago the government crossed into Sudan to attempt another Iron Fist operation to try and get the LRA out of Sudan. They have managed to get them out and into Uganda, Acholi land of which Kitgum is inclusive [sic]. Normally when the rebels cross like this the atrocity they do is terrible ... people are without hope because they are imagining that if the few rebels who remained ... can do mass killings like they did in Lira ... what will happen when they are many? Sister, the situation needs nothing but prayers.

Several months later the bishop himself was taken prisoner, but released unharmed. He and Margaret have chosen to stay with their people despite the danger, but have sent their children to school in Kampala. They are a couple who know the meaning of both calling and sacrifice. Many of those who cause them to live this knife-edge existence are themselves prisoners to those who have forced them to fight.

War and slavery feed off each other, both breeding poverty, and much of Margaret's letter was outlining simple projects which could alleviate the bleak conditions endured throughout their area.

> We have 44 pastors in the diocese ... they are
> really in great need. They are living with the dis-
> placed people in camps without salaries because
> the people are in abject poverty and cannot man-
> age to pay them. They come to beg for money
> from us who do not even have anything to offer
> them.

She was asking for financial aid to buy five grinding machines, one for each region so that maize distributed by the World Food Programme could be ground and sold to create a little income for food and schooling.

Perhaps our reaction is to think that giving money just plasters over the cracks; and indeed to some extent that is true. But close your eyes for a moment, and imagine life without a supermarket within easy reach; without a bank card; without those things which you consider important to access easily. If you live in a rural area so that your access, though easy, may take time, try to imagine what it would feel like to be afraid because the journey is dangerous.

If we pray 'Thy kingdom come, on earth as it is in heaven', our lives must include finding a way to help loose the chains of injustice, untie the cords of the yoke and set the oppressed free. It must include sharing our food with the hungry and providing the poor wanderer with shelter. It must include clothing the naked and spending ourselves on behalf of the hungry.[2] Whatever way we can.

Let's look back at some of those who have risen to this challenge.

Wilberforce, Butler, Ellis and Esther

William Wilberforce became the leader of the abolition movement
under William Pitt the Younger in 1787. Two years later he made a
speech that the newspapers praised as being one of the most eloquent
ever to have been heard in the House. One reported that, 'The gallery
of the House of Commons was crowded with Liverpool Merchants;
who hung their heads in sorrow—for the African occupation of bolts
and chains is no more.' But it was a premature announcement, for
not until 1807 did Parliament vote overwhelmingly in favour of
abolishing the slave trade, and even then slavery remained a reality
in the British colonies. Another twenty-six years were to pass before
slavery itself was abolished through the Slavery Abolition Act of
1833, a mere three days before the great Wilberforce died, having
truly laid down his life for his brothers and done what he was created
to do.

Josephine Butler was another nineteenth-century reformer
whose heart propelled her into destiny.

> Josephine was encouraged by her father, not only
> to think for herself, but also to believe it was her
> Christian duty to improve the lot of the people in
> her orbit. She couldn't help but contrast her own
> comfortable, protected life with the appalling pov-
> erty and deprivation to be found elsewhere ... At
> one point it filled her with doubts about the exis-
> tence of a loving God. How could there be such
> huge inequalities? Why did God allow his creatures

to suffer or tolerate such blatant abuses of power?
Why was his church so uncaring and ineffectual?[3]

Josephine went on to fight for twenty years for the repeal of the
Contagious Diseases Acts of the 1860s. These gave the police the
power to subject any lone woman suspected of prostitution to a brutal internal examination to check for signs of venereal disease. The
physical consequences of this were multiple, including miscarriage
or permanent internal damage causing sterility, not to mention the
emotional effects. Meeting destitute girls in a Liverpool workhouse,
whose only source of income was prostitution, convinced her that they
were not wicked and licentious, but the victims of circumstance and
of predatory men.

Josephine Butler became a great and courageous crusader on
behalf of such women, openly challenging the responsibility of men
towards them and sacrificing much time with her family; but she
was also beautiful, and had to endure much heckling, crude abuse
and innuendo when she spoke in public. Her husband, George,
had released and encouraged her in her calling, yet they had to
endure rumours of a failing marriage and obscene drawings of her
sent through the post. They also had to bear long separations as she
travelled the country to make known her cause. Not until 1833 did
she hear the reading of a bill to repeal discriminatory Acts, from the
Ladies' Gallery of the House of Commons, at 1.30 a.m.

Deeply moved, she went out onto the terrace overlooking the
Thames.

> The fog had cleared away and it was very calm under the starlit sky. All the bustle of the city was stilled and the only sound was that of the dark water lapping against the buttresses of the broad stone terrace ... it almost seemed like a dream.[4]

One of the most remarkable things about Josephine Butler was that all this took place following the tragic death of her little girl Eva, an adored daughter born to her and George after three sons. The accident took place at home when the child, rushing to greet them on their return, fell through the collapsing banisters to her death. Josephine's story is magnificently inspiring, although it's also daunting in a way. 'I could never find that sort of strength and courage,' we think. But if you have been stopped in your tracks by tragedy like me, these sorts of stories can help us reach for hope that recovery is possible, and remind us that our calling can't be cancelled by circumstance.

Many of my own forebears were Quakers, and worthy of mention are James and Mary Ellis, who retired in 1848 from a successful worsted manufacturing business in Bradford to move to Letterfrack in Connemara. They were deeply distressed by reports of the famine in Ireland, and the relief work they set up was an individual response to try to alleviate the terrible poverty and starvation caused during the famine. The many letters written by Mary reveal the frightening deprivation of this time; she describes the conditions they found on a visit soon after their arrival. The cabin they entered was,

... about nine feet by six, with no furniture ... but
a little stool, about six inches high ... so down we
sat against the wall, and close to our feet, two of the
gentlest little bairns, about three and four years old,
with their feet almost in a little bit of the fire.[5]

She describes their meal of cockles and then the family's story of
misfortune:

... six years ago they had two cows and were doing
well, when the famine came; one cow went after
another, the last for £2 10s. Then her husband fell
ill and never since have they had food enough to
eat. But the semi-nudity! The three poor little creatures had each a strip of woollen rag stitched upon
them, but all in strips, not covering either a limb or
any side of their body, yet they were all children one
could love well ... They had lessened their cabin
this last week to sell two sticks for sixpence. There
are two little skeletons in another cabin, I think too
far gone to be restored.[6]

The Ellises lived in Letterfrack from 1849 to 1857, and accomplished much that has long outlived them. Having built a family
home, James began by employing eighty men to drain the bog land,
plant thousands of trees and construct walls, gardens and roads. Next
came a school/meeting house, dispensary, shop and temperance hall,

along with cottages for his employees. Mary visited the poor, distributing money to urgent cases of distress from a private fund.

Today Letterfrack is a thriving community and, 150 years later,
the schoolhouse still stands as a legacy of the Ellises' commitment
to it. Connemara West is a college linked with Galway University
where students train in practical crafts such as furniture-making, and
behind the imposing buildings one enters the National Connemara
Park and its visitor centre which tells the Ellis story. On holiday with
my parents in 2004, we met the principal and were given a tour of
the college. What a testimony to the lasting fruit borne by people
who grasped hold of their destiny through allowing compassion to
give birth to action!

Like history, the pages of the Bible are liberally scattered with
such noble people. We can think of Esther, a humble girl who was
plucked from obscurity to become one of the greatest of Jewish hero-
ines. Unlike many, her family had remained in Persia after most Jews
had returned from their exile to Jerusalem. An orphan, we first meet
her cooped up in a harem of young virgins from among whom the
capricious king will choose a queen to replace Vashti, rejected for failing to obey his every whim. Esther is judged pleasing to the king and
begins a life as queen. Some years later, her uncle, who has brought
her up *in loco parentis*, reveals to Esther his discovery of a plot to
exterminate all Jews; a plot instigated by the most senior politician in
the land, Haman. A crisis of this magnitude demands a response, and
Mordecai asks Esther to appeal to the king. Approaching the king
without being summoned risked the death penalty, but Mordecai is
firm. 'Don't think you're special enough to be spared if our people

are destroyed,' he tells her. 'In any case if you don't intervene on our behalf, someone will....'[7]

What a moment of choice for this young girl, until now a submissive and acquiescent character who had always sought to please, whether it be Mordecai, Hegai the chief eunuch, or the king himself. She could so easily have declined the request, fearing for her life. But instead, a new Esther seems to rise up; an Esther ready to risk everything; position, status, reputation, and even her life. She asks Mordecai to call a fast and participates in it with her maids. At the end of the three days she is received by the king, despite the contravention of protocol, and the story of the salvation of the Jews steadily unfolds from thereon.

Common to all these people, biblical and historical, is selflessness; they are ready to give everything up for the sake of justice and righteousness. 'If there is a right place for us, I think my chief desire is that we may be in it, even if it be in exile.'[8]

Nor do they seek fame; '… we have no inclination to be published. As long as we live in the remembrance of our friends, and under the protecting care and approbation of the Best of Friends, we do not care how obscurely we pass on.'[9] They are not so much asking: what is your will for my individual life, with its inevitable subtext of wanting to be special; but more: what is your will and what is my part in it? Of course, each individual is uniquely handcrafted, and so to be special is a given. The question is how we will seek to employ whatever makes us special in favour of others; that is to truly live out our calling and purpose.

Many are the saints and heroes who have done what they were created to do. Some, like Wilberforce and Josephine Butler, are well known, but many, like the Ellises, are virtually unknown. We can conjure many names to mind: The Earl of Shaftesbury, perhaps the best-loved benefactor and politician of the nineteenth century, whose tireless compassionate work on behalf of the poor and oppressed earned him the affectionate title of 'The Poor Man's Earl'; Florence Nightingale; Bishop Hannington; David Livingstone; the roll-call is long.

In our own times, the procession continues. Martyrs, politicians and ordinary people, made extra-ordinary by their response to a call from deep within, make up this royal procession that winds its stately way through the pages of our history. I leave you to contemplate your own heroes.

Interestingly, all these men and women had a deep faith in God; of James Ellis it was written: '... his life showed that Christianity was, with him, a living principle, and we believe it may be truly said that "he feared God and hated covetousness"'.[10] During Wilberforce's early years in Parliament, 'he did not involve himself at first with any great cause. A sudden conversion to evangelical Christianity in 1785 changed that and from then onwards he approached politics from a position of strict Christian morality.'[11] Of Josephine Butler it is written: 'Her belief in a loving God simply would not let her remain silent in the face of such injustice.'[12] This despite the moments of doubt she had experienced.

Doers of the Word

Poverty and injustice abound in the far-off lands of the developing world but they dwell much closer to home as well. We have all encountered the homeless in our cities, and when we do, how do we react? Do we walk by on the other side like the priest and the Levite, or do we stop and talk like the Samaritan?[13] Are we in too much of a hurry to stop today? Are we put off when we discover that the poor are not always overwhelmed with gratitude when we intervene on their behalf? That they might shout abuse at us, fail to keep an appointment or lie?

It's challenging to examine our hearts for what attitudes lie dormant there. Justice for the poor and endangered, the fatherless and the orphans is one of the great golden threads of the Bible. To omit compassion, and its translation, into some action on behalf of the poor, is to forgo fully living out our true destiny. The Bible says that he who oppresses the poor shows contempt for their Maker, but whoever is kind to the needy honours God.[14] Elsewhere it tells us: '… faith by itself, if it is not accompanied by action, is dead'; and: 'Do not merely listen to the word, and so deceive yourselves. Do what it says.'[15]

During our years in Paris, I discovered that my heart was a stony place. To my shame, my heart was full of fear and resentment about the poor. They didn't shape up when we helped them! They stole our blankets, they urinated at our front door and at our garage door (which became so corroded that it had to be replaced!); they smuggled alcohol into the Christmas party, and urinated there in the church too; and they shouted at the person who was preaching. So what? So … my heart was revealed to be seriously wanting. This last person (who shouted at Charlie as he preached) was an Angolan, who had seen his own family felled by gunfire in his homeland. Somehow, he had made his way to France, and turned to alcohol to treat the pain. He told us his name was 'le docteur Zaza', and perhaps, before pain drove him mad, he had indeed been a teacher as he claimed. He would sit quietly at the back of the church, but erupt unpredictably into a heart-rending plea, as he stumbled down the central aisle: 'Papa! Papa! Papa Charlie, je vous aime!' An interruption to a service? But this means the service will end late! Oh, but how we grew to love him, and our stony hearts slowly grew soft; towards him and towards the many poor whom we encountered.

When adults are poor, children are too. In 2017 'there were approximately 36.9 million people worldwide living with HIV/AIDS.... Of these, 1.8 million were children (<15 years old)'.[16] In the world's poorest countries, 1 in 4 children are child labourers.[17] 'Among the world's migrants are nearly 20 million refugees—some 10 million of whom are children—who have been forcibly displaced from their own countries.'[18] 'There are up to 150 million street children in the world today'.[19]

We live in a global age. No longer can we plead ignorance as a reason for apathy. Poverty, plague, slavery and war are not happening by accident, and they demand a response.

Many agencies exist to respond; the catchphrase 'Think globally, act locally' was never better illustrated than by the launching at the beginning of 2005 of the Make Poverty History campaign. This was a coalition of more than 120 organisations, joining in a massive, concerted effort to tackle world poverty. The campaign called on world leaders to pursue fair trade, cancel unpayable debts and provide more and better aid. The monthly debt repayment of many nations in the developing world exceeds what they receive as aid, so some of the wealthiest and most powerful nations were beginning to think globally and act locally.

Another arena urgently requiring reform today is the environment, for the relentless abuse of our ecosystems by the wealthy nations is also inextricably linked to poverty. Poor communities inevitably put their surrounding environment under stress. In turn that stress impacts negatively on the lives of those communities, producing a vicious cycle. Nothing illustrates the link between the environment and poverty more starkly than the catastrophic tsunami of December 2004, which has been followed by further devastating tsunamis, cyclones and hurricanes since. The amplification of suffering in the wake of these disasters comes about because poverty forces people to live in areas that are highly dangerous to life. Thanks to corruption, often itself the child of poverty, planning restrictions are ignored. This leads to natural coastal defences, such as coral reefs and mangrove forests, being destroyed to make way for densely crowded and poorly constructed dwellings, such as those we saw swept away like a million matchsticks all those years ago on Boxing Day.

The environment is very much the issue of the moment, yet radical action is low on government agendas, and despite the 2015 Paris Agreement, powerful voices deny the reality of global warming.[20]

Climate change is also low on the majority of church agendas, for green issues have traditionally been left to secular evangelists. But not completely. The Christian global conservation movement A Rocha—the Rock—was born in southern Portugal in 1983. Over thirty years on, it has established active projects in twenty nations and is gathering momentum as growing numbers of people wake up to the environmental crisis.[21]

And now the children are rising up in protest about the world they will inherit from us. In 2018, Greta Thunberg, then fifteen, started the first school strike for climate control outside the Swedish parliament. Since then she has given a TED talk, addressed the UN Climate Change Conference and the World Economic Forum in Davos, and continues to pop up periodically in the limelight. Like Malala before her, she has quickly become a household name and hero.

Her actions have sparked a global protest movement of school strikes about climate change. In March 2019, children from 2,233 cities and towns in 128 countries walked out of school to protest. She is a hero to other children, such as Levi Draheim from Florida, at eleven the youngest of twenty-one plaintiffs in a lawsuit against the US government, an action launched in 2015 by Our Children's Trust and Earth Guardians. He lives just thirteen feet above sea level and is acutely aware of the effects of global warming.

Poverty, plague, slavery and war demand a response from governments, NGOs and the church, but they demand a response from you and me too. The very best way to think globally and act locally is to ask, 'What can I do today?' What relief agencies and missions does your church support? What provision for the poor has been made in your town? Does the need exceed the provision? Could you be involved in helping with an existing project or setting something up?

During our first year at St Aldates, about a dozen different people brought Isaiah 58 to our notice, each one saying in his or her own way that they felt drawn to reaching the poor in Oxford. More than this they felt that there was a call from God to make sure the walls of our newly refurbished church didn't send a message of 'we're all right in here,' but were permeable, with doors open to welcome everyone. It's so easy for a church building to shut people out.

In 2005, ignited by a social worker who was a member of the church at the time, the ministry of ACT![22] was founded, and has grown and evolved to become an on-the-ground compassionate service to the marginalised which has gained the respect and support of the city and its council. ACT! includes housing ex-offenders; offering discipleship care; and operates a much-expanded prison visiting programme, taking in the four prisons in the area. Currently, a call and vision for providing care and relief for marginalised women is being considered as those involved dream and scheme about how to turn vision into reality.

All these things use up hours of prayer and thought and longing and planning. None of them has been birthed without struggle and often tears. But all of them carry intense joy with them too. Loosing the chains of injustice is part of our destiny, but a costly part. Jesus said that greater love could not be shown than by laying down our lives for our friends; he referred to himself, but he was also giving us a mandate.

Patrick Macdonald is one young man who has recognised and responded to this mandate. Himself fatherless from the age of twelve, Patrick's world was turned upside down when, at seventeen, he met individual homeless children on the streets of Bogota, Columbia. The impact this made on him was so great that he returned to England vowing to pour his life into the relief of children at risk. Twenty-five years later, Viva Network, founded by Patrick in 1994, is a flourishing and ever-expanding organisation that seeks to link agencies working on behalf of children worldwide. In Patrick's words, 'We are essentially a network of networks … Viva could be called The International Association of Evangelical Work Among

Children in Need, and our aim is to link Christians working with such children around the world.'[23]

It all began with one child who broke Patrick's heart; one child, with a life and a calling of which he would in all probability be robbed. And it is with this awe of each life being crafted together in the womb of his or her mother that we must all begin. Statistics, so plentiful today, will blunt our compassion as they overwhelm us, but the face of a single child looking into our eyes will keep it alive.

You and I may think we can't do much, but too often that stops us doing anything. A smile and a kind word are better than nothing, and if our hearts are set on the pursuit of justice, we may be surprised by how far we are taken. To what extent are you or I free to rub shoulders with those whose existence is rough and difficult; who have lost their children, partner or spouse; who live with a history of abuse or violence or illness or addiction? Or have we somehow created a cocoon that shields us from anything too sad or shameful? I've come to believe that unless we make contact with the poor and deprived in even the simplest way, we won't become who God created us to be.

Time to put the book down again and ask God about all this. Perhaps you hear his winsome voice calling you to show his love to the poor, and join the nineteenth-century Reformers, the twentieth-century heroes and the justice-seekers at the dawn of the twenty-first century?

God's Retirement Plan Is Out of This World

The Appeal of Heaven

There have been times when I think we do not desire heaven, but more often I find myself wondering whether, in our heart of hearts, we have ever desired anything else.

- C. S. Lewis, *The Problem of Pain*

I believe there is nothing more needed by humanity today ... than the recovery of a sense of 'beyond-ness' in the whole of life to revive the springs of wonder and adoration.

- John V Taylor, *The Go-Between God*

There's an old story that does the preaching rounds: heaven is where the food is French, the police are English, the love is Italian, and it's all organised by the Swiss; hell is where the food is English, the police are French, the love is Swiss, and it's all organised by the Italians. I don't think our caricatures of one another will be that simply enshrined for eternity!

Nor do I think the fancies of the cleric and great wit Sydney Smith will necessarily be indulged: 'My idea of heaven is, eating pâté de foie gras to the sound of trumpets.'[1] Nor yet do I think it will be where we finally get our own way as some other wit has said: 'Heaven: A place where the wicked cease from troubling you with talk of their personal affairs, and the good listen with attention while you expound your own.' My first brush with heaven was when I waved goodbye so prematurely to Samuel, though I waved not with peace or confidence but with a raging heart.

> Do not go gentle into that good night,
> Rage, rage against the dying of the light.[2]

Dylan Thomas wrote these words with the impending death of his father, and raged for old men, wise men, good men, wild men and grave men. I raged for an infant who would never become a man. Something I theoretically believed in drew close, unpalatably close, and some thinking had to be done when the storm subsided.

Many writers and divines have expressed themselves on this subject, each articulating in his or her own way longings and feelings that in the end are perhaps inexpressible, for none of us knows much about the subject after all. C. S. Lewis writes the following:

All the things that have ever deeply possessed your soul have been but hints of it—tantalising glimpses, promises never quite fulfilled, echoes that died away just as they caught your ear. But if it should really become manifest—if there ever came an echo that did not die away but swelled into the sound itself— you would know it. Beyond all possibility of doubt you would say, 'Here is the thing I was made for.' We cannot tell each other about it. It is the secret signature of each soul, the incommunicable and unappeasable want, the thing we desired before we met our wives or made our friends or chose our work, and which we shall still desire on our deathbeds, when the mind no longer knows wife or friend or work. While we are, this is. If we lose this, we lose all.[3]

Of necessity the majority of what we can say about heaven has to be gleaned from apprehensions; and since man began to write he has sought to capture those apprehensions, be he poet, philosopher or theologian.

We shall rest and we shall see, we shall see and we shall love, we shall love and we shall pray, in the end which is no end.[4]

Bring us, O Lord God, at our last awakening into the house and gate of heaven … where there shall be no darkness or dazzling, but one equal light, no

noise nor silence but one equal music. No fears nor
hopes but one equal possession, no ends nor begin-
nings, but one equal eternity…[5]

One thing we do know heaven will be is the constant presence
of Jesus more fully known:

Christ is the desire of nations, the joy of angels, the
delight of the Father. What solace then must that
soul be filled with that hath the possession of him
to all eternity.[6]

There are others who have visions of an open heaven, like
Handel, whose vision inspired the writing of the 'Hallelujah Chorus'
at the end of *The Messiah*. 'I did think I did see all heaven before
me and the great God Himself'.[7] The outstanding twentieth-century
evangelist extraordinaire Michael Green requested the 'Hallelujah
Chorus' to be played as he died, and again at his funeral, for he was
one who understood the reality of heaven and was ready to go there.

And there are many who testify to having glimpsed or visited
heaven during a near-death experience. Some such stories are fanci-
ful, some are more thought-provoking, some are arresting, but in any
case, no indisputable view of heaven can be constructed from such
accounts since they are so subjective and personal.

One account that made an impact on us is that of Prossy Mulinde,
who became John's wife until she died in 2000 … for the second time.
Yes, that's right! Here's the story as recounted by John one day as we
sat in the lunch bar of a P&O ferry, crossing from Dover to Calais; the

contrast between our drab surroundings and John's evocation of the brilliance of heaven created an unforgettable memory.

In 1988, John, and a team which included Prossy, were conducting an evangelistic campaign, praying much and knocking on doors; not altogether welcomed by the communities in Uganda where they were working. They had been reminded by one of their number that God was far more interested in their availability than their activity. One night as they spent themselves in prayer for several hours, someone found Prossy, bent over in prayer, leaning against the wall; but she was stone cold. She had not moved for a long time. Slowly it dawned on the company that she had died, and with the terrible realisation some began to wail and scream, responding to death in the conventional way. John pleaded with them to be quiet, fearing the noise would aggravate the people of the area. But they also knew they would be accused of killing her, so their prayers for her to come back to life were fired with extra passion. It was now nearing midnight. The hours passed with unabated pleading, but Prossy remained motionless and cold. As dawn began to steal across the sky they realised they would need to report her death, and so laid out the body in preparation for medical and legal inspection. No one in the group wanted or dared to undertake this, and in desperation John cried out from the depths of his being for the help of the Lord. His eyes were closed as he pleaded with his God.

Suddenly his body jolted as Prossy rose in a single movement from where she had been immobile for eight hours and fell into his outstretched arms. Her lips were moving weakly and, in shock and amazement, the group saw that she was alive. They brought her some water and after a time she whispered, 'I have received a grace from the Lord.' They were the only words she uttered for a week. She was twenty-one, and in the December of that year she and John were married, for John had come to a certainty that she was to be his wife in the very instant that he caught her risen body. For many years she would not speak of the experience, except to repeat that God had given her a grace. From this time on she consistently communicated the need for unity, and when she addressed the leaders of the church at a troubled time, they spent twelve hours at a stretch with her, sensing the very presence of God—they seemed rooted to the place, each dealing deeply in their hearts with God and utterly oblivious to his neighbour. Several came into full-time ministry at the church as a result of that day.

Prossy and John had four children, as well as adopting a street child and parenting the two children born to Prossy during her teenage years; years of terror and of flight from the Amin and Obote regimes which had unleashed random violence and killing across the country. Like many, she had spent at least a year living wild and on the run during this time.

Prossy's second death occurred a month before she was due to visit Europe, but not before she had at last given testimony to her experience of seeing heaven opened. Like many who have such experiences she speaks of light, but she also speaks of understanding the urgency of salvation and of being questioned about her life. Her message is both sobering and motivating.

Heavenly Insights

By far the most reliable insights about heaven, however, are to be found in the Bible. There are five things I want to draw out as encouragements to us in our call to be people whose final destination is heaven, and whose lives should be lived as pilgrims with that perspective, in the world but not of the world, as Jesus prays for his disciples in the High Priestly prayer of John 17.

The first is that heaven is another world, another dimension that is much more real than earth. This is quintessentially captured in the words of Aslan to Susan, Lucy, Edmund and Peter in *The Last Battle* by C. S. Lewis: 'You are—as you used to call it in the Shadowlands— dead. The term is over: the holidays have begun. The dream is ended: this is the morning'.[8]

Today, disillusioned by the failure of modernism, materialism and technology to satisfy the cry of deep to deep in our spirits,[9] many are turning to the non-material world for hope and help. Heaven is in another dimension, and it is our true home, so it can succour us even as we make our pilgrim's progress through all the sloughs of despond and the lodgings at doubting castle of our days on earth. Heaven is in fact where we truly exist:

> We were made for God. Only by being in some respect like Him, only by being a manifestation of His beauty, loving kindness, wisdom or goodness, has any earthly Beloved excited our love. It is not that we have loved them too much, but that we did not quite understand what we were loving. It is not that we shall be asked to turn from them, so dearly familiar, to a stranger. When we see the face of God we shall know that we have always known it ... in Heaven there will be no anguish and no duty of turning away from our earthly Beloveds. First,

because we shall have turned already; from the portraits to the Original, from the rivulets to the Fountain, from the creatures He made lovable to Love Himself. But secondly, because we shall find them all in Him. By loving Him more than them we shall love them more than we do now.[10]

The Old Testament expresses this other-worldliness in terms of geography; it is high up and holy, the dwelling place of God. 'Lift up your eyes to the heavens';[11] 'The heavens, even the highest heaven, cannot contain you';[12] and the psalmist says: 'for as high as the heavens are above the earth,' and compares this difference in altitude between the heavens and the earth with the difference between God's capacity to love and ours.[13] The same idea is repeated in Isaiah:

'For my thoughts are not your thoughts, neither are your ways my ways,' declares the Lord. 'As the heavens are higher than the earth, so are my ways higher than your ways and my thoughts than your thoughts'.[14]

Secondly, heaven is a place of communication and provision. When the ark is brought to the temple that Solomon has built, he prays to the Lord, 'Hear from heaven, your dwelling place, and when you hear, forgive.'[15] In Jacob's dream at Bethel, he sees a 'stairway resting on the earth, with its top reaching to heaven … There above it stood the Lord.'[16]

Heaven is a place the Israelites know as a place that God speaks from, as when he gave the Ten Commandments to Moses.[17] In Jacob's dream God spoke from heaven, reiterating the promise first given to his grandfather, that Canaan would be given to their descendants who would be like the dust of the earth.[18] It is also a place that God hears from,[19] and a place that God provides from; he told Moses that he would rain down bread from heaven for the grumbling people under Moses' charge.[20] The phrase 'bread from heaven' reminds us that Jesus is the bread of life, and that man shall not live by bread alone.[21] This can be real provision in a day when old boundaries have been uprooted and anything goes, just as it was for the wandering Israelites.

Thirdly, heaven is for children. We are told that heaven belongs to little children,[22] and that we can't gain entry to heaven unless we become like little children.[23] Small children are trusting, ingenuous, simple and easily pleased. They have not yet learned how to be proud, devious, self-seeking or manipulative. Jesus was always welcoming and giving his attention to people whom everyone considered a nuisance, so whatever our need or anxiety, we can come to Jesus if we come with the trust of a child.

Fourthly, heaven is a reality that is revealed when the veil is drawn back. We see this several times in the Bible, either clearly stated or strongly implied. The only place in the Old Testament where it is expressly stated that heaven is revealed is at the beginning of the book of Ezekiel.[24] The prophet proceeds to capture in words a series of the most fantastical sights and events that lie for us by definition in the realm of fantasy, for he is describing things that come from another dimension. It is interesting that Philip Pullman, in his powerfully successful trilogy, *His Dark Materials*, whose message is that God is an evil dictator, seems to have drawn heavily on the images of Ezekiel for some sections of his novels, although his purpose is the very opposite of encouraging us to look forward to the certainty of heaven:

Balthamos said quietly, 'The Authority, God, the Creator, the Lord, Yahweh, El Adonai, the King, the Father, the Almighty—those were all names he gave himself. He was never the creator. He was an angel like ourselves—the first angel, true, the most powerful, but he was formed of dust as we are, and dust is only a name for what happens when matter begins to understand itself. Matter loves matter … the first angels condensed out of dust, and the Authority was the first of all. He told those who came after him that he had created them, but it was a lie … And the Authority still reigns in the Kingdom, and Metatron is his regent.'[25]

If it's true that Pullman has found inspiration in Ezekiel, this is an outright challenge to the nature of God and of Jesus. It's disturbing to read a reversal of what Ezekiel seeks to convey; a description that recalls Lewis' *Screwtape Letters*, but which is written with a very different objective. It's disturbing that the Bible should be plundered in this way. But it's not the first time, and it won't be the last; indeed Pullman continues his deconstruction with the recent publication of *The Book of Dust*,[26] the first in a new trilogy.

By implication, other characters in the Bible have heavenly experiences: Moses disappears for forty days up Mount Sinai to the accompaniment of signs including fire, darkness, gloom and storm;[27] the prophet Isaiah has an overwhelming vision in the temple;[28] King Solomon and the priests, on the occasion of the ark being brought to the temple, can't perform their service because the temple is filled with a cloud which is the glory of the Lord, in other words his presence;[29] and Joshua encounters the commander of the army of the Lord as he prepares to lead the Israelites to victory over Jericho, surely his most challenging and frightening experience to date.[30] These are all instances of the touching of two worlds, the elision of two kingdoms; what we often call 'a thin place.'

With the advent of Jesus in the New Testament, heaven is opened again at his baptism, variously recorded in all four Gospels as being opened or torn open to reveal the Holy Spirit descending on him in the form of a dove. A voice comes from heaven confirming the identity of Jesus. Similarly, although the language used is not that of being opened, heaven is clearly close as the skies grow black to herald the death of Jesus and the earth quakes. After the resurrection, the disciples see Jesus taken up into heaven.

Others see heaven opened; Paul speaks of being taken up into the third heaven, or paradise, and hearing inexpressible things.[31] Perhaps referring to this, or maybe to his conversion experience on the road to Damascus, which must be included in this category of illustration, he later tells King Agrippa at Caesarea that he has done all that he has done in obedience to the vision from heaven.[32] Somehow, what Paul had seen in and from heaven had filled him with an incomparable courage that had led him through violent persecution, deprivation of all kinds, and prison. Equally extraordinary is the record of the death of Stephen.

> Stephen, full of the Holy Spirit, looked up to heaven and saw the glory of God, and Jesus standing at the right hand of God. 'Look,' he said, 'I see

heaven open and the Son of Man standing at the right hand of God.'[33]

For Stephen, Paul, and pre-eminently Jesus, heaven touching earth announces the supernatural in terms of pain as well as power. You and I, who struggle to regain our balance when life has torn the rug from beneath our feet, or to retain it when loss is part of our daily experience, can perhaps paradoxically be encouraged by this truth, and the knowledge that pain is part of the human condition, not something we are chosen for or deserve.

Others have powerful visions of Jesus: Daniel sees a vision following a twenty-one-day partial fast, and the apostle John sees a vision while in prayer on the Island of Patmos where he has been exiled for his faith. Later on he says he saw heaven standing open.[34] Both were dedicated seekers of God; if the aftershock and fatigue of trauma have saddled us with sloth or cynicism, I pray we might be inspired, encouraged and strengthened by all these sightings of heaven.

But even those who are not particularly searching for God, be they believers or not, can experience heavenly happenings. Speaking through Isaiah, God says, 'I was found by those who did not seek me.'[35] The Roman centurion Cornelius is an example of this. Described as a God-fearing man who cares for the poor and is familiar with prayer, he receives a message from an angel.[36] Although he had a form of faith, we know from the ensuing story that this encounter radically altered his life.[37]

Lastly, Jesus brings the kingdom of heaven wherever he is. He himself tells his hearers that the kingdom of heaven is near, is at hand. So what, after all, is this heaven? Well, it is where we belong, Paul tells us.[38] Our citizenship is in heaven, he says.

'We talk about heaven being so far away. It is within speaking distance of those who belong there.'[39] It's the final destiny of our mortal being but, at the same time, Jesus makes it clear that eternal life begins on earth: 'Now this is eternal life: that they know you, the only true God, and Jesus Christ, whom you have sent.'[40]

Heaven is where the dwelling of God intersects with earthly existence. Of course it will be but intermittent until we go through the gate of death, but we can look for it and expect to see evidence of it during our lives; where the kingdom of heaven comes there is healing, forgiveness, reconciliation and the wiping away of tears. God is calling us to have a heavenly perspective, and to live out our days in the light of that perspective. In other words, he calls us to be those whose values are not rooted in anything that can't be taken with us when our days on earth are done. He is looking for people who hold lightly to wealth, possessions and reputation; people for whom possessions are enjoyable but incidental, things they are stewarding rather than owning.

Writing to the Corinthians, Paul compares our human body to a seed and the body we will have when we are raised from the dead to the plant that grows from that seed. So he turns on its head our typical notion that earthly things are much more reliable and substantial than heavenly things. 'The body that is sown is perishable, it is raised imperishable ... it is sown in weakness, it is raised in power'; then he repeats himself, as if doubting that we have really understood: 'For the perishable must clothe itself with the imperishable, and the mortal with immortality.'[41] Then, he says, repeating himself for the third time, it will be true that death will have been swallowed up in victory. These are wonderful verses, strengthened by being repeated three times; for one of the hardest things following the death of someone is to believe that these things are really true; that far from being gone, the person has really arrived.

Strength through Brokenness

In the summer of 2004, the son of a friend took his life very unexpectedly. He was thirty-five. Receiving the news, I broke down; in part because the memory of my own cousin doing the same thing at about the same age swirled about me again. Outside there were tears, but inside there were screams of protest, as the chaos of complicated questions swam at me like a dense net threatening to close in and inextricably entangle me. Not long afterwards, I met my friend and was absolutely stunned by her serenity. Here is her story:

> God is a covenant-keeping God of mercy and grace. We underestimate God's sovereignty and faithfulness; nothing happens without God being there. He's never surprised, never caught out. I recently met to pray with an Armenian pastor friend of ours and his wife. During the prayer time the Lord showed me a picture of a broken heart. At the time Stephen had just moved out to his own home and things were going well for him. Also at that time the Lord drew my attention to scriptures concerning the protection our faith can lend to another's life. He reminded me of his covenant with Abraham, and of the promise of rest given through the book of Hebrews. He

reminded me how important it is to have a clean heart and that even the guilty can escape, through God's grace in our lives. And he reminded me that children can be sanctified through the faith of a parent, as it says in 1 Corinthians 7:14. It was this verse that God said he would continue to tell me until I received it. When Stephen died, I heard the question, 'Whose report will you believe? Will you be like the disciples at the foot of the cross feeling that everything on which they had staked their lives had failed, or like the disciples on the road to Emmaus who were transformed from utter defeat to radiant hope in an instant of recognition?' I have been given an incredible lightness of spirit and strength from God. A friend who was praying for us was shown a vision of Jesus with Stephen in his arms, and I heard the words, 'I'll show you this as many times as you need to see it.' I saw the thief on the cross, and knew that we have no idea what happens as earthly life ends. If God is a long time answering, you have no idea what he's doing … in the process of answering, he refines us.[42]

She, the bereaved mother, was a tower of strength to others in the very centre of her own grief.

Let this rare but precious testimony to the truth of Paul's words encourage us to ask that we might know something of the reality of heaven in our earthly lives, so that we can somehow be able to be a source of strength and comfort to others in their loss. Paradoxically, it is through our weakness and brokenness that this strength so often comes. Without this experience of death coming so near, my friend would not have been able to comfort her son's distraught friends. I too know that I will see Samuel again one day, but I could not write about heaven if he had not been wrenched from me so suddenly.

> Be sure that the ins and outs of your individuality are no mystery to Him; and one day they will no longer be a mystery to you. The mould in which a key is made would be a strange thing, if you had never seen a key; and the key itself a strange thing if you had never seen a lock. Your soul has a curious shape because it is a hollow made to fit a particular swelling in the infinite contours of the divine sub-stance, or a key to unlock one of the doors in the house with many mansions. For it is not humanity in the abstract that is to be saved, but you—you, the individual reader, John Stubbs or Janet Smith. Blessed and fortunate creature, your eyes shall behold Him and not another's. All that you are, sins apart, is destined, if you will let God have His good way, to utter satisfaction … your place in heaven will seem to be made for you and you alone; because you were made for it—made for it stitch by stitch, as a glove is made for a hand.[43]

11

Freedom from Shame
Called to Forgiveness

But while he was still a long way off, the father saw
him and was filled with compassion for him; he ran to
his son, threw his arms around him and kissed him.

- Luke 15:20

God forgives me with the compassion of his eyes, but my
back is turned to him. I have been told that he forgives
me, but I will not turn and have the forgiveness, not
though I feel the eyes on my back. God forgives me,
for he takes my head between his hands and he turns
my face to his to make me smile at him. And though
I struggle and hurt those hands, for they are human
though divine—human and scarred by nails—though
I hurt them they do not let me go until he has smiled
me into smiling, and that is the forgiveness of God.

- Austin Farrer, *Said or Sung*

In the months following Samuel's death, I suffered frequent bouts of guilt. Different images would invade my imagination and cause me to wince, sometimes to physically recoil, and my stomach to contract. Nearly always, these images would provoke anguished sobbing. What were they?

I would see Samuel lying alone on the floor of a bedroom at a conference centre, arching his back and screaming; a tiny baby who could neither crawl nor walk, yet who managed in his discomfort to turn a full 360 degrees in the space of half an hour. We had gone, in the first week of our Californian visit, to a conference up in the mountains and I had made a bed for Samuel on the floor, having no Moses basket or travel cot. This was obviously the safest place to leave him, but how could I have left him at all, however short the time? Why, oh why had I not simply carried him in my arms to the session? Shame can still pierce me that I had chosen to be more interested in what someone was saying than in my new and precious son. Did something that I could have prevented happen to him during that half hour? By holding him to me and rocking him, I could have calmed his agitation, reduced the frenetic expenditure of his energy, and perhaps prevented him from becoming too weak to overcome what lay ahead.

I would see Samuel, screaming in the aeroplane cot that lay on the table just inches away from me, and myself, lying back in my seat, exhausted. Why didn't I realise he was dehydrating? Why didn't I drink more water myself? Why didn't I give him water?

I would see a hot, stuffy changing room in a Bristol clothes shop, where I was squeezing my post-natal body into a truly horrible trouser suit, because I thought I needed new clothes for the trip to America. Why didn't I stay at home with my newborn son, the answer to my prayers, who was so much more fulfilling than any new clothes could ever be? When I got home, he was distressed, and if I hadn't gone out, he wouldn't have been.

I would see myself holding a bottle of powdered baby milk that I had made up in desperation for Samuel. He seemed to be perpetually hungry. My milk seemed watery and in short supply. It was the only bottle of milk he ever had. Did it kill him?

Ravi Zacharias, evangelist and author of many books, says this:

> What a vortex of human emotion swirls around this subject of guilt! We come up against it in our families. We battle for it in our courtrooms. We philosophize about it in the classroom. We try to explain it with psychology. We shout about it from the pulpit. We wrestle with it in private. So pervasive and deep-seated are its ramifications that some in professional counseling have gone so far as to say that guilt is the cornerstone of all neuroses.[1]

We have various responses to guilt. The first is to be persuaded that it doesn't exist. Our postmodern culture, in which there are no longer any absolutes, no boundaries, and whose philosophy is that we may believe, say and do as we like, provided we do no harm to another, tends towards the notion that guilt is imaginary and completely unnecessary. If right and wrong are purely subjective notions, I can claim not to be guilty when my behaviour troubles you, because I am being faithful to my personal creed. Yet we all know that, while we may subscribe to this because it seduces us with its promise of freedom, it raises problems. In the year 2000 the UK lowered the age of consent for homosexuals to sixteen. Why should we not therefore in time, as our understanding of freedom grows, lower the age of consent for everyone, whatever their orientation, to fourteen, to twelve? If the child is consenting, there is logically no problem. Yet we all know there is a problem, because to be human is to recognise certain universal truths that supersede time and culture, which means that we do not operate solely on the basis of logic. One of these truths is that children should always be protected, yet today a considerable number of children and young people are being 'given the freedom' to explore their gender identity, which often seems to mean adults bending over backwards to facilitate lifelong changes at an age long before we think people are old enough to vote, to drive or to have sex. Another truth is that it is wrong to kill, yet the euthanasia debate continues to rage. While end of life questions have become far more complex with the increase in life expectancy, and medical advances in prolonging life, it can seem that our desire for freedom means we think we should have the right to end our own life.

To deny the universal existence of personal guilt will only imprison us more securely.

So, though we may attempt to deny the guilt we feel over certain thoughts, actions and inactions, we know at a deep subconscious level that guilt is real, and our feelings confirm this. It's one of the earliest issues raised in the Bible. Having succumbed to the temptation to eat the one thing that was out of bounds, two things immediately happened to Adam and Eve in consequence. First, instead of being entirely comfortable with their nakedness as previously, they became embarrassed and ill at ease and spent the afternoon initiating the world of fashion by making designer fig leaf outfits. Disobedience had spawned shame. With shame comes disgrace, says the book of Proverbs.[2] Second, hearing the Lord approaching as evening fell, they hid.[3] I'm sure they didn't discuss what to do; guilt triggered their spontaneous reaction. And so we hide from the One who will demand an explanation.

Centuries later, King David—mighty general, lover of God, and forebear of Jesus—allowed an idea to take root in his mind as he strolled on his roof in the evening sun and caught sight of the beautiful Bathsheba bathing.[4] An overpowering desire took hold of him, and he knew he could use the power of his position to transform it into reality. James writes that, after desire has conceived, it gives birth to sin; and sin, when it is full-grown, gives birth to death.[5] In the story of David and Bathsheba, the first death that is caused is that of Bathsheba's husband, Uriah. David needs to conceal his paternity of the child now awaited as a result of his desire.

Unmasked by the prophet Nathan, a terrible remorse seizes David as he acknowledges his guilt. 'I have sinned against the Lord.'[6] In Psalm 51, he pleads for mercy, asking to be washed and cleansed, wishing to be whiter than snow, and likening his pain to that caused by the breaking of bones. To admit guilt for wrongdoing is to accept the existence of a higher law than our own, so in a culture that has tried to dispose of God, we can then begin to understand a profound resistance to the notions of guilt and sin. David knows that he has sinned against several people: Uriah, Bathsheba, their baby, his household, even the army out fighting the enemy on his behalf. But he knows too that his principal sin is against the law of God, and that it is from God that he must first seek forgiveness.

This he finds, but Nathan prophesies the consequences of what has happened: the baby will die as well as Uriah; next, someone close to him, unidentified at this point, will commit adultery with his wives; and calamity will come upon him out of his own household. Seldom, if ever, can we claim that our choices affect only ourselves. It's important for us to understand that forgiveness doesn't ensure a fairy tale life; good actions have good consequences and bad actions have bad consequences as the life of David so strikingly illustrates.

A second way that is used increasingly to dispose of guilt is to mock and belittle Christianity. The media act as an effective vehicle for this, and we might say that a church which repeatedly fails to stand up for integrity, honesty and dignity has only itself to blame. One can think of a dozen documentaries, soaps and series that surreptitiously invade and influence our thinking. If faith and morality are no more than a matter of personal opinion, we are unlikely to be disturbed by the faint discomfort of guilt.

This reached a zenith with the broadcasting on BBC2 in January 2005 of *Jerry Springer: The Opera*. It generated miles of print, both prior to and after the screening, and occupied as much air space. The most honourable offering in all this for me came from Antony Pitts, who was a senior producer for BBC Radio 3 until he resigned as a result of this broadcast. He describes how he was persuaded by Mark Thompson, the director-general of the BBC, to watch the show before it was screened, although he had flagged up that many news sources had made it clear that the show contained 'elements that were clearly blasphemous in any ordinary understanding of the word'.[7] His conclusion after watching it was that, 'the blasphemy was far, far worse than even the most detailed news reports had led me to believe'.

He cites some examples:

- The introduction of and dialogue with the Jesus figure containing all kinds of abuse, insults, profanity and deliberate mockery of the Lord's Name.
- The ridiculing of the figure of Jesus on the cross, dressed to imply sexual activity.
- The repeated mockery of the wounds (stigmata) of Jesus, linked to acts of crudeness.
- The singing of 'Jerry eleison' as a contemptuous travesty of an act of worship.

He goes on to write out the current legal definition of blasphemy:

Every publication is said to be blasphemous which contains any contemptuous, reviling, scurrilous or ludicrous matter relating to God, Jesus Christ or the Bible, or the formularies of the Church of England as by law established.

This definition covers the written and spoken word.

He ends his letter of resignation by quoting the Latin inscription on Broadcasting House:

This Temple of the Arts and Muses is dedicated
to Almighty God by the first Governors of
Broadcasting in the year 1931, Sir John Reith being
Director-General. It is their prayer that good seed
sown may bring forth a good harvest and that the
people, inclining their ear to whatsoever things are
beautiful and honest and of good report, may tread
the path of wisdom and uprightness.

And he signs off, 'My prayer is Kyrie eleison.'

So far have we departed from this noble dedication that it is not
in the least surprising that the nation that feasts on such spectacles
should feel absolutely no need to be accountable to such a God.

A third way we smother guilt is by justifying our actions. How
we are perceived by others is for most people an all-consuming cause
and can lead us to sail close to the wind where truth is concerned.
In the public arena this is often evidenced in the political realm, by
exaggerated claims or promises, and also, shamefully, in the church,
by cover-ups that lose their cover.... Reputations are ruined, but
too often there are no admissions of failure or guilt, and the truth
continues to be disputed.

In 1 Samuel 15, we find Israel's first king, Saul, who has received
clear instructions from God through the prophet and priest, Samuel,
modifying those instructions according to his own understanding.
Saul's excuse is that he took plunder from the enemy in the form
of sheep and cattle, in order to sacrifice them to the Lord, but a
few verses earlier we have been told that he kept everything that
was good, while destroying everything that was weak and despised.

Samuel calls his bluff and utters the memorable words, 'To obey is better than sacrifice … rebellion is like the sin of divination, and arrogance like the evil of idolatry,'[8] announcing that Saul's kingship is over. Saul admits that he has sinned, and that it was because he was afraid of the people. He asks for forgiveness and to resume his kingship, but in a dramatic scene, Samuel says it is too late and turns to leave. We may imagine his robes whirling as he turns, and tearing as Saul grasps at them, revealing a man who could not hear the word of the Lord.

> You have rejected the word of the Lord, and the Lord has rejected you as king over Israel … The Lord has torn the kingdom of Israel from you today and has given it to one of your neighbours—to one better than you.[9]

Of course this is not the first time that Saul has overridden Samuel's instructions. Not long before this incident, he had acted as priest, which was not his role, and been rebuked by Samuel in a similar way. He had also shown early signs of his deep sin of jealousy when his son Jonathan had achieved a great victory for the Israelites. Later he became uncontrollably jealous of Jonathan's friendship with David and of David himself. Saul was a person who repeatedly tried to cover up his guilt, and it led in the end to his death. The frightening thing about his exchange with Samuel, in which he learns that the kingship is to be taken away from him, is that his last thought concerns what others think of him. 'I have sinned', he says. 'But please honour me before the elders of my people and before Israel.'[10]

Please maintain my reputation even if it is a whitewashed tomb. The final verse of the chapter says that the Lord was grieved that he had made Saul king over Israel. Let's reflect on this incident for a moment. This man cared far more about the opinion of men than the opinion of God. He had smothered his guilt in that greatest of all sins, pride. C. S. Lewis expresses this well:

> You may remember, when I was talking about sexual immorality, I warned you that the centre of Christian morals did not lie there. Well, now we have come to the centre ... the utmost evil is pride. Unchastity, anger, greed, drunkenness, and all that are mere fleabites in comparison. It was through pride that the devil became the devil. Pride leads to every other vice: it is the complete anti-God state of mind.[11]

Yet another way in which we deal with guilt is by concealing rather than denying it, and living in fear of discovery. We hide it by appearing to be in control. Thus we cannot go very far in friendship, because if we do we may be discovered and we will certainly have to disclose ourselves. Abraham's grandson Jacob is a vivid example of a devious life, from wheeling and dealing with his brother to tricking his elderly father and scheming against his father-in-law.[12] Deceiving his father led to wronging a nation, because deceit is a monster that needs feeding, and to hide guilt will always have repercussions on others as we create a web of lies to cover our tracks. Deceiving his brother meant he had to flee and lose contact for many years, being absent at his mother's death. When eventually the moment of confrontation between the estranged brothers arrived, Jacob was in anguish all night, wracked with fear before God that the wrong he had committed so long ago would be avenged against his children.

Jacob found mercy because he came to God; thousands don't because they have neither looked for nor found him, or they have believed the lies of our culture. Christianity is the only world religion whose voice cries out for people to deal with wrongdoing, to admit guilt, ask for pardon and come to God to receive it. But its voice is growing faint in a culture that is casting off all restraint and proactively seeking to silence the voice of Jesus.

Accepting Responsibility

Living through those early months after Samuel's death, I knew the reality of guilt. While I was assured repeatedly by paediatricians and other medical authorities, both immediately following his death and later when I became pregnant with Jack, that I was not responsible for what had happened, I knew that there were moments of inadequacy as a mother, as exemplified by some of the scenes rehearsed at the beginning of the chapter. These things were not to do with legalities; they were not subject to human judgement. They were rather a question of conscience between me and my God. How might the sense of shame and failure in one generation affect their parenting of the next?

I have spoken to numerous parents of the pain of seeing their children walk away from the Lord, but who in their pain have responded with a sense of resignation. There is almost unbearable pain in seeing a child suffer, whatever the cause. Of course, we cannot make an equation: I did this so my son did that. But behind our pain and for some our resignation ('Well, it is what it is …') can lie an awareness and acceptance that somewhere along the line, because we ourselves as parents are damaged and bruised, we may be at least partly responsible for our children's suffering or rejection of our faith. In a way it would be strange to think otherwise. But in a culture whose narrative is that guilt is unnecessary, we feel guilty for feeling guilty. Yet knowing our guilt is real simply exacerbates our internal tension.

I want to make a plea for guilt to become part of our parenting; that is, for us to openly admit that we may bear some responsibility for the stories in which we find ourselves. Perhaps this seems scandalous in a culture which denies or suppresses guilt. But that's not the end of the story; if we turn to the heart of the gospel and ask ourselves why Jesus submitted to the agony of the cross, we remember that the answer is to provide a way for us to find peace with God. To bear away our sins. To pay the debts we could never pay ourselves. To enjoy the destiny and freedom of forgiveness.

Jean Vanier, the founder and director of L'Arche, an international ministry to the disabled, with whom he worked, lived and learned how to love, writes: 'The yearnings of Jesus … are to undo the chains that bind us up in guilt and egoism, and prevent us from walking on the road to inner freedom and growth.'[13]

If we will but let these misgivings tumble out of us and say, first to God, but also to those whom we have hurt, 'Yes, I didn't recognise those teenage confusions; yes, I was too strict about your clothes; yes, I did allow my anger to lacerate your soul when you weren't even really the cause of it. My work situation, my relationship with your father at the time, my fatigue all demolished my self-control; I was so wrong; please forgive me', then we will find not resignation but resolve waiting for us. My plea is of course not for us to admit guilt alone, but to restore it to its proper place within forgiveness; forgiveness we both ask for and freely offer.

What so often happens is that the spring of prayer within us dries up because we have not felt that a confession of guilt is appropriate. And our culture, and sadly so often the church too, has tacitly approved our conclusion. The fruit of all this is multiple. There is alienation between the generations; thousands of young men and women wander in the wilderness for far too long because we have adopted the false theology that we can do nothing except wait. And thousands of children, while growing up surrounded by other Christians and immersed in church culture, are passengers rather than passionate, because they don't feel forgiven for their teenage tantrums, they hear gossip and criticism of others at home, and they see church disputes, conducted through interminable meetings, that in addition deprive them of their parents' time. The pleasure and the glory of forgiveness are hidden from us because we have been persuaded that we don't need it or owe it.

I had to verbalise my sense of guilt about Samuel's death and my shortcomings as his mother with Charlie, with friends and before God before I could come to a place of peace.

Part of the road back to wholeness for my daughter Hannah involved my recognising how little of her struggle I had truly understood; the extent to which I had expected her to be more mature than her years; the subconscious expectations I had laid on her as a pastor's daughter (because of what people would think of us); the pain I had inflicted through my frequent outbursts of anger. I may have been in pain, but pain doesn't justify anger, nor striking out in uncontrollable rage ... and wasn't there the nagging feeling of guilt lurking behind all this because we had torn her from her home and nation at the vulnerable age of fourteen and expected her to feel as excited as we did? I had to confess all of these things to God, and I had to confess all of these things to her. I had to ask both of them for forgiveness, and they both granted it. I doubt if I could write about guilt if these things had not happened.

I can still see Jack flinching as I raised my hand threateningly. We had a volatile relationship during those teenage years of his in Paris. Like the majority of teenagers, he would while away hours listening to (not very suitable!) music and doodling when he was meant to be doing '*les devoirs*' (homework). Neither reasoning nor persuading nor cajoling seemed to produce any reaction, so I resorted to physical persuasion with him too. I say this to my shame, but I say it because I know I am not alone. I am not alone as a parent, and I am not alone as a Christian. I did it because I was afraid. I was afraid he would not be able to reintegrate into the British education system when the time came. We all have different fears, but not one of them justifies being violent with our children. We had always practised saying sorry as soon as possible in our family, but asking for forgiveness for the same thing too often weakens the ability to forgive, and a time came, some years later, when I had to have a conversation with Jack and wrap up the business of the guilt I felt concerning this turbulent period of our common life.

The pain of all this was only mitigated by the sweetness of forgiveness which had freed me to pray for him with energy and passion. If we suppress our guilt as parents, whatever method we choose to obliterate it, so will our children. We are, after all, their role model.

Once, at a student meeting at St Aldates, the theme of the evening was learning to pray for one another. It was more a workshop than a teaching, and those of us on the team wandered around the groups to offer help or advice if needed. I asked one girl what she had asked for prayer for. Sex and lust, she replied. In your head or your body? I asked. Both, came the answer. I found out that she was a Christian and made an appointment with her. Without a place to admit guilt, make confession and receive forgiveness, where might this sweet young thing have ended up? Probably stumbling through life and not enjoying the freedom and abundance promised by Jesus.[14]

Charles Spurgeon wrote, 'We are certain that there is forgiveness, because there is a gospel, and the very essence of the gospel lies in the proclamation of the pardon of sin.'[15] Part of our calling is to ask for and give forgiveness with liberality. It's worth pointing out that the system often breaks down, not only because we have done away with guilt, but also because we can't forgive ourselves. We somehow imagine our sin is simply too big or complicated for even God himself to handle. But the glory of the gospel is that 'if we confess our sins, he is faithful and just and will forgive us.'[16] Just pause for a moment to take in the enormity of this: only Jesus offers real freedom from the real burden of guilt. Nothing is beyond the reach of his forgiveness, and if God forgives us, who are we to withhold forgiveness from ourselves?

'It is always the case that when the Christian looks back, he is looking at the forgiveness of sins.'[17] Sometimes those who have the greatest perceived need of forgiveness are those who best understand it. Luke 7 recounts the story of the sinful woman (which means prostitute) who came to the Pharisee's house where Jesus was having dinner and knelt weeping at his feet, drying them with her hair and pouring perfume on them. How very inappropriate and embarrassing! What exactly is your relationship with this woman? And how extremely rude to gatecrash our dinner party. But she who had so little had so much, for she knew that forgiveness was her only hope and she had found out where to get it. As this same story reveals, the more we are forgiven, the more grateful we are, and the more loving we become, for we are amazed to be acceptable after what we have done. This story reminds me too of Ben, an ex-offender who has recently joined our congregation. He once did something terrible, but he now exudes love because his life, like that of the sinful woman, has been turned inside out through meeting Jesus and finding forgiveness. There is logic as well as awe in the fact that the gospel thrives in prison. 'Forgiveness is the answer to the child's dream of a miracle by which what is broken is made whole again, what is soiled is again made clean.'[18]

Individual guilt is one thing, but wider expressions of guilt can be found where the individual has no tools for recognising or handling their guilt. Such expressions may be far from peaceful. Take for example the Rhodes Must Fall protest in 2015. Originating in Cape Town as a call to end white supremacy, it was echoed by other South African universities, as well as institutions elsewhere in the world. One of those was Oxford, home to a statue of Rhodes in Oriel College. Impotent in the face of our personal guilt, we can try to atone for corporate guilt to somehow make peace with our inner guilt by externalising our feelings. In this case the felt inner guilt was perhaps a recognition of the injustices in an institution of privilege, and an imposter syndrome telling the students involved that they didn't deserve the privilege they were enjoying.

On a much wider scale altogether we in the West carry the big cultural weight of post-colonial guilt, and Germany still struggles today with guilt from the holocaust, and residual shame from the harshness of the Treaty of Versailles. On an equally wide scale, in a *Guardian* article, the Foreign Secretary Jeremy Hunt and Bishop Philip Mount-Stephen write about how the influence of post-colonial guilt adversely affects recognition of the widespread persecution of Christians around the world; mainly, it should be added, in poorer, non-white nations.[19]

Corporate guilt is real, though complex to address, and many live with it, albeit mostly at a subconscious level. But it's our personal inner guilt, whatever its cause, that we have the opportunity to treat. So let's come back to you. I wonder if something here is awakening a sense that you may need to say or do something? Just take a moment to imagine how it would feel to lose the burden of something you may have carried for years, like a heavy weight inside you....

To ask for forgiveness, seek counselling or ask for prayer for help in a struggle with shame can be like passing through the Narnian wardrobe door into a world of wonder. I would steer well clear of communicating by email which can easily seem impersonal or be misunderstood, but if you need to make a visit or a call, or write a letter, go for it. It's a decision that can change your life.

12

Guilty Pleasures
Healing Our Histories

And then I felt sad because I realised that once people are
broken in certain ways, they can't ever be fixed, and this is
something nobody ever tells you when you are young and
it never fails to surprise you as you grow older, as you see
people in your life break one by one. You wonder when
your turn is going to be, or if it's already happened.

- Douglas Coupland, *Life after God*

A bruised reed he will not break, and a
smouldering wick he will not snuff out.

- Isaiah 42:3

'Woman, where are they? Has no one condemned you?'
'No one, sir,' she said. 'Then neither do I condemn you,'
Jesus declared. 'Go now and leave your life of sin.'

- John 8:10–11

I was introduced to Laura by our vicar. There was a background that made it more suitable for me to help, it seemed. I soon found out why. Laura was attending an Alpha Course,[1] although she had already decided that Christianity was the way for her some years previously. Now she had completed her training as a nurse and was working part-time. She spent the rest of her time earning a considerably higher salary as a sex worker. She had met and fallen in love with John at college. She had also fallen into bed with him, a common tale within the church as well as without. One thing led to another, and Laura soon discovered that John was working as a male escort and becoming an increasingly wealthy property owner from the proceeds. Now seduced rationally as well as physically, she had entered the world of sex work under John's tuition and was doing rather well herself, owning one house in Oxford and renting another out to students; students whom we can assume were blissfully ignorant of the financial affairs of their landlady.

Laura saw no contradiction between her work and being a Christian. Indeed, she became rather annoyed if I posed questions on Christian morality, and told me repeatedly what a lot of good she was doing, bringing a few moments of intimacy and comfort to a succession of mostly lonely men in their fifties and above. She insisted she was completely unaffected emotionally, and described to me her very business-like approach: a room set aside exclusively for this work in her house, its own sets of linen and towels and so on. She conveyed the impression of a very clean and tasteful business. She was only twenty-three years old, the same age as one of my daughters. We met for six sessions of studying the Bible together, because despite her assurances that she was contented with life and in love with John, she was on a quest for a love much safer and more secure than that which she knew with John.

Laura had, because of her earlier experiences of growing up with believing parents, some inklings of this true love, and perhaps they were sounding from deep within her, reminding her of a far-off place and awakening the universal nostalgia of the human being. But she was feisty and argumentative; committed to nit-picking the text of John's gospel and striving to reconcile it with her chosen way of life. At the same time, there was part of her that longed to settle down in a more conventional way with John, and she was prepared to go to any lengths to secure such a future—except the lengths that demanded she confront his lifestyle, and therefore face the contradictions of her own.

One Sunday she brought John to St Aldates. He lived in London and was also attending a church where some were building bridges of love and friendship with him in an admirable way. Laura warned me to be careful what I said to him, so I was careful with my words, but they were not received in the way they were offered and, unwittingly causing offence, the game was lost. From that moment on, Laura became unreachable on her mobile and invisible in church and, after several weeks of leaving messages, I gave up the chase.

I have no idea what happened to John or Laura. In my perfect dream world, they integrated into the church he was attending on the outer edges of London and eventually broke out of their prison into freedom and healing. I am sure my words could have been more carefully chosen; but I am sure too that they fell on the ears of one so insecure that the chances of being misinterpreted were high if not inevitable.

They were a sweet but ensnared couple, typical in many respects of so many of their generation, and part of the cultural move towards normalising sex and escort work. Indeed we don't just normalise it, we embrace it, and publish articles about it in the glossy weekend magazines of national papers alongside other serious subjects like the humanitarian work of Bill and Melinda Gates.[2]

Paul says that the body is not meant for sexual immorality, but for the Lord. 'Do you not know,' he continues, 'that your bodies are members of Christ himself? Shall I then take the members of Christ and unite them with a prostitute? Never! Do you not know that he who unites himself with a prostitute is one with her in body? For it is said, "The two will become one flesh."'[3]

By this he shows his understanding that the sexual act represents much more than bodily union, and that to become one flesh with someone has consequences well beyond the relatively short time it takes to do so. I recently heard that a missionary who is a household name uses the following visual aid to press the point: she beats up two eggs in a bowl together, holds it out to the assembled youth and says, 'Try and separate them.'

All through human history mankind's sexual appetite has caused him to over-indulge, so to speak. There is barely a hero of whatever realm of society or whatever epoch, whose biography does not include amorous escapades and adventures. After the deprivation imposed by the years of the Second World War, there grew up a generation who revolted against their parents' hypocritical observance of a Victorian moral code and, casting all caution to the winds, threw themselves, mind, body and soul into the new 'permissive society'.

Defining events in the corporate life of that generation, the so-called Baby Boomers, legitimised a new code of conduct. Woodstock, the upstate New York concert in 1969, was one of those events, ratifying free love in the collective consciousness, though other landmarks had appeared earlier. The poet laureate Philip Larkin puts it thus:

> Sexual intercourse began
> In nineteen sixty-three
> (which was rather late for me)—
> Between the end of the Chatterley ban
> And the Beatles' first L.P.[4]

The end of the Chatterley ban refers to the result of the Old Bailey obscenity trial launched in 1960 when Penguin Books decided to publish D. H. Lawrence's erotic novel *Lady Chatterley's Lover* in paperback, thus putting an effective end to the censorship that had forbidden its publication in the UK.

At the same time the rising star of the Beatles was a significant element in the establishing of a profound cultural change that would irrevocably influence the nation's approach to sexual mores, leading us through the decades to today's culture-wide status quo of individual freedom to create our own sexual identity and practise our own moral code—as long as we do not harm the other in so doing. These defining influences of the 1960s are captured by Ian MacDonald:

> As British Pop Art and Op Art became the talk of the gallery world, a new generation of fashion designers, models and photographers followed Mary Quant's lead in creating the boutique culture of swinging London.... Long-standing class barriers collapsed overnight as northern and

cockney accents penetrated the hitherto exclusively
Oxbridge domains of television, advertising and
public relations. Hair lengthened, skirts shortened
and the sun came out over a Britain rejuvenated,
alert, and determined to have the best of times.[5]

Inhibitions were further relaxed by the Beatles' public experi-
mentation with drugs and their explorations, geographically and
otherwise, into the worlds of mysticism and Eastern religions. Old
convictions were sneered at by those feeling the refreshing wind of
liberation. Of course, a liberal approach wasn't really invented in
the 1960s any more than sex itself. Researchers point out that the
generation born roughly between 1925–45, dubbed the Builder or
Silent generation, depending on which side of the Atlantic they were
born, was the generation that showed the biggest ever age-bracket
rise in the divorce rate as they reached mid-life in the 1970s. The
women of this generation were chronologically the first mature
female generation to take the pill, and 'between the 1950s and the
1970s they and their male peers reported the highest increase in the
number of sexual partners of any previous generation in history'.[6]

It is not that no one had ever hinted at a sexuality smouldering
below the surface—take Marilyn Monroe and Elvis Presley, born
in 1926 and 1935 respectively, for example—but hinting had long
been as far as it went, at least publicly. Social norms in behaviour
were more or less observed across the board in this generation, thus
keeping at bay anything that might seriously threaten the status quo.

By the late 1960s there was a little cloud on the horizon
called postmodernism. Foucault, Derrida and Leotard, the new

existentialists, were publishing their ideas, and the West as a culture was beginning to realise that the answer to life's conundrums, toils and troubles did not lie in the economic prosperity or technological progress championed by the modernist era. It seemed clearer and clearer that the answer was that there wasn't an answer.

This meant that any answer could be an answer; indeed, any answer was validated simply by being expressed, and so anyone could believe, think and act as he chose to without infringing commonly held absolutes.

> The 'Billy Graham years', spurred by the austerity, and socio-economic retrenchment that marked post-war reconstruction, and by a certain selflessness springing from these things, had yielded to the tidal wave of the sexual revolution, and by 1970 there had been a mass rejection of mainstream Christian faith and values, shown by a near 50% decline in church recruitment during the previous decade.[7]

The way was thus opened for an out-and-out race to be the most outrageous; and the last five decades have seen a gradual but determined erosion of all the boundaries of once tacitly accepted modesty and decorum. So it is that we can read near-pornographic synopses of the latest film, be it about gang rape, sadomasochism or sexualised cannibalism, not in a magazine that we all recognise as adult literature because it is sealed up on the top shelf, but in the pages of our staid and respectable national newspapers. In the same way, the visual arts, from television to theatre, from museums to Netflix, and using the whole reach of the internet, have unlocked Pandora's box where sexuality and sexual practice are concerned. We have become a thoroughly sexualised society, in which sex sells everything from cars to computers, and where children are often forced to grow up before they've had a chance to enjoy childhood, too often becoming the sexual victims of their elders.

The prophet Isaiah, speaking to the apostate Judah in the eighth century BC says, 'Woe to those who call evil good and good evil, who put darkness for light and light for darkness, who put bitter for sweet and sweet for bitter.'[8]

Our evolution in the ethical arena is one thing, but its consequences are another. We live now in a world of rights, which is the logical child of an individualist culture. We have demanded the freedom to do what we want when we want and how we want and with whom we want. But we live also in a world of enormously increased poor mental health, a world of addiction to a whole gamut of substances and behaviours, and a world of increasing confusion about identity, sexual and otherwise. Our freedom and our rights have not delivered contentment and well-being.

Jordan Peterson, the cult celebrity Canadian clinical psychologist, argues that it is recognising our responsibilities rather than reclaiming our rights that brings inner peace. Like anyone who dares to question political correctness and the aggressive stance of its proponents, he has attracted an enormous following of both friend and foe. But all would agree that he speaks courageously to power.

Moral misconduct is no longer immediately obvious and identifiable, as it was only a few decades ago. Boundaries have melted away and right and wrong have been discarded or blended into 'my code of conduct.' So it can be argued—and indeed sometimes is—that we are an improved version of humanity. Of course, in many ways we are—the unpartnered or unmarried mother of a child is no longer judged and ostracised; the mentally unwell or disabled are no longer rejected and hidden; the gay and lesbian communities are welcomed and legislation to protect them from harm has been created. And as I write, strenuous efforts to understand and provide for that small percentage of people who find themselves struggling with gender dysphoria are being made.

But nothing is black and white. Despite the welcome rejection of an old hypocrisy in the realm of sexuality and behaviour, we hear many stories of misery and unhappiness, of self-harm, and even of suicide, the ultimate extreme response to extreme despair. So how are we to think?

The Idolatry of Sex

In nearly forty years of ministry, my experience has been that a significant proportion of emotional or psychological disturbances find their roots in the sexual history of the individual. That is to say, that a person suffering from nightmares, or another who consistently fails to make durable relationships, or a third who cannot escape compulsive behaviour, sexual or otherwise, is more than likely to have had their initial sexual encounter in a less than conducive context. Many have suffered abuse as a child, or fled from demoralising or demeaning surroundings, such as violent or alcoholic parents, into the arms of someone who did not meet their real need, which was to be loved and comforted. It often takes many years to discover that love is not spelt s-e-x, and the pain and guilt are compounded with the passing of each sexual encounter.

In recent years we have been inundated with revelations of abuse inflicted within the church, political or entertainment worlds. Old men in their sixties and seventies are being brought to account for the sins of their youth, and while justice is served, it's a disturbing canvas.

The Old Testament story of Amnon and Tamar illustrates the truth that sexual encounter outside God's design will so often breed hatred rather than love.[9] Amnon was one of David's many sons, and the story recounts that one day he fell in love with his half-sister. 'Amnon became so obsessed with his sister Tamar that he made himself ill. She was a virgin, and it seemed impossible for him to do anything to her.' His friend Jonadab, described as a shrewd man, devises a ploy whereby Amnon can seduce Tamar. Feigning illness, he orders some lunch to be cooked and brought to him by her. Arriving with the food, Tamar finds herself not only suddenly alone with her brother, who has swiftly dismissed all his attendants, but instructed to feed him in the intimacy of his bedroom. 'But when she took it to him to eat, he grabbed her and said, "Come to bed with me my sister".' Not so ill after all, perhaps? Protesting vigorously, Tamar says such a thing would be not only wrong, but bring disgrace upon her, and tries to reason with Amnon, saying she is sure the king will allow them to marry if they ask. 'But he refused to listen to her, and since he was stronger than she, he raped her. Then Amnon hated her with intense hatred. In fact, he hated her more than he had loved her. Amnon said to her, "Get up and get out!"' Deep fury is born in Absalom, Tamar's brother, also son to David, and two years later he murders Amnon in revenge for Tamar's disgrace and desolation. The story records, 'This [had] been Absalom's express intention ever since the day Amnon raped his sister Tamar.'

Of all the many obstacles to being what God intended us to be and doing the things we were made to do, the idolatry and enslavement of sex, roaring like an escaped lion and seeking whom it may devour, as Peter describes the devil,[10] is surely one of the most fearful and successful. Its effects are seldom limited to what takes place between two individuals. Pregnancy, abortion, misery and broken relationships can follow; and as the story of David illustrates, sexual habits and practices often pass from one generation to another.

Certain individuals have been well aware of the power of sex and sought to exploit it under the guise of religious thought or the ideology of freedom.

One such was Alice Bailey, a leader of the Theosophy movement,[11] who wrote many books on the subject, and was one of the first authors to use the term New Age. Her writings formed a springboard for the lavish religious buffet spread that has come to be known as the New Age Movement. It is sobering to recognise that Bailey received a Christian education, and as a young woman was involved in evangelical work with the YMCA and the British Army; her books reveal a mind that has been seduced by a potent cocktail of truth and falsehood. For the Christian her teachings are at best confused, at worst dangerous. Among the topics she addressed were the destiny of nations and prescriptions for society in general. So it's not surprising that in a plan, or mandate, widely thought to have originated in her writings, though heavily influenced by her mentor, Helena Blavatsky, she outlines ten strategies to promote a society liberated from the restrictions of faiths in general and Christianity in particular:

1. Take God out of school. Without reference to God he will become irrelevant.

2. Break the traditional Judaeo-Christian family concept. Discourage communication between parents and children about faith.

3. Remove restrictions on sex. Sex is man's greatest expression of enjoyment, and Christianity seeks to rob people of it.

4. Man must be free to enjoy any expression of sexuality. All forms of sexual expression are desirable so long as no one is being abused or harmed.

5. Work to provide abortion on demand. Women must be free to abort unwanted children.

6. Everyone develops 'soul-bonds'. Everyone should be free to follow his instincts, and marriage should be no obstacle to the creation of a new sexual relationship. Divorce must be readily available.

7. Defuse religious radicalism by silencing Christianity and promoting other faiths.

8. Use the media to influence mass opinion. Mould mass opinion to be receptive to these values.

9. Debase Art in all its forms, and make it obscene, immoral and occultic.

10. Endeavour to persuade the church to endorse these strategies, and to accept the principles enshrined in them.[12]

This is very hardcore, and it's difficult not to recoil from its extreme language. Unsurprisingly its authenticity is debated, nevertheless little comment needs to be made on the way in which so much of it has become reality over the last half century.

It's tempting to lie down and give up in the face of such monstrous notions, and under the weight of death and crime and misery that floods our newspapers and news programmes. Youths are knifed to death in our streets and we seem unable to stem the tide of slavery. We're reminded of Jeremiah's lament: 'Death has climbed in through our windows and has entered our fortresses; it has removed the children from the streets and the young men from the public squares.'[13]

But for all the destruction and consequence of our foolish choices, there is good news; there is redemption, and it's found in the person of Jesus, who gave up a life in which he had caused no harm, and made no foolish choices. It was a perfect life, but he freely allowed it to be cut short in his prime for you and for me. God came to us in the flesh of Jesus … just think about that for a moment; this is a better story than any of the superhero tales. It's the rescue that really happened, the reality that we are always searching for in our fairy tales and fantasies. Redemption is found in encountering the One who remembers our sins no more,[14] who sweeps away our offences like a cloud, our sins like the morning mist,[15] and who says that he has removed our transgressions from us as far as the east is from the west.[16] This last picture used to make me worry that it would only take a day's plane travel to come upon the shameful mountain of my sins and follies, and dread discovery and retribution, until I realised that the psalmist wasn't using the Date Line to calculate the distance between east and west!

During our ten years in Paris, I saw many people set free from the chains of sexual addiction or pain that had caused them to walk with a limp for years or skewed their every attempt to build a fruitful life. I think of Christina, a mature mother of two grown children, but long ago abandoned by their father. As the child of café owners serving long-distance lorry drivers, she had been used to serve them more than coffee, and this with the acquiescence of her parents. Slowly, in the safety of our small group of wounded women, we brought these haunting ghosts into the light, one by one. She spoke to Jesus of them, and listened to his Spirit until she heard the truth that she was not responsible for them, and the spell of the lie was for ever broken. There was no hurry, and there were many tears, not all of them shed by her, for the things we had to hear from one another were hard to bear. In time, Christina remarried a gentle man called Thomas and her life was slowly rebuilt.

Don't let the spectre of past experiences of brokenness and pain anchor you to a place where you can only dream about being free, being at peace and starting again. When your heart cries out in recognition of deep calling to deep, but your body and your disappointed hopes and longings say no, not for you, please believe that your heart is right. Jesus is calling you:

> Are you tired? Worn out? Burned out on religion?
> Come to me. Get away with me and you'll recover
> your life. I'll show you how to take a real rest. Walk
> with me and work with me—watch how I do it.
> Learn the unforced rhythms of grace. I won't lay

anything heavy or ill-fitting on you. Keep company
with me and you'll learn to live freely and lightly.[17]

The writer to the Hebrews tells us that hope is an anchor for us,[18] and Isaiah promises that those who hope in the Lord will renew their strength.[19]

Dear reader, if you are reading this weighed down by any regret that lingers from encounters in your past, or the pain caused by them, please reach out for hope and make that superhuman effort to believe that freedom and a future can be yours. You are loved with a perfect love, just as I am and as Christina was and is. You really are.

13

When Death Strikes Early

*Bereavement—Accepting
the Unacceptable*

*No one ever told me that grief
is so visceral and so voracious in
its capacity to consume memory,
confidence and concentration....
Anguish and lament. Sorrow and
soundless scream. Protest and passion.*

- Stephen Oliver (ed.), *Inside Grief*

*Is it nothing to you, all you who
pass by? Look around and see. Is
any suffering like my suffering
that was inflicted on me?*

- Lamentations 1:12

On a bright October morning as we took a coffee break in our kitchen, enjoying the autumn sun that streamed through the windows, there was a knock at the door. Outside stood a policeman; 'Are you Reverend Cleverly?' This established, he continued. 'There's been an accident. Do you know a Joanna Braithwaite?' We not only knew her but loved her. She was our PA, and a friend we had come to love dearly. She was an EA really, full of initiative and creative ideas and solutions. As he began to explain that Jo had been knocked over on her bike by a concrete cement mixer on her way to work, and that the only contact details they could find on her person were us, he stopped abruptly to listen to an incoming call on his pager. 'I'm sorry,' he said, 'she's passed away.' Yet again the world was upended, something unthinkable had happened and my heart crashed against my ribs as I shouted 'No! No! No!' over and over.

Minutes later we were on our way to the hospital in a police car to identify Jo's body. Her parents (with whom we have since become dear friends, bonded through this loss beyond words for them, which connected with our own loss all those years earlier, the more poignantly because our children shared a birth date) lived, and still do, in France, and it fell to Charlie to break this unbreakable news to them. They hadn't seen her for some five months …

A few years before this, picking up my phone to answer a call from Charlie, I could tell from his tone that something was terribly wrong. 'We need to go and see Dan and Suzie; the scan was bad.'

To their great joy, Dan and Suzie were expecting their third child, a little sister, they had already discovered, for older brothers Jack and Josh, now eight and six. Sitting in their kitchen we listened to them telling us that the scan had revealed that the left side of the baby's heart was grossly under-developed. This is hypoplastic left heart syndrome, an extremely rare condition with devastating implications. While in utero, and therefore dependant on the mother for sustaining life and providing nourishment, the baby thrives and will be as active as any normal baby. But from the moment of birth, when the baby must sustain his own life, and therefore depend on his lungs and heart, the clock is ticking and death is inevitable. The only question is how many days of life will be eked out by a failing organ.

Over the previous twenty years, surgical procedures had already become much more sophisticated, enabling the re-direction of the flow of blood into and out of the developed half of the heart in order to sustain life. But even with such surgery, no child suffering from this syndrome had yet lived beyond fifteen, and the doctors had clearly communicated, as they are obliged to, that quality of life is usually poor and the normal activities of a growing child, particularly those of movement, such as running and jumping, severely restricted.

Dan and Suzie had come home from what should have been a routine visit to the maternity hospital to face one of the most agonising questions a parent can ever have to face. The question before them was whether to subject a tiny, vulnerable infant to punishing and painful surgery in the hope of giving her a chance to live a life, with no guarantee that it would be easy or prolonged, or whether to allow her to drift away to eternity after her birth without surgical intervention, in however many days it took. They had time to think about it, but this made it no easier.

Today they were in no state to do any thinking. Like us, many years earlier, their world had been turned upside down in a matter of minutes. The first sign that something was terribly amiss had been the sudden influx of medical staff into the room where the scan was taking place and the look on the consultant's face.

We sat clutching our cups of tea and weeping with them. Trying to grasp the enormity of the day's discovery, we prayed, but our voices felt faint and it was hard to find faith in the wake of so much medical information.

There followed four long and difficult months for Dan and Suzie. Their family and friends rallied round, and heaven was most certainly stormed by many on their behalf, but still it was a lonely path as they journeyed to a decision about what to do when little Jessica Rose was born. Trips to Great Ormond Street Hospital and lengthy consultations with surgeons and specialists came and went; so did long conversations with friends, and private times of prayer and wrestling together. In the end they opted for surgery. It seemed unthinkable to choose not to offer Jessica every possible chance to live a life on earth.

The birth was relatively easy physically, and Suzie was up within hours to go and join her little infant who had been whisked straight to Great Ormond Street. If the last four months of the pregnancy had been difficult, what followed was a much greater challenge. The operation was announced successful, though the sight of their daughter wrapped in cling film around her open sternum (since the little chest was too small to sew up over the swollen heart immediately) with needles, tubes and monitors everywhere, was almost too much to bear. It was 15 January, and Jessica was three days old.

Long winter day succeeded long winter day, but slowly, so slowly, little Jessica recovered. Her tiny heart kept beating. Three weeks later she was transferred to the John Radcliffe Hospital in Oxford, and it was there that we first saw her. Tiny, pale, perfect and beautiful.

Breathtaking. Another three weeks later, what had seemed impossible happened. Jessica went home, and the family was reunited; Suzie was radiant. We all wept tears of joy, relief and amazement.

They had several weeks as a family. Suzie brought Jessica to church, and on another day I met her out shopping, the perfect little bundle, with her bright eyes, wrapped up warm in her pram. But on 14 April, another phone call came.

'Charlie, I have to tell you that Jessica died this morning.' No! No! NO! A familiar engulfing wave of rejection rose up from deep inside me; a powerful human emotion in which it's as if one's whole being is activated in some strange way to defend from danger. Truly, death is the last and greatest enemy. Jessica had finished a feed and simply and suddenly died as her heart ceased to beat. She was in her mother's arms.

A week later the church was packed with people who came to say goodbye. It was a momentous and overwhelming funeral. Just as we had declared all those years ago that God was not on trial, so, in different words, this eternal truth was again proclaimed. Dan chose to sing 'St Patrick's Breastplate'; a choice to declare his faith with defiance to any, human or spirit, who would sneer at a loving God in such a context. All were amazed by his clear and unfaltering voice which lanced our working hearts; for any who were present and unsure about God, this courageous act must certainly have been a challenge.

Suzie, pale but composed, spoke with a serene authority. Every word counted. Among them were these: 'I used to say as a joke that I wanted a little girl so that I could plait her hair and buy her shoes. But I had time to do neither.' Charlie guided the grieving company through each part of the service: that the veil between heaven and earth, usually so sturdy, seemed but a film, was perhaps partly because his own heart knew dearly about such things. As the service came to an end, Dan and Suzie projected a photographic record of Jessica's life while the old song rang out:

> Not from sorrow, pain or care,
> Freedom dare I claim …
> This alone will be my prayer,
> Glorify your name.[1]

If anyone had not been undone so far, they were now. For myself, the appearance of the little white coffin before the beginning of the service threw me in a way I was completely unprepared for. I did not know so much grief could still be inside me, but the wells of human emotion are very deep, and from time to time the cover is removed. The years rushed up in an instant to meet me and bring back that other far away funeral.

A question has lingered with me since that day: did Jessica fulfil more of a destiny in three short months than many a mortal who walks the earth for three score years and ten and (increasingly today) well beyond that? If it is true that before you were formed in the womb, God knew you, that before you were born you were set apart;[2] that all the days ordained for you were written in his book;[3] several thoughts follow. Firstly, we might suggest that the quality of our life is more significant than the quantity. We live in a culture which has effectively put away death. Corresponding to a post-Christian age where there are no longer any common absolutes, there are fewer and fewer individuals who will profess themselves ready to die for the name of Christ, as the martyrs of old so readily did. From this we might suggest, secondly, that finding out what God set us apart for, what we have been made for, is of much greater importance than securing a well-ordered life and bank balance. Thirdly, we might question common definitions of happiness. Paul gives us an interesting perspective on this issue:

'For to me, to live is Christ and to die is gain. If I am to go on living in the body, this will mean fruitful labour for me. Yet what shall I choose? I do not know! I am torn between the two: I desire to depart and be with Christ, which is better by far; but it is more necessary for you that I remain in the body.'[4]

Not your average perspective in the West today! I once met a friend of one of our daughters who has a large tattoo of a Huguenot cross on her back, with Paul's words, 'For me to live is Christ, to die is gain', inscribed in Greek around the outer edge of the circle. That at the time tattooing was a controversial subject, or that the dove dives neatly into that intriguing spot that joins back to buttocks, I chose to ignore. I felt I was meeting someone who had understood something deep.

Despite our Western aversion to death and self-sacrifice, we can't deny that in an age of terrorism we are witness to the willingness of a number of people, mostly young, to lose their lives for the sake of a cause. We live in an age of an increasing number of extraordinary psycho-dramas: from time to time, extremists combine mediaeval barbarity with the internet and assassinate random hostages when their equally random demands are not met. The whole world holds its breath when we experience this kind of war without rules. For the hostages caught up in these terrifying events it is, of course, a question of their life and purpose being brutally cut short, not one of embracing death. But for those who do the cutting short, death clearly is a welcome option should the opportunity present itself, or should they lose control of the game.

If this was not crystal clear to the world before 9/11, it has certainly become so since that day, universally regarded as a hinge of history. Perhaps the definitive difference between such 'martyrs' and those who die for their faith in Christ is captured by Paul: 'If I give all I possess to the poor and give over my body to the hardship that I may boast, but do not have love, I gain nothing.'[5]

Many are those whose lives have been cut short by accident, illness, murder or assassination. We can think of mass shootings in (usually) US high schools; of the (thankfully only occasional) story of children being born and kept in degrading captivity and slavery, their existence unknown; or of the sixty-nine young people murdered by the far-right terrorist Anders Breivik in 2011. There are too many such stories, the fruit of unspeakable psychosis. All of these are terrible and untimely losses that should be mourned. Lives of promise and potential cruelly cut short.

God's Purposes Fulfilled

There is, however, another category of lives cut short, where we might consider that though young in years such individuals have somehow completed what God created them for.

We can think of David Brainerd who lost his life to tuberculosis at the age of twenty-nine after ministering to the American Indians for five years, from 1742–47. Or of Martin Luther King, assassinated in his prime as he fought for racial justice and equality hundreds of years later in the 1960s.

We can think of David Watson, to whom I referred in an earlier chapter, who succumbed to cancer at the age of fifty; of John Wimber, notorious for his persevering stance on healing and practice of praying for it, who likewise died of cancer at the age of sixty-seven.

The list is in fact endless, for history is liberally scattered with noble characters who inspire courage, devotion and admiration of all that can be most glorious in a human being.

Had they lived on, all of these people would certainly have added to their achievements, yet we can sometimes be aware of an unspoken consensus that in some way they fulfilled their destiny. Perhaps we can say that though they did not fulfil their potential, more profoundly, they did fulfil their purpose. Why might we think this? Perhaps because what the human spirit perceives in such persons is a reflection of the nature of Jesus, who supremely fulfilled his purpose in the space of thirty-three years. All these people have, to one degree or another, become mature, attaining to the whole measure of the fullness of Christ.[6]

Thinking of Joanna again, is it possible that in some strange way she had fulfilled God's call to her? Was the mercy of God somehow operative here, through the unbearably thoughtless action of a driver making an illegal manoeuvre to reverse into a sideroad? Minutes later, she died in the arms of a Christian doctor who was herself cycling past on her way to work as the accident happened, and who spoke of the extraordinary eye contact they shared as Jo took her last breath. She was thirty-four. The death of anyone so young is hard to bear, and there are no real answers to the anguished cry of 'Why, O Lord?'

'Why is it so hard to face your own death or the death of loved ones? It's so hard because we think this broken world is the only world we're ever going to have … but if Jesus is risen, then your future is so much more beautiful, and so much more certain, than that.'[7]

If we turn to those whose lives have been snuffed out before they have barely begun, like Samuel and Jessica, the question becomes much more delicate and complex. It is a question that can't really be answered for: who knows what the lives of these two tiny infants would have unfolded to reveal?

What I do know is that the loss of Samuel woke up my own soul to the realisation that I was here for a purpose, not here just to amble aimlessly through my days. It may be that many are propelled into reconsidering their ambitions and lives by just such a lightning strike of tragedy.

It's like an alarm bell sounding, that puts a person on red alert, triggering a search for meaning and purpose. Thus, the outcome of one person's life might be activated by the cutting short of another's. This is what happened to Jesus' disciples. His death and resurrection catapulted a bunch of men who struggled to grasp what was going on, whether at the feeding of the five thousand or the transfiguration, into a group of powerful evangelists, preachers and prophets.

Every tragic loss of life has the potential to open up or close down the fruitfulness of other lives. The death of someone we love crushes, paralyses and immobilises us; it empowers doubt, releases hopelessness, robs us of energy and makes us sit down by the wayside in tears, unable to go on. A graphic picture of such dejection was sealed in the memory of many during the 2004 Olympics: the sight of the marathon runner Paula Radcliffe sinking to the ground, later saying, 'There was just nothing in my legs.' It's a good description of how the body can respond to trauma, and after the death of Samuel, I felt like this for a long time.

But in this season of what felt like a suspension of life itself, something deeper was going on. This disruption of my former plans would not be allowed to crush my spirit and make me give up on what I knew I was called to, and what I would therefore say God made me for; namely together with Charlie to serve whatever expression of church we found ourselves called to at different stages of our lives. Sometimes tragedy, whether clothed in death or other garments, does stifle faith and deprive a person of the energy to trust God and believe he can hear our cries of pain and despair. But often it does the very opposite.

During our time in Paris, we met the Beise family. Jim and Angela first came to Paris with their baby, Brian, to work with Youth With A Mission in 1987. While living in Paris they had their second and third children, Melissa and Rachel. Returning to the States to further their training, their fourth child, Michael, was born. But Michael was born with a composite of disabilities.

Thus began a journey of multiple operations for Michael, disrupting their family life and taking them on a very different route from the one they had imagined. Nevertheless they decided to return to France all the same, and arrived in 2000. This was not going to divert what they understood to be their calling. Meeting Michael and watching the dynamics of this extraordinary family provoked further questions for me over the subject of a life's purpose. Michael could not be said to be living what most of us would deem a normal life, and nor could his family; yet the tapestry of this family's communal life was far richer and more filled with meaning and purpose than many a family life untroubled by such a challenge. Could it be that Michael is in fact fulfilling his purpose and that, because of him, so is his family; and many others too, who come within their orbit and are brought up short by what they see in this family?

In 2003, Angela sent me the following piece of writing about Michael:

Recently my son Michael's therapist/teacher said something to me that shook me to the core of my being. It took me a few days to process her comment and to begin to understand my own reaction. Michael is eight years old and has a rare genetic syndrome called 18Q-minus. We moved to France three years ago, with our four children, to work as missionaries. We have been surprised to find that there are few schools for disabled children, and none where they can be mainstreamed. In our area of Paris alone there are 300 handi-capped children on a waiting list for a school place. We have searched in vain for three years for a place for Michael. Fortunately, we have a teacher who comes to our home twice a week to teach him.

On this occasion we were talking as she left our house after a therapy session about this question. She has been proactive in helping us in our search, and was telling me about a couple of schools in the area that exist specifically for children with Down's syndrome. She encouraged me to apply, although Michael does not have Down's. Then she made the shocking, or what should be shocking statement. 'Schools for Down's syndrome children are starting to take children with other syndromes, since Down's is becoming so rare. Now that tests can tell so early in pregnancy that a baby has Down's, fewer people are choosing to complete the pregnancy.' I walked back into my house trying to unscramble my reaction to her statement.

Michael has benefited greatly from the incredible advances in medical technology. He was born with a cleft lip and palate, and feet that required extensive surgery. I am grateful for amazing doctors, and technology, that have so beautifully met his needs. But today I wondered whether technology was also robbing us of an important element of society.

In the days that followed I tried to imagine a society void of dis-abled people. What if this technology reaches a stage at which any or all babies with special needs can be eliminated? What would society look like if everyone were 'normal', if we never had to make provision for people who are slow, or deaf, or blind, or lame, or crippled? What if we could eliminate the 'weak' altogether? The question that haunted me was this: Do disabled, imperfect people contribute anything to society? Do we need them in order to be balanced, healthy and whole?

I didn't have to look any further than my own family to start finding answers. My children are among the most selfless, giving people I have ever known. I am in awe of them. They have made sacrifices, too numerous and too big to calculate, for their handicapped sibling. One might think that this would make them bitter and discontented with life. In fact it has done exactly the opposite. They are thankful and giving, and tolerant of difficult and unlovely people. Could it be that these 'imperfect' people somehow balance society as a whole? How would love and compassion be developed among people who were exclusively surrounded by beautiful and intelligent people? My children treasure nothing more than a smile or kiss, sometimes just eye contact from their little brother. Sometimes I see my husband kiss our son's often expressionless, crooked little face and my heart nearly bursts with a love and joy I can hardly contain.

As I continued to ponder the future with its possibility of a 'perfect' society, a verse from the Bible kept coming to mind. 'Do nothing out of selfish ambition or vain conceit.'[8] I can think of no other reason to eliminate a disabled child than either of these things. To parent a disabled child will require many ambitions to be laid aside. Large sums of money may have to be spent on therapists, doctors, medical bills and equipment. The child will become the focus of most of your time and energy and will determine what you can and cannot do in many situations. He can bring limitations to the dreams you can pursue. He can bring more sleepless nights than most parents will ever have to endure. Parenting seasons will be unusually long, and grief will last the lifetime of such a child. Parents not only grieve the child they 'lost' at his birth but grieve as they watch him struggle with tasks that normally come easily to a child of his age. They grieve when he realises he is not like other children, and when they see him in physical or emotional pain. They will certainly die to selfish ambition.

What about vain conceit? That will die too. It's often embarrassing to have a child who cries out in public for no reason, doesn't always behave appropriately in social settings, looks different, and acts differently. He will never be top of the class, or a good athlete. Most of what this child's parents will do will be for the benefit of another individual.

I wonder if in time when our advanced technology has succeeded in eliminating the weak and needy, whether our scholars, theologians, poets and politicians won't ponder the question: How did our society become so selfish and loveless, so intolerant and so driven by individual gain? Will the 'perfect' society be a place where any of us would want to live?

I am one parent of a child with special needs who is better because this child came into my life. Would I have chosen this road? Never in a million years. Am I grateful for the changed person I am today? You bet. Would I trade one sleepless night, hour in a hospital, penny spent on medical bills, or minute spent in a therapist's office? No chance. All heartache considered, I'll take the 'imperfect' society.[9]

The current evolution of European and US law in this area poses a serious threat to many lives being lived out fully. Joanna Jepson, ordained in the Church of England, was operated on for a cleft palate as a baby, and gained notoriety following her high profile campaign many years later to bring abortion back into the national arena for debate. Her reason was that, had her life begun at a different time, it might not have begun at all.

'We are losing part of our community,' she says, 'and it's a vital part. I am raising awareness, and that is as much for women as it is for those babies who might be aborted.... Are we OK with abortion being the thing we celebrate as a point of freedom for women and women's choice? Really, is that as good as it gets?'[10]

Like many sensitive topics the temperature (and the tempers) can rise dramatically in any discussion of abortion, or termination if we prefer. But there's no getting away from the sharpness of those words. And it's not a one-size-fits-all question. Nevertheless the responsibilities involved in creating a new life, albeit accidentally, and the rights of the unborn never seem to be debated along with the rights of women (and men). It's politically incorrect. And it's magnificently incoherent ...

My friend Colette, mother of twenty-one-year-old Katie, who has Down's syndrome, and is at college, says:

For the first eighteen years of my daughter's life, I had simply acknowledged that prenatal screening for babies like her took place, and that some women chose not to continue the pregnancy. In fact, I had had personal experience of this. It happened when Katie was about three years old and had recently had open heart surgery at Great Ormond Street Hospital, where amazing surgeons had saved her life for the second time. A lady I knew, who had also known Katie for a while, returned from a holiday to say that while overseas, she had had an abortion because she had found out that her baby would be like mine, and she chose to tell me this, while Katie sat happily playing with her toys at our feet. One life saved, another ended, the same medical profession, the same genetics.

It felt wrong, it felt like a negative judgement on my baby's life, but it was her 'choice', and so my objections were difficult to put into words.

Fifteen years later, I read responses to a consultation by the National Screening Committee, concerning the introduction of a new, more accurate screening test for Down's syndrome, NIPT. And suddenly, there were the words that explained my feelings. Did introducing this test comply with our Equality legislation?

And so I started on a journey. I have met many parents and siblings along the way who also recognise prenatal screening for Down's syndrome for what it is, facilitating discrimination. I don't blame people who don't recognise it, or who don't want to, it took me a while. But once you see it, you can't unsee it. And once you have tried explaining it to someone with Down's syndrome, who doesn't understand the nuances of 'choosing not to keep the baby', you can't turn back, or at least I, and several others like me, can't.

So we press on together, combatting this discrimination. Are all foetuses equal? Well it turns out they aren't.

Choosing babies based on their characteristics is a very dangerous slope. Allowing other people to ascribe humanity to a particular group is also a dangerous situation to be in, but that is what we are currently doing. 'Oh, I am pregnant!' she celebrates. 'When's the baby due?' say her friends. 'A boy!' says dad, following the scan. 'It has Down's syndrome,' says the doctor, 'what would you like to do? I can book you (and the baby?) in for a termination next Tuesday.'

Based purely on the baby's genetics that will lead to some unknown level of learning difficulty, and may lead to some medical complications, women are told there is a decision to make. And this is not just any old decision, this is a decision to continue or end a human life. Surrounded by fear, lack of preparation, outdated perceptions, and, dare I say it, disability discrimination, 90% of women unsurprisingly choose termination, and yet would be horrified if termination was suggested based on the fact the baby was a girl. Yet both being female and being disabled are protected characteristics under the Equality Act.

I believe we are far more than our genetics. If this is true, what are we doing?

So my friends and I are out to change attitudes, to help people see the positives in a life with Down's syndrome, and see those with Down's syndrome as human, but also to try to highlight where we, as a society are going. That this is discrimination is clear. Whether we as a society wish to accept, and have the NHS facilitate, that form of discrimination, when we rightly legislate against it just minutes later, after birth, is the big question. At this stage in the progress of genetic medicine that poem, 'First they came for the Jews', has never been more apt. 'First they came for those with Down's syndrome, but I did not have Down's syndrome, so I did not speak out ...' Let's hope and act, so it doesn't end the same way.[11]

Her words are strong, but she has a right to be strong; she speaks from experience, not theory.

Questions of purpose and destiny are complex and philosophical, and there are no simple answers.

Theologians from Augustine to Barth have analysed, expounded and pronounced on the subject. My goal is to raise rather than answer questions, and hopefully provoke in you the desire to live a life that is full of adventure and compassion. I believe that God lovingly creates every human being to walk through an exciting and unique existence on the earth with him. Equally, I believe that because the world has refused his leadership and Lordship, multitudes are wandering in the desert, without focus, without purpose, searching unsuccessfully and increasingly despairingly for meaning in a world that grows more dangerous as it grows more sophisticated. In this way they bypass what they are appointed for.

You were created unique and called to purpose and life in all its fullness, which is what Jesus said he had come to give.[12] Let yourself be inspired by the stories of martyrs and heroes, of men and women who were longing for a better country, a heavenly one,[13] and so were free from the various forms of slavery in which this world so often imprisons us. Every day is unique and every day counts. Three decades redolent with purpose and meaning better describe a life fully lived than six without. Be inspired even by the little ones who spent so short a time on earth yet made such an impact upon their parents, families and communities. Allow yourself to be moved by the brief life of Jessica, the unfinished story of Michael, the truncated life of Joanna, and the inspiring story of Katie, and let them call you to find life in all its fullness, and to flourish in it.

14

Pain, the Gift Nobody Wants
A Theology of Suffering

*God lets himself be pushed out of the
world onto the cross. He is weak and
powerless in the world, and that is
precisely the way in which he is with us
and helps us.... The Bible directs man
to God's powerlessness and suffering;
for only the suffering God can help.*

- Dietrich Bonhoeffer, *Letters
and Papers from Prison*

*God whispers to us in our pleasures,
speaks in our conscience, but shouts
in our pains: it is his megaphone
to rouse a deaf world.*

- C. S. Lewis, *The Problem of Pain*

Paul Brand was an exceptional missionary doctor, whose book about his life captivated me.[1] Born to missionary parents in India, at the age of nine he was sent to England for his education, already familiar with dysentery and malaria at this young age. Perhaps this, and the loss of his father when he was only fifteen, determined his choice of medicine as a career, qualifying as a surgeon during the Second World War. He returned to India after the war and, following a visit to a leprosy sanatorium, began to explore the reasons for the deformities developed in those with the disease, eventually discovering that most of their injuries were the result of pain insensitivity, and not directly caused by the leprosy itself. From here he became an internationally recognised pioneer leprosy surgeon, receiving many awards and honours during his lifetime.

Brand came to appreciate the importance and value of pain, and to see that it is vital for the preservation of health in anyone leading a normal life. He gives horrifying descriptions of the results of insensitivity in those with leprosy or a congenital absence of pain, and goes on to reflect about the pursuit of pleasure in our Western society, questioning whether it can, like leprosy, produce equally horrifying results in the psyche as well as the body, because of our insensitivity to its effects.

I was not only captivated by Brand himself, but also by the profound message his life and work carried. If we become insensitive to things that hurt us we will suffer damage that we'll be unaware of, sometimes until it's too late. The parable for our modern world made a deep impression, and made me reflect on the importance of pain.

That pain and suffering are universal and unavoidable has been implicit throughout this book, and woven into many of the stories, but I want to unpack the question a little further in this chapter, since the pain of suffering and its seemingly random nature are often the final fence at which people fall in their exploration of Christianity.

Clearly there are different kinds of suffering: there is suffering we bring on ourselves; suffering that comes to us through the deadening of our consciences—which is the kind best illustrated by the leprosy image; suffering caused by natural disasters; suffering caused by relational breakdown; and suffering caused by sickness. Dictionary definitions focus on serious physical or mental pain (to which we should add emotional pain), distress and hardship.

So suffering is a vast topic, which has almost limitless forms. It has been explored and wrestled with throughout the history of man, and is still the subject of many debates, books, personal exploration and autobiographies. Surely in our modern age, with our medical and technological sophistication we should be able to eliminate much of it? But no. Suffering remains in its many forms. So let's look at some of the underlying causes of it, and at how we might survive and even thrive and grow through our trials and tragedies.

I want to do this through the lens of the book of Job, a man described as 'blameless and upright', one who 'feared God and shunned evil.'[2] The book of Job opens up a whole new dimension of understanding about suffering, which largely and paradoxically concerns the fact that it is not given to us to understand it at all in terms of rationality. But it's a book that helps us to know that it's integral to our humanity. My goal here is to try to help us make peace with a component of human life that we can neither properly comprehend, nor avoid. But before we do this it's worth taking a look at the cultural background against which we wrestle with our suffering.

'The vast majority of the church worldwide has a theology of prosperity rather than a theology of suffering.'[3] As humanity increasingly subscribes to a humanist vision of how the world works and succeeds, and steadily pushes back the boundaries of survival through technology and medicine, so in equal measure we have slowly rejected failure of any kind. For the twenty-first-century human the ultimate failure is to die, and so we find ourselves in a world in which we speak of passing, of passing on, but seldom of dying. Passing where? Passing on to what? Further evidence of our unwillingness to embrace death is the mantra, 'It's time to move on' from grieving. There's an urge to distance ourselves from the reality of death and all it signifies as fast as possible, in the belief that if we ignore it, it will go away and take its pain with it.

At the same time we are confronted with the reality of suffering on both a global and a personal scale. Terrorist events pepper the second decade of the twenty-first century. The most recent development in the communal global experience of terror has been the capacity to live stream multiple murders as they happen, and it will be some time before the effects of this on the communal psyche become known; but we can be sure there will be some.

When an attack happens, the response is often worldwide, immediate and intense. Personal suffering can certainly hold the same intensity for the individual as war and terrorism hold for the community. I well remember speaking to a woman at a conference who, asking for prayer, said to me, 'This time a year ago, my husband left me, and fifteen years ago our son went missing while backpacking in Australia....' There was nothing to say in response to such information. There are no immediate answers, and any attempt to give one is likely to be in the Job's comforters category; his so-called friends who, as we shall see, tried to account for his suffering in a very unhelpful way. By far the best response is either silence or a comforting arm or our own tears, depending on the context.

One thing all this means is that we often experience a profound inner tension and conflict, between the reality of suffering, and our corporate humanist reflex to 'sort it.' Maybe you are thinking, 'Wait a minute, Christians don't think like this.' But oh yes, they do. Because we all subconsciously reflect the corporate cultural consciousness. I remember being at a large Christian conference, in a crowd of about 5,000 people, as we were all invited to pray for a mother fighting advanced cancer. It felt uncomfortable, and as if we were challenging God to defy the prayers of such a large crowd ... trying to outnumber him somehow. Months later I attended the funeral of this mother, and discovered that the experience at the conference was only one of a number of such events attended by the family in search of healing. I don't for a minute question the choices of this family. Of course, when we believe absolutely in the power of prayer, and in the power of Jesus to heal, why should we not try everything we can to bring relief from pain and suffering to all concerned? It's natural and completely understandable, and times of extreme distress can lend us an almost superhuman energy for survival.

But like other similar stories, the experience caused me to reflect on this instinct for survival at all costs, and whether sometimes it may cause us subconsciously to deny the reality of our suffering, and unwittingly forgo precious weeks or months of peace and treasured memories in its pursuit.

We can tend to build a theology by selecting biblical material that supports what we want to believe, and influences the way we spend our precious resources. Failing to embrace the Bible in its entirety can have tragic consequences; and church history is shamefully littered with examples of false doctrines arising from the practice of selective Bible reading, each of which has led ultimately to great unhappiness and/or disunity. A terminally ill person may die despite receiving prophetic assurance of healing. Or we might think of the closed Brethren of the 1970s and '80s, during which time the denomination effectively became a sect, excluding from membership people who were judged to be mingling with 'the world'. Or of the prosperity gospel, with its message that if you serve God well he will make you rich, which is still very much alive in some church contexts. Such are the fruits of faulty theology.

I am persuaded that suffering is an indispensable component of our Christian faith. How could it not be, with a Saviour who laid down his perfect life on behalf of all mankind? 'The crucible for silver and the furnace for gold, but the Lord tests the heart.'[4] At first sight this seems harsh, but even a moment's meditation will lead us to reflect on the beauty of refined gold, and very possibly on the way our own suffering and loss has refined our character, modified our opinions, and smoothed our responses. We may be reminded of the Japanese art of *kintsugi*, which repairs broken artefacts with gold, creating an even more beautiful item.

A friend of mine, describing her father's last months, said of him, 'Everything was stripped away; ministry, health, freedom, but what was left was something of great beauty. He was not diminished in his illness, but grew larger.'

This is exactly what befell Job; everything was stripped away—livelihood, property, family, health—an unbearable weight of loss, but a picture from the Spirit of God to help us understand that not only is suffering not the worst thing that can come to us, but that through it we may become more like Jesus himself.

'And we all, who with unveiled faces contemplate the Lord's glory,' writes Paul to the Corinthians, 'are being transformed into his image with ever-increasing glory, which comes from the Lord.'[5] He follows this immediately with the famous 'jars of clay' image, 'to show that this all-surpassing power is from God.'[6] We are 'hard pressed … perplexed … persecuted … struck down,'[7] but it is God who keeps us operational. The *kintsugi* image returns to mind, as does the more prosaic version found on greetings cards: 'Blessed are the cracked, for they let in the light!'

Job is widely considered to be the first book of the Bible to be written, despite its place after the Pentateuch and the historical narratives. This makes it a prelude to creation itself, underlining the notion that suffering is inherent to existence. Job asks the questions most of us ask at some time or another:

'Why did I not perish at birth, and die as I came from the womb?'[8]

'Why is life given to a man whose way is hidden, whom God has hedged in?'[9]

'What strength do I have, that I should still hope? What prospects, that I should be patient?'[10]

'Is there any wickedness on my lips?'[11]

'If I have sinned, what have I done to you, you who see every-thing we do? Why have you made me your target?'[12]

'Your hands shaped me and made me. Will you now turn and destroy me?'[13]

This is a far from exhaustive list of Job's questions around suffering; and his questioning expresses well our confusion too, when confronted with apparently random suffering. We struggle with it, knowing instinctively that this isn't the way things are meant to be. And yet at the same time we believe in a God who is completely loving, completely in control of history,[14] and intimately concerned with the details of our lives.[15]

So how can we integrate our personal suffering and the weight of humanity's suffering with our faith?

Looking to Job's example, he is someone who desires to know the presence of God, and we can be too. Only a man or woman who has learnt to recognise God's presence and learnt to trust him could say, as Job did, 'The Lord gave and the Lord has taken away ... shall we accept good from God, and not trouble?'[16]

Moses also understood the need to know God's presence. Speaking of the Israelites' troubled journey towards the Promised Land, he says, 'If your Presence does not go with us, do not send us up from here.'[17] We must want to be in the Father's presence, just as Moses wanted to be, and find the kind of worshipful setting that suits our personality and taste. This is not about being choosy, it's about being who God created us to be. Some of us respond to quite repetitive contemporary songs and hymns of worship; some to hymns ancient and modern, some to classical choral or requiem music, and yet others to the soaring heights of classical music that is not necessarily explicitly spiritual. Hopefully you are situating yourself somewhere along this spectrum as you read. The essential thing is to find space and time to connect with the presence of God, but so often we are more energised by serving God than by being with him.

Why is being with God more important than serving him? Because when lightning strikes and we are not familiar with the close presence of Jesus, we are utterly undone and at sea. Of course suffering, whether sudden or gradual, undoes us for many reasons other than the state of our devotional life, but as Job's initial response reveals, familiarity with the Father can steady us in the storm.

Without this, prayer can become an obstacle rather than a door to hope, because there's too much that doesn't make sense, and the pain is overwhelming. And so our hearts can become hardened; more often because of this pain and sickness of heart, mind or body rather than because of wilful rebellion.

So central to human life is this subject that C. S. Lewis treated it in two books, *The Problem of Pain*, a seminal exploration of its meaning, and the much more personal record of his own experience following the death of his wife, *A Grief Observed*. In the former, he included an appendix written by R. Havard, M.D., which stated:

> Mental pain is less dramatic than physical pain, but it is more common and also harder to bear. The frequent attempt to conceal mental pain increases the burden: it is easier to say 'My tooth is aching,' than to say, 'My heart is broken.'[18]

Half a century on from this comment, we supposedly live in an age which has overcome all stigma relating to mental health issues, yet even as I was writing this chapter a young friend who suffers from depression reflected how difficult it still is not to spiral down into shame and the fear of being found out.

Fear easily hardens our hearts while pain, though it may harden our hearts, can also call us towards God. In *The Problem of Pain*, Lewis writes:

> The human spirit will not even begin to try to surrender self-will as long as all seems to be well with it. Now error and sin both have this property, that the deeper they are the less their victim suspects their existence; they are masked evil. Pain is unmasked, unmistakeable evil; every man knows that something is wrong when he is being hurt … We can ignore pleasure. But pain insists upon being attended to.[19]

Clearly we need to unpack this a little. We've already noted that not all suffering is caused by sin, and Job is a prime example of this truth. Yet at the same time, many can testify to being woken up, and experiencing a life-changing *volte face* because of the advent of serious suffering. As Christians, we are filled with a longing to reconcile our experiences of suffering with a loving God who is just in all his ways, and to help others do the same.

Francis Schaeffer said, 'If a belief system is true, then it is fully livable for anyone in any culture, in any demographic group, at any time point in history.'[20] Disciples of Jesus believe that Christianity is that belief system, and on a good day are eager to follow Peter's exhortation; 'Always be prepared to give an answer to everyone who asks you to give the reason for the hope that you have.'[21]

A justification of the ways of God to men—a theodicy—is a legitimate task for the Christian, and in Job, the search to do this takes place entirely within the household of faith. All the participants are fully committed to belief in one supreme God who is unquestionably just in all his acts. It's taken for granted that somehow the goodness of God and the existence of evil are both absolutely real and coexist. So our task is somehow to find a place of peace within this framework; to embrace a theology of suffering without rejecting God.

Here in Job, the problem of suffering is not dealt with abstractly but through one man's suffering. Evil and suffering (the impact of evil on a person's life, as amply demonstrated in the catastrophes that Satan unleashes upon Job) is really evidence *for* the existence of God, not against it, because we recognise it as a contrast to what we know as good. The recognition of evil is dependent on the existence of good.

Sickness reminds us of being well; war reminds us of peace; cruelty reminds us of kindness. Evil is good that has been corrupted, spoilt, broken, yet so many conclude that because there is abundant evil in the world, God either doesn't exist or is weak, malicious or indifferent to our suffering.

So in a way, evil is only a problem for the person who believes in an all-loving, all-powerful God. Therefore, it's a problem for the cast of Job. If God doesn't exist, then suffering isn't a problem, it's just the way things are.

The Causes of Suffering

We can ask then, what causes suffering?

Firstly, moral evil relates to the way people behave. The biblical teaching that a man reaps what he sows in this life is a central theme of Job, repeatedly emphasised by his so-called friends. Eliphaz for example insists that Job is being disciplined.[22] And yet Job's story illustrates that troubles and benefits seem not to be distributed to mankind by an even-handed justice. We have to accept that Job's righteousness is genuine, because God himself testifies to it.[23] It's both comforting and surprising that we can be these things and still find suffering is our lot, so Job's experience provides a balance to the Deuteronomic covenant in which Yahweh sets two ways before his people—life through obedience or death through disloyalty[24]—and which is echoed in Paul's words in Galatians; 'A man reaps what he sows'.[25]

Job helps us understand that life is more complex; the wealthy and apparently happy man may actually be miserable, while the poor and apparently deprived man may be peaceful.[26]

Incidentally, this is yet another illustration of the need, or obligation really, to embrace the whole Bible so that we avoid becoming either over-indulgent or over-harsh with ourselves or others.

At the same time, we know that much suffering in the world is the result of the way we use our free will. Free will means we have a choice of action in every situation, and every choice we make has consequences or costs. 'Every mistake comes with a price tag.' I can think of mistakes I have made that have had costly consequences … what about you?

A second cause of evil originates from nature itself, either in the form of disease and sickness or in the form of natural disasters.

Let's look at them separately as we ask why God allows these things to happen.

First, sickness and disease: a popular response is that it's just the way things are; put more bluntly, the evolutionary process is simply weeding out weaker genes. This is the view of famous atheist Richard Dawkins:

> In a universe of blind physical forces and genetic replication, some people are going to get hurt, other people are going to get lucky, and you won't find any rhyme or reason in it, nor any justice. The universe we observe has precisely the properties we should expect if there is, at bottom, no design, no purpose, no evil and no good, nothing but blind pitiless indifference.[27]

This seems so very bleak. In response, let's turn to the opinion of the apologist Sharon Dirckx:

> The Christian response would be that this is not just the way the world is. There is a brokenness at the level of our physical bodies that has not always been present. When people said 'no' to God they also dragged along into their rebellion their very skin and bones, their very heart and brain, their very muscles and marrow. It is as though

> our disconnect from God entered the physical-
> ity of every person ever to live, whether religious
> or irreligious.... When someone becomes ill ...
> it is a general consequence of living in a world
> in which our very bodies are not as they should
> be because humankind is out of sync with their
> Maker.[28]

For the atheist, humans are the answer to the problem of pain: 'For the first time in human history [people] possess the means—provided by science and technology—to ameliorate the human condition, advance happiness and freedom, and enhance human life for all people on this planet.'[29]

But Christians will want to help people whether they believe in God or not, because they can, but primarily because they are made by him. So for the theist, God is the solution *through* human beings—medicine, technology, counselling, NGOs, aid workers and more. We know that contrary to what the humanist mani-festo implies, science can't solve every health problem, because of the complexity of the human body and the limitations of human beings; and untreatable illness is a reminder of the brevity and frailty of our human lives.

Before we leave the topic of sickness that has as its underlying cause humanity being out of alignment with God, it's important to return to the idea of consequences and costs to our decisions; we must remember that some illnesses *are* caused by lifestyle choices, an obvious example being substance abuse of any kind. In the West, an obsession with food, whether over-eating or starving ourselves, is the cause of a great deal of sickness, and tragically even of death in some cases. Despite this, the Bible tells of a God who is close to the broken-hearted, who doesn't disregard the weak, whatever the cause of their broken hearts or weakness; a God who strengthens the weary and points us to a story bigger than our own. Just as the book of Job does. But we'll come to that.

Let's take a brief look at the other kind of evil originating from nature, that of natural disasters.

There are three common explanations for these. First, some argue that cataclysmic events sustain the planet. For example, volcanic ash contains minerals that produce fertile soil valuable for agriculture. Volcanic eruptions are seen as being the fine-tuning of the planet that sustains life, only becoming a natural disaster when loss of life occurs.

The second explanation is that nature itself is broken and reflects our human rebellion against God. Paul writes in the book of Romans, 'We know that the whole creation has been groaning as in the pains of childbirth right up to the present time'.[30]

And flowing from this comes a third explanation, which is that we ourselves have become disconnected from nature in the same way that we are disconnected from God. Genesis portrays the closeness of the first humans with the creator but also with the creation. Many animals are alert to natural signals, and can recognise for example the approach of a storm. We all know how dogs retreat in a thunderstorm, and how cattle head for high ground in flood or tsunami conditions. 'The animals take cover; they remain in their dens. The tempest comes out from its chamber, the cold from the driving winds.'[31]

We've noted that man is responsible for the consequences of his choices. One of the choices which has the biggest and worst impact is the choice not to share our wealth, which of course leads to oppression of the poor; and one of the chief ways in which the poor are oppressed is through social conditions. Municipalities and cheap high-density housing are swept away like so many matchsticks in a catastrophic flood or storm, because of inadequate infrastructure. Such things account for the much higher death toll in developing countries when disaster strikes …

Not only do nations not share their wealth, but many nations plunder the earth's resources, which is widely considered the primary cause of climate change leading to global warming … and has led to the increase we are seeing in climate-related extreme weather events.

So we see that moral evil and natural evil are inextricably related; a case in point being Cyclone Idai that tragically swept through Mozambique, Zimbabwe and Malawi in 2019, turning the land into sea at the cost of hundreds of lives, thousands of homes and much more besides; and triggering the inevitable outbreak of cholera caused by lack of sanitation and adequate food and medical supplies. The cause was the cyclone, the cost was death, disease and sickness; but another cause was poor housing quality, the result of the unequal distribution of wealth between the global north and the global south. While we can't take personal responsibility for such cataclysmic events, we can recognise the corporate human responsibility implicated in them, and acknowledge the overwhelming injustice that such events reflect.

Perhaps this is a good moment to pause and consider the immeasurable weight of suffering unleashed by natural disasters ... and to ask God whether you could do or give anything, however small, in addition to praying for the poor and dispossessed.

As we see, the causes and responsibilities around suffering are complex and can be confusing. Turning back to Job now, there is a further element of complexity when we find that Job's calamity had its origins with both God *and* Satan. The opening conversation is initiated by God as the angels 'present themselves before the Lord,' and are joined by Satan.[32] Yet Satan's presence with the angels is provocative; it is as if he is throwing down the gauntlet, so perhaps it is he who is the real initiator of this conflictual conversation. It's a very 'human' conversation in a way:

God: Have you noticed my servant/friend Job? He's really amazing, an exceptionally godly person.

Satan: Well of course he's amazing, you've made life a total breeze for him. You've given him everything from wealth to health. But I bet if tragedy struck it'd be a different story.[33]

So, tragedy strikes in unimaginable dimensions.

Enter Job's so-called friends who adopt the role of counsellor. But their arguments are very limited by their human reason; for example: 'Obviously God wouldn't allow such traumas to befall a righteous man so he must have sinned and therefore he needs to repent, turn around, say sorry, change direction'.[34]

Much of what Eliphaz, Bildad and Zophar say about God is true, and substantiated by scriptures across the breadth of the Bible, but all of it is wrongly directed at Job; both interpretation and application are profoundly wrong. It's yet another reminder of the vital importance of embracing the Bible in its entirety, while accepting that comprehension will be a lifelong journey. We may point the finger at Job's friends, but aren't we also very quick to want to sort out suffering, and somehow make sense of things that make no sense? We easily judge by what we see instead of what we hear, as these men did, and can even have an internal reflex of wondering what the person may have done wrong: the believer whose unbelieving spouse isn't showing the slightest sign of interest in the things of God; the devout couple with a prodigal teenager; the sincere father struggling to make ends meet. During our years in Paris, when we were living on one salary and bringing up four teenagers (who were all at International schools with the children of diplomats and civil servants, so experiencing constant peer pressure about clothes, appearance and equipment) we remember the sense of shame at having to ask our mission agency if they could fund the purchase of new tyres for the car. It was a huge struggle to make ends meet, and we were conscious that the mission agency might have raised an eyebrow about our budgeting on receipt of this request.

The fact is that tragedy and suffering are no respecters of situation or spirituality. Joseph made all the right decisions but still went through the darkness of being accused of sexual harassment and sent to prison.[35] Likewise Job, and his response to trauma was exemplary; he tore his robe and shaved his head, which are both expressions of anguish and mourning, but he also 'fell to the ground in worship.'[36]

Deliverance eventually came to Job, not from the godly way in which he handled his trials but from the manifest visitation of God's glory to him. Carefully considered, this is a very freeing thought, in that though we may fail to respond to our trials as we would like, our failings will not remove God's compassion.

Job's journey is full of mood swings, which tells us it's OK to say lots of things we may have been taught not to say or to suppress. He moves between the deep depression of chapter 3 (I wish I'd never been born) to extraordinary revelations of truth.

> Even now my witness is in heaven; my advocate
> is on high. My intercessor is my friend as my eyes
> pour out tears to God; on behalf of a man he pleads
> with God as one pleads for his friend.[37]

Somehow he sees deep into the spiritual realm and far into the future, articulating the truth that the role of the resurrected and ascended Jesus is to pray, to intercede.[38]

We find strong language of despair, where Job voices his anguish, and says he would prefer death to what he's going through.[39] We find too the contradictions of the person in pain, as Job says, 'Though he slay me, yet will I hope in him', in the same breath justifying himself: 'I will surely defend my ways to his face.'[40]

Apparent immunity to pain, or what is sometimes called 'victorious' living in the context of deep suffering can be unreal and inauthentic. Three months after the loss of Samuel, a couple at the church we were then members of cheerfully inquired on a Sunday, 'I expect you're feeling better now?'

To be real with people means humbling ourselves, opening ourselves and becoming vulnerable. It means taking off our masks. It means asking for help. To be real with God means raving and ranting, screaming out our pain, as both Job and David did, and asking God questions. Job, says God, was justified in questioning him. 'You have not spoken the truth about me, as my servant Job has.'[41]

This is God making clear that he welcomes Job's questioning of his justice because Job's integrity is more pleasing to him than the judgemental approach of his friends.

So where does this leave us as we consider the mystery of suffering? It calls us to the art of waiting; it challenges us to think of ourselves as God thinks of us: 'My dove in the clefts of the rock, in the hiding-places on the mountainside, show me your face, let me hear your voice; for your voice is sweet, and your face is lovely.'[42] This is just one of the many expressions of God's love for us that are strewn like flowers through the pages of the Bible.

And so we come full circle; let me remind you what I said a few moments ago: the book of Job opens up a whole new dimension of understanding about suffering, which largely and paradoxically concerns the fact that it is not given to us to understand it at all in terms of rationality. But it's a book that helps us to know that it's integral to our humanity, and as we've seen, there are vast areas of human misery which are neither personal, nor remedial, nor redemptive. They just are, and are often beyond explanation. They are a mystery.

They are a mystery while we live in what Paul, referring to our physical bodies, calls our earthly tent. But human suffering recalls God's suffering as his son laid down his life on the cross. And the suffering of Jesus *is* redemptive, for though we wait, we know that just as he came back to life on the far side of the cross, so one day he will return and make all things new.

This is beautifully expressed in the title song of the new St Aldates worship album, *Until You Do*:

> Through every trial, through every fear,
> Through every tear we can't conceal,
> God we look to You.
> Through every storm,
> Through every pain,
> Through every grief we can't explain,
> God we look to You.
> You became a Man of Sorrows that we might
>   know joy,
> You have treasured every tear drop,
> And said that You'd restore.
> You will not forget Your people,
> You'll make all things new
> Until You do, we choose to trust in You
> Until You do, we choose to worship You[43]

These are some of the lyrics, and I encourage you to listen to the whole song, for it will move you.

My hope in stirring the deep waters of suffering is that wherever you sit with it as you read, something here will soothe your soul and help you in your sitting; that something here will enable you to release long suppressed pain if you have been taught that 'you don't need to be upset;' that something here will light up God's immeasurable love for you if that light has grown dim because of suffering; and that something here will free you to reach out with compassion and acceptance of another's suffering. And then, just in case you're reading this because indeed in your exploration of Christianity suffering was the last straw and the final fence that couldn't be jumped, I hope with all my heart that you might be able after all to soar over it.

15

The Voice of This Calling
Life in All Its Fullness

'The men where you live cultivate five thousand roses in one
garden—and they do not find what they seek!' 'That is true,' I
said. 'And yet what they are seeking may be found in a single rose
or a drop of water.' 'So it can,' I answered. And the Little Prince
went on: 'But the eyes are blind: one must look with the heart.'
- Antoine de Saint-Exupéry, *The Little Prince*

Christ plays in ten thousand places,
Lovely in limbs, and lovely in eyes not his
To the Father through the features of men's faces.
- Gerard Manley Hopkins, *Poems and Prose*

Then there came a swift flash like fire (but it burnt nobody) either
from the sky or from the Lion itself, and every drop of blood tingled in
the children's bodies, and the deepest, wildest voice they had ever heard
was saying: 'Narnia, Narnia, Narnia, awake. Love. Think. Speak.'
- C. S. Lewis, *The Magician's Nephew*

Turning up the volume, I raised my voice and accompanied Andrea Bocelli with abandon, singing at the top of my voice. The difference between us was that he was singing earthly love songs and I was singing heavenly ones. He sang to an audience of probably hundreds of thousands, and I was singing to an audience of one. Rain lashed the windscreen in the darkening air as I drove down the motorway, returning from a conference at which I had officially taken on a leadership role within one of the numerous prayer networks around the world. It was a moment to remember and a journey of great joy. I was laughing and crying and singing, and it had so much more to do with a brief and breathtaking glimpse of the big picture of my life than with the responsibility I had just taken on. Ha! So I did get to sing with somebody famous after all! It all depends on your perspective....

In this final chapter, I want to point to pathways for finding your voice and discovering your song.

Postmodernism, the great answer to the failures of modernism, has done away with overarching narratives in which our own little individual stories have a place. As a culture, we in the West claim that there are no longer any absolute truths, which means there are no universal signposts to guide us along the twists and turns of life's road. The questioning of the supernatural during the Enlightenment, perhaps a logical consequence of the Wars of Religion, was followed by Hume questioning the existence of God, Rousseau arguing for a society based on rights not responsibilities, and Kant proposing ethics deriving from human rather than divine sources. These things laid the foundations for today's deconstructionism, a 'pale Galilean Jesus and a distant God,'[1] and flung wide the door to usher in the god of humanism.

The result is a belief in nothing, or perhaps more accurately, as G. K. Chesterton pointed out, a belief in everything. There is no overarching truth that everyone must believe, yet the range of options of lifestyle choices and belief systems is dazzling, so that I can gaze at New Age crystals at the same time as working out in health and fitness clubs, arrange my home according to the principles of feng shui, go clubbing at nights and engage in Buddhist meditation when I wake up in the morning. Christianity takes its place among these as just another private lifestyle choice.[2]

But in all of our hearts lies a longing for a Sacred Romance. 'It will not go away in spite of our efforts … to anaesthetise or ignore its song…. It is a Romance couched in mystery and set deeply within us. It cannot be categorised into propositional truths … any more than studying the anatomy of a corpse would help us know the person who once inhabited it. Philosophers call this Romance, this heart-yearning … the longing for transcendence; the desire to be part of something larger than ourselves, to be part of something out of the ordinary that is good.'[3]

Deep down you and I know our life has a purpose. We know there is something greater and grander than the dimensions of our body and the reach of our personal life experiences.

Often when I am talking to or praying for someone, I encourage them to be 'seated in heavenly realms'[4] with Jesus. It's mysterious; how can we be 'seated in heavenly realms'? I think what Paul is saying is that when we have discovered Jesus to be real—been 'made alive with Christ'[5]—we can access a different perspective on our life—we can look down on our circumstances rather than up from below them. A bit like the moment the plane bursts through the cloud and visibility is gloriously restored.

Life will often take us through dark places or a patch of thick fog on the road, and when it does and we can't grasp at all what's happening or why, we are easily tempted to give up. A verse I love is: 'For anyone out there who doesn't know where you're going, anyone groping in the dark, here's what: Trust in God. *Lean* on your God!'[6] It's the same message as Paul's, with a different image—if you can't see don't be alarmed, just switch on your fog lamps and proceed with caution. The road won't disappear, and there are still errands to run, acts of kindness to do, encouragements to give, and days to live.

Anyone who has encountered the risen Christ becomes involved in the coming of God's kingdom. Such a person by definition carries the presence of Jesus. This is the great distinctive of the Christian faith. Jesus said, 'If anyone loves me'—and to encounter him is to love him—'… My Father will love them, and we will come to them and make our home with them.'[7] God, who became human in Jesus, takes up residence within us by his Holy Spirit. Think about that for a minute. It's a pretty amazing idea, right up there with any sci-fi or fantasy literature or film that you could think of—and there's plenty of it, because the human heart yearns relentlessly for 'happily ever after.' On a good day, being host to Jesus in the form of the Holy Spirit can provoke the question: 'There's something about you; what is it?' And Paul uses the analogy of perfume for God's presence, though he is well aware that not everyone will like it.

> But thanks be to God, who always leads us as captives in Christ's triumphal procession and uses us to spread the aroma of the knowledge of him everywhere. For we are to God the pleasing aroma of Christ among those who are being saved and those who are perishing. To the one we are an aroma that brings death; to the other, an aroma that brings life. And who is equal to such a task?[8]

Not me! But to know God is to carry his presence. We see that some won't like it, but it's not the perfume that's off; the smell is perfect but it contains a message, the scent of a far-off country, just as the smell of a rose or a lily can transport us in an instant to the country of our childhood. For some the message is the answer to the question they've always been asking, but for others the message reacts with the deceitfulness of the human heart; with anger, rage, malice, slander, greed, idolatry, immorality, impurity, unbelief or any number of other gods that may control it. And a powerful malodourous stink results. For yet others, it's much less black and white; from somewhere in the recesses of the corrupted heart comes the distant memory of a better scent, drawing its owner towards the magnetic person of Christ.

That's how it was for me. In his majestic and timeless poem 'Little Gidding', T. S. Eliot puts it like this ...

With the drawing of this Love and the voice of
            this Calling
We shall not cease from exploration
And the end of all our exploring
Will be to arrive where we started
And know the place for the first time.
Through the unknown, unremembered gate
When the last of earth left to discover
Is that which was the beginning;
At the source of the longest river
The voice of the hidden waterfall
And the children in the apple-tree
Not known, because not looked for
But heard, half-heard, in the stillness
Between two waves of the sea.
Quick now, here, now, always—
A condition of complete simplicity
(Costing not less than everything)
And all shall be well and
All manner of thing shall be well
When the tongues of flames are in-folded
Into the crowned knot of fire
And the fire and the rose are one.[9]

I believe the drawing of this love and the voice of this calling are operative from the instant of life's first cry. I grew up with loving and nurturing parents within an Anglican framework. I came to know a reasonable amount about God and Jesus, but my knowledge was not personalised until my early twenties.

Through the Narnian Wardrobe

At the age of nineteen I came to Oxford to study at what was then the Oxford Polytechnic. I came because I was dissatisfied with the college where I had started my studies to become a teacher. At this college I had been approached by some students who said they were Christians, but far from drawing me by their winsomeness, they alarmed me with their dowdy clothes, thick stockings and severe hair styles. Paul says 'I have become all things to all people so that by all possible means I might save some.'[10] I don't think he meant that he would compromise his faith or principles in his desire to reach others, but rather that he would do his very best to find some common ground and gain a hearing. Legalism in any shape or form of course has the opposite effect, and although I didn't know what legalism was at the time, I did know that I felt constricted and stifled in the meetings these girls took me to. In any case, my heart was dry at the time, and I was not yet alive to the pulse of faith. I certainly didn't fancy the dress code it appeared to offer.

So I essentially ran away to Oxford so that I could be in the same place as a good friend of mine, who was beginning life as a student.

Here in the city of dreaming spires, our relationship evolved from friend to lover over a period of time, not only because we were young and sexually hungry, but also because we were needy. What we really needed was to hear the voice of this calling and be drawn by this love, but like so many who have a vague apprehension of God inherited from family or school, the sound of the voice and the drawing of the love was dulled and diluted by the passion of the present.

This friend and I first encountered each other at the age of five during a beach picnic in west Wales, where our families had met while on holiday. Years later, I would learn that his early years were a distressing period for his parents, who eventually divorced. Every summer several families would congregate for the 'Welsh Holiday' and a decade or so later there was the inevitable rush of pubescent fervour, largely due to the sudden and virtually simultaneous activation of everyone's hormones. I found myself pursued by my friend, while at the same time completely deserted by my appetite and intelligence, owing to an uncontrollable passion for his cousin. So at that stage I was unimpressed by his fireside conversation and his subtle attempts to put his arm round me! Such are the vagaries of the adolescent world.

Two years into our Oxford years it was time for my boyfriend, a language student, to spend a year abroad, which meant a separation. This was something I dreaded, being by this time unhealthily dependent on the relationship that had developed between us. I think he probably saw the year as a welcome escape, though he would not have been able (or dared?) to articulate such a thought at the time. The truth was that without boundaries or a firm foundation, our situation was cloying and claustrophobic and brought us very little satisfaction or happiness. We had frequent arguments and brief separations, and my pleadings were certainly counterproductive. All the same we limped on, and I made several visits to his rather austere little apartment in Strasbourg. Occasionally since, when I have found myself visiting a less than fragrant *cabinet de toilette* in Paris, a powerful memory of

Strasbourg days and the *Rue de Berne* loo has swept over me. These were the heydays of Bob Dylan and Leonard Cohen, and their mournful compositions suited us well. Despite an uneasy truce and our volatile existence together, my boyfriend and I were making plans to cohabit once he returned to Oxford for his final year. By now I was living in a potentially perfect flat right in the centre of the city, and it seemed obvious that we should share it when the time came.

The time did come, but it wasn't the time I thought. Another still in the memory file is of my boyfriend standing at the bottom of the stairs that led to the flat and saying, carefully and clearly, 'I don't really want to live with you anymore. I'm too young, it's too soon.' Not for the first or last time in my life, my stomach performed an involuntary somersault as I searched for a reply. But as is so often the case, I eventually came to see that God was in this apparent catastrophe. My young man's decision was not up for discussion, and he'd clearly done some careful and conclusive thinking. So now I had to get my skates on and do some fast tap dancing if I was going to be able to transfer my place for post-graduate studies. The thought of remaining in the same city among the same friends felt unbearable.

A hurried application led to an open door into a teacher training college that ironically had turned down my application some years earlier, and after a silent and almost ceremonious separating of all our personal effects, helped by my father (who was certainly most relieved by this development), I was on my way to Cambridge, a tormented muddle of thoughts and emotions, to begin a new life.

A new life was indeed exactly what awaited me, but I had no idea as yet just how new. A strange thing had happened in our God-fearing and upright family the previous year: my younger sister had 'become a Christian'. What an absurd idea and arrogant claim! Surely she was already a Christian, having been born into a good church-going Protestant family? My father and I often exchanged amused remarks with each other at my sister's expense, knowing of course that normality would return once the dust had settled. All the same, I was apprehensive about finding myself anywhere near a bunch of fanatics as I moved to her city, though at the same time I craved security at any price.

I was not only apprehensive about my present move, but almost perpetually on the edge of irritation; I had discovered that my sister and her friends prayed for me and was annoyed by such cheek.

Something happened, however, which began to change my life before I was aware of it, and the change was to prove momentous. Having nowhere to live, I was taken in by three students who shared a tiny little house, yet were apparently willing for me to sleep in their minute sitting room until I found accommodation. This in itself impressed me, but I was perhaps even more struck by the orderly lives led by these three sweet girls. Nothing could have provided more of a contrast with the lifestyle of my Oxford flat, where washing-up only took place if the kitchen was completely devoid of clean implements, and even then it was usually partial. Housework never took place. Parties were a regular event and an inordinate amount of alcohol was consumed. I can remember stumbling into the bathroom on many occasions and thinking as I threw up that this wasn't really what I enjoyed. Now, I was in a very clean place, in every sense of the word.

In the months that followed, I went through an intense time of questioning and debate, sometimes with myself and often with one or other of the many Christ-followers into whose orbit I had come, as if through the Narnian wardrobe. I still went to parties too and maintained the old lifestyle, afraid that too much exposure to my new friends would make me strange. I didn't hide my pain and confusion, however, nor the fact that I was intrigued if not captivated by the Christians. They were unfailingly patient with my untutored ways and unending questions. With one, I would sit until way into the small hours, chain-smoking and pressing every question with intensity. All the time, the subject of the resurrection of Jesus, at first very faint and indistinct, loomed nearer and clearer, until one night as I was drifting off to sleep in my new-found accommodation, a student house much less inviting than my first port of call in Cambridge.

It was 23 January 1974. Suddenly, my room was undeniably and completely filled with what I knew to be the presence of God. It was thick, but didn't prevent me instantly sitting bolt upright, my heart crashing against my ribcage, and then falling to my knees beside the bed. 'All right, Lord,' I said, 'you win.' Not the most appropriate or respectful response to the King of kings, I realised with hindsight. But something so life-changing was taking place that searching for eloquence didn't cross my mind. Deep down, I knew that the months of debate and heart-searching and wrestling with apologetics (up to this moment in the role of devil's advocate) were reaching a climax and resolution. In those few moments, the birth, death and resurrection of Jesus became for me the pivotal facts of history, and I knew that because of this epiphany my life would never be the same; that its direction would almost certainly radically change, and that Jesus would become its driving force. And that had implications.

The first of these was to inform my ex-boyfriend of my new-found status in life. We had remained in touch periodically, and had just come to the end of a self-imposed six-month moratorium on phone calls and long letters. So I sat down to write to him and describe the passage from cynicism to certainty; I urged him to read the enclosed copy of C. S. Lewis' *Mere Christianity* and to go and buy a Bible and read the four Gospels at one sitting. Then we would review the situation. For by now, with the passing of time and the freedom of living without me, he was not so sure that he wanted the break to be definitive. Phone calls, discussions and heated debates ensued. Majestically awkward meetings between him and my new-found friends were arranged by me in the first flush of excitement about Jesus. I manoeuvred and manipulated, all to no avail, and it was only when I grasped the truth that God alone could change his heart, and let go with a certain relief, that the lock was sprung. He did buy a Bible and he did read the Gospels; and then he went to church and heard that God is the same yesterday, today and forever, and that Jesus still calls people to follow him. And something happened to him too....

That's another story, which led in turn to our marriage—for yes, this friend, boyfriend, ex-boyfriend was indeed Charlie—and in due course to the birth of two daughters, and then in 1981 our son Samuel. And so terribly soon afterwards to the greatest and most unexpected upheaval in our lives, when Samuel died a week after our arrival in California.

Disappointment and Renewal

A year earlier, we had organised a placement in the beautiful city of York, at a church rapidly becoming well known in evangelical circles thanks to the ministry of a remarkable man, David Watson, then the vicar of St Michael-le-Belfry. David died of cancer in 1984 but already in 1981, the work that he and his wife, Anne, were doing was becoming known because of their radical devotion to the teaching of Jesus and their refusal to make religious compromises. They were hungry for more of God and were prepared to take the rough with the smooth. They had chosen to live in community with their two young children and took three or four students into their rambling and rather large vicarage, committing themselves to live together as a family. Inevitably this was not without its tensions in a world which had long dispensed with such outmoded ideas. Nevertheless, many doors opened up to David to teach and communicate the things he had been privileged to learn with his family and household.

Our Oxford days had found us fairly consistently mixing with the theatre crowd, and a character who had particularly struck us was an American called Geoffrey, a theology student at Keble. We were attracted by his quiet and cultivated air and warmed to his thoughtfulness. A firm friendship had been established and maintained, the years had passed, we had been invited to one another's marriages, and now Geoffrey lived in York with his wife and two small daughters. It was to their beautiful home near the city centre that we came to learn from this vibrant church.

As young Christians, these were heady days. We had discovered Jesus; now we were discovering his church, and it is no exaggeration to say that we fell in love with her. We had both grown up in the traditional Anglican church to one degree or another, but had never entertained the notion that church could involve one's affections. Neither of us had had any idea that faith could be expressed in ways so much more immediate than those we had known to date. It was clearly going to be a good time from every point of view. It was also a time that coincided for me with a longing for another child—quite normal for anyone in these early years of building a family. What was perhaps less normal was the strength of my desire for a son, which became almost obsessive as my thoughts were more and more taken up with it. Acutely aware of my body, I became certain I was pregnant, but joy and excitement turned suddenly to fear and anxiety when bleeding began.

To this day, I can recall my early morning walk to the doctor's surgery. It was a dismal winter day and the sky hung low over the city as it cranked into life again. Like the dense traffic, I hugged the city wall, blackened by centuries of dust and dirt and more recently the emissions of fuel. Equally clear in my memory is the doctor's verdict: 'Mrs Cleverly, although you had a positive pregnancy test, we are almost certain that your condition is not that of a normal pregnancy, but very probably a hydatidiform mole.'

A what?! My stomach was somersaulting, and I fought to control it as I asked the doctor, 'What do you mean?'

He carefully described a medical condition in which the egg is fertilised but simply begins a chaotic and formless multiplication of cells, therefore excluding any possibility of a normal pregnancy. He advised me to consult my GP on our return home to Bristol, as I would almost certainly need a 'D&C'[11] in preparation for starting again. I walked slowly back beneath the black city wall with a despondent heart and a sinking stomach.

The following week was a special week at the church, called 'Renewal week'. Word had spread far and wide over the years about the extraordinary life and liveliness that was to be found at St Michael's.

The worship was exhilarating, David's preaching captivating and edifying and, most intriguing of all, people testified to being healed when prayed for at the end of services. Some prayed in the tongues of angels, and some seemed to faint with all the excitement—or was it really that? At any rate, the scene as the Sunday service drew to a close bore so little resemblance to what might loosely have been called Anglican that it inevitably attracted a great deal of attention. Like all such things it was a mixture of the genuine, the glorious and the rather weird. Despite this, there was an undeniable hunger in the air.

Renewal week was born to help meet this hunger and included all sorts of seminars, services and plenary sessions. Idly discussing this plethora of church activity, in which Charlie was fully involved thanks to his placement, I felt suddenly that I must go to the healing service that was one of the week's focal points. Sitting in the crowded church beside a friend, I listened as it was explained that all were welcome to go forward for prayer, but that it was not the time for explanations or counselling; only prayer. Although I had felt I must come to the service, I now felt persuaded that my needs were so insignificant compared to the vast majority of those present (in particular my friend who was undergoing tests for multiple sclerosis—this seemed so overwhelming and dramatic that my own fears shrank momentarily to almost nothing) that I decided to sit tight and watch; and pray.

'You must go forward.' The voice was almost audible and I turned round to see who had spoken, as I rose sheepishly from my seat to take my place in the queue that was inching towards the altar. 'I so hope no one has seen me,' I thought. In those early days, it was still difficult to admit need publicly. I felt awkward and out of my comfort zone but was distracted from my self-consciousness by the need to plan for my arrival at the altar. It wouldn't do to be prayed for by a man, since my need was very personal. I couldn't tell a man that I was bleeding.

'I'd like to be prayed for by a woman,' I said firmly, praying that no questions would be asked. I was directed round the large altar rail and found myself at a space, looking into the kindly face of Anne Watson.

'My insides are in a mess and we'd like to have another baby,' I said lamely, and dropped to my knees. Anne began to pray, quite quietly and authoritatively. I don't remember all she said, but I remember that it was quite a long prayer and that, as she prayed, I felt the tension and anxiety drop away from me and a sense of peace settling on my shoulders like a comforting blanket. I also remember that about half-way through, her prayer became prophetic. At first praying for my consolation, she now began to speak of the son we would have and of how he would be a servant of the living God all the days of his life.

She drew to a close and, raising my head, my eyes met hers as she smiled, her expression full of tenderness. Turning, I made my way back to my seat, hope coursing through me like a mountain river leaping into life after winter's ice. Instinctively I knew something had happened but I wasn't sure what. My anguished confusion had been transformed into certainty born of faith quite suddenly. I knew that I was experiencing grace and kindness from God. I was going to have a child and, what's more, a son who already had a calling.

Returning home elated, I recounted the service to everyone, but omitting that all this had left me with a new conviction, despite the doctor's solemn advice. Several weeks later, I was sitting in our GP's surgery in Bristol, explaining my condition and the need for a D&C. Dr. Stanford was a kindly man with a keen sense of humour.

He had once told me, when I was afflicted by a severe and persistent cough, that the only thing that would cure it was heroin and he wasn't allowed to prescribe that. At another routine appointment, awaiting the birth of our daughter, and well past the due date, he nodded his head in the direction of the mantelpiece, indicating the bottle of cod liver oil. 'A good dose of that would start you off,' he said. 'I made my wife take it every time. Marvellous stuff.'

Now he looked at me thoughtfully and there was quite a long pause before he answered. The pendulum clock ticked loudly and there was an expectant silence. My eyes roamed over the heavy antique furniture, anxious to avoid hurrying him with my stare.

'Hmm,' he said slowly. 'Well, I think we'll have a scan before we make any decisions.'

And so it was that some days later, this time in hospital, the radiologist said the unthinkable. 'You have a twelve-week foetus in there, and as far as I can see everything is perfectly normal.'

'Well,' I recognised Dr. Stanford's avuncular tones as he entered the room, 'lucky we weren't too hasty, eh?'

Thus, as far as I was concerned, a miracle had happened and I was bearing a child known and called by God. His future was assured and his paths prepared by heaven. All of this served to consolidate in a remarkable way our relatively fledgling faith, and the dark days of winter gave way to a spring and summer of joy and laughter as my belly slowly swelled and we awaited the arrival of Samuel, already named because, like Hannah, I had asked the Lord for him.

When Samuel died we were flung into the normal vortex of grief that any parents would experience, but we also had to wrestle with the confusion of having received a promise that in our eyes had been cut so unexpectedly and cruelly short. But for now our time of trial had not yet come and the weeping and wrestling lay ahead of us.

This is still my conviction: every child has a potentially assured future and his paths mapped out by heaven. Every child is designed and known by God:

> For you created my inmost being; you knit me together in my mother's womb. I praise you because I am fearfully and wonderfully made.... My frame was not hidden from you when I was made in the secret place, when I was woven together in the depths of the earth. Your eyes saw my unformed body; all the days ordained for me were written in your book before one of them came to be.[12]

You can't get much clearer than that. So why are the ordained days of so many cut short? Every day we hear of lives being cut short by accident; every day war and disasters fall upon the earth and its inhabitants. Why an omnipotent God permits these things is the very crux of the ancient dilemma of suffering that we looked at in chapter 14.

My purpose throughout this book has been to reassure you that God is there even in such life-changing storms, and that he calls you and loves you. 'I have come that they may have life, and have it to the full', said Jesus.[13] Hope is a powerful force, and it helps us set a steady course through turbulence and make it through.

I pray God would awaken your hunger to know him and to live for him, and that you would come through prayer and communion with Jesus to love him so fiercely that you feel you could die for him, as well as live for him. Many have known this place. In our own city three bishops, Cranmer, Latimer and Ridley, gave up their lives for the sake of Jesus as they were burnt at the stake. Latimer encouraged Ridley with the famous words: 'Be of good cheer Master Ridley; we shall this day in England light such a candle as can never be put out.'[14]

Search out and read the stories of those who have decided to go wholeheartedly for the call of Christ: martyrs of every century and every nation.[15] Remember that more people are giving their lives for Christ now than at any other period of history. Seek out the company of like-minded souls: 'Do not be misled: "Bad company corrupts good character."'[16] The people you choose to spend time with will shape your life to an extent.

Don't let your personal story obscure the grand story in which you have a unique role. Are you worried about your calling? About whether you will marry or not? The Lord of the universe is more than able to fulfil your life, whether single or married, in ways more wonderful than you can imagine today. Paul puts it like this: 'With all wisdom and understanding, [God] made known to us the mystery of his will according to his good pleasure, which he purposed in Christ, to be put into effect when the times reach their fulfilment—to bring unity to all things in heaven and on earth under Christ.'[17] You have a place in this, and whether you find the fullness of life that Jesus said he came to earth to give us depends on whether you decide that following him, whatever that may mean, now or in the future, is far and away your greatest priority.

Statistics point overwhelmingly to faith being found in the first half of life. The mind is more open, courage is intact, possibilities are infinite, we can still change the world. In later years, disappointment can wield more power than hope, and eat away at the notion that our life can be full of meaning and purpose.

'I'm the King of Salem,' the old man had said.

'Why would a king be talking with a shepherd?' the boy asked, awed and embarrassed.

'For several reasons, but let's say that the most important is that you've succeeded in discovering your destiny.'

The boy didn't know what a person's destiny was.

'It's what you have always wanted to accomplish. Everyone, when they are young, knows what their destiny is.

'At that point in their lives everything is clear and everything is possible. They are not afraid to dream and to yearn for everything they would like to see happen to them in their lives. But, as time passes, a mysterious force begins to convince them that it will be impossible for them to realize their destiny.'[18]

Energy declines, horizons close in, ambitions shrink and we can be tempted to simply live out our days as best and comfortably as possible.

Dear reader, if like me you have come to the second half of life, don't be deterred. It is never too late; the pages of the Bible are strewn with stories of late starters: Abraham, Moses, Jacob, Zechariah, Elizabeth, Simeon, Anna ...

Many years ago we met a couple called Tom and Joan Beak. They were over seventy when they felt God speak to them and tell them they were to start—yes, start!—a ministry in Togo. They didn't even know where Togo was and had to find an atlas. But just like Abraham, they obeyed. They found Togo and went there, and founded the

'Ministry of Jesus' which has outlived them and is still flourishing, over thirty years later.[19] Indomitable, Tom and Joan moved on. To retire, as would be proper at their age? Not a bit of it. They ventured off in the opposite direction and purchased a 420-acre farm about an hour away from Quito in Ecuador! In 2005 I heard from them again. Then aged 89 and 84 respectively, they had completed their second project, the building of a training and retreat centre on the farm called The Meeting Place. And they were on the move again: 'We expect to leave the house fully furnished, and take away only our personal things, books, family mirrors and silver etc., so we will be starting again from scratch,' they reported. The Lord, they say, hasn't finished with them yet! 'He says we can have a vacation and then he has other work for us to do. What can one say? Only Yes, Lord!'[20]

Such stories should shake us free from slumber and apathy. But they shouldn't trick us into thinking our lives will only be worthwhile if we do something equally hardcore. The point is not what we do, or where we go, it's that we choose to follow Jesus in these things. We can make this choice at any time … and there's no deadline while we live.

Pause for a moment and take a deep breath. Decide to consider, or reconsider, what you were made for. Ask God, and like the persistent widow,[21] keep asking until he answers. And then set out to be who you were born to be, with renewed hope and energy. The Spirit of God is at work in the world, drawing with this love and calling with this voice. And he is drawing and calling you.

'How can I set about this?' you ask. Well, it depends where you're starting from. If this is something you've never really considered, you may want to ask for help. Whether you identify as a Christian or not, it's helpful to hear what others might think you were made for, and to hear their stories of God's working in their lives. If you're thinking, 'Yes, I want to live a life that counts', then you, likewise, do the same. Pastoral leaders and spiritual directors[22] are good people to seek advice from too.

Of course, most important is to ask God himself for help! Set some time aside to listen to him speaking through the Bible; and speak to him. Have this very important conversation. From the very beginning, God has been looking for, even longing for, our company; 'Where are you?' he asked Adam.[23] And he spoke to Moses face to face as one speaks to a friend.[24] It's also wise to take a kind of audit of your situation; what do your current circumstances tell you about yourself, your giftings and abilities? Are you contented or restless in them?

If you are young, you know money can't buy you love; you know that nation rises against nation and kingdom against kingdom. You see famines, earthquakes and war.[25] You see that the love of many is growing cold. You see the unrest, division and polarisation across Europe and the West, and you hear the growling of Russia and China. You understand that the perpetual conflict in the Middle East has more to do with ancient tribal tension than seeking settlement, with spiritual forces than political negotiation. You understand that many have chosen to serve Mammon rather than God because the returns are quicker and initially more gratifying. You know that the time to choose is here.

Some of us need to listen to our children and our grandchildren.

As a Baby Boomer born in the post-war generation that threw off the traces of the discipline necessarily imposed by war, I believe that our generation owes those who follow us an apology. Not an official statement but a request for forgiveness. I am part of a generation that popularised sex, if one may so express it; a generation that approved divorce and abortion; a generation that revolted against ancient boundaries; and our descendants are reaping the multiple consequences of all these things.

Yes, I was influenced by the philosophers of my time. At the tender age of seventeen, I spent a year in France, discovering the amazing psychedelic reaches of Sartre, Camus and company, as I took a philosophy course. I also took an extraordinary boat trip across Lake Victoria the following summer with some friends during the four years my parents spent working in a school in Uganda. My back propped against the deck, my flesh basking in the sun's warmth, and my spirit delighting in the wide horizon of my future, I devoured *The Second Sex*, principal work of Simone de Beauvoir, the existentialist and long-term lover of Sartre. Like a sponge I drank in what I took to be a key to understanding as she traced the development of male oppression through historical, literary and mythical sources, attributing its contemporary effects on women to, 'the systematic objectification of the female as a positive norm'. 'Yes, I agree!' I thought, and decided under an African sky to be her disciple. Unbeknown to me at that rather pompous moment, the God who formed me in my mother's womb had other plans, as the book in your hands has revealed. I was to become a disciple of Jesus Christ, not Simone de Beauvoir, though of course she was a significant contributor to the cause of feminism, and a remarkable child of her time.

Sometimes God gives us an epiphany which strengthens and reaffirms our faith; a kind of glimpse into the unseen world. Paul, to whom this happened, says that, fourteen years before he wrote the Second Letter to the Corinthians, he had an experience of God that he was not permitted to tell.[26] I believe many people are given insight through such moments of epiphany, perhaps in part because of my own experience—I once received a kind of vision that I have never really spoken of in detail, though obviously of a completely different order to that of Paul!

In 1990, at a conference in Switzerland that had gathered some 300 people, the speaker said at the close of a talk, 'There's someone here called Anita,' and once I had identified myself (with what must have seemed to him a frustrating delay; I was sure there must be someone else present called Anita!), he continued by speaking of difficulties that lay ahead of me but would not overcome me. During that same conference I had another experience—of a sobering glimpse into the future concerning persecution. At the close of one evening we were requested to remain silent as we returned to our rooms for the night. Filing out of the hall to only the sound of footsteps, a powerful vision that I have never forgotten came to me. It had to do with persecution in Europe becoming as real as it is in Iraq, or Syria, or Yemen. It felt very real and very frightening, but paradoxically my love of Christ and my certainty that I would always follow him, whatever the cost, flowed into my being like oil. That night my faith was incrementally strengthened, and I have never forgotten it.

As you've journeyed with me through the ups and downs of my life, and through my reflections about different aspects of life as a disciple of Christ, it's my prayer that faith and hope will have risen in you, whatever your reason for reading. It's my prayer that you too would have experienced somewhere in these pages an epiphany, a sudden insight into the ways of God.

It might be an experience something like this:

> It was deep January as I set off on my daily morning walk with the dog. I try to get out before the children are up for breakfast, so it was still dark as I walked through the woodland not far from where I live. It's a great opportunity to seek God and pray without distraction, and on this morning I sensed God wanting to show me something. At a particular spot among the trees I felt he was asking me to be still and look up. As I stopped and lifted my eyes, I noticed almost immediately the white sky above the tree canopy. I stood for a while, asking, 'Why have you asked me to be still?' Suddenly I was aware that despite it seeming so dark all around me, the dawn had broken as I walked, though I had not noticed. It came to me that God was showing me that the challenges we often face may represent the dark night, and when surrounded and weighed down by those challenges without being still before God and offering him our worship, we may miss the breaking of the dawn. As I stood still and silent before him, looking up at the brightening sky, encouragement flooded my heart as my circumstances regained their true perspective, like the view through a camera lens coming into perfect focus.[27]

It's my prayer that like me your faith would have been strength-ened, or its dwindling embers sparked into flame again, as you read. Or even that faith might have been conceived within you. Maybe you came out of curiosity, or maybe you came because you have been, or are, in a dark night of loss or suffering, or because someone you love is in such a night. I hope so much that however you came, as you lay this book down, you will find you can look up and see the gleam of dawn—the promise of a bright morning ahead.

Notes

Preface

1. Sudden Infant Death Syndrome, now called The Lullaby Trust.

2. C. S. Lewis, *The Silver Chair* (Fontana Lions, 1980) 25–27.

3. Lewis, *Silver Chair*, 27.

4. Philippians 2:7, Colossians 1:17.

Chapter 1: Unless a Seed Fall to the Ground

1. 2 Corinthians 5:1.

2. 1 Corinthians 15:42–44.

3. Romans 8:38–39.

4. W. B. Yeats, 'The Second Coming', *The Collected Poems of W B Yeats* (Wordsworth Editions Limited, 1994).

5. Leona Von Brethorst, 'I Will Enter His Gates' © 1976 by Maranatha! Music. The original lyrics are 'I will enter his gates with thanksgiving in my heart'. In the moment I substituted 'presence' for 'gates'.

6. Mark 15:34.

Chapter 2: Double Blessing

1. Isaiah 40:30–31.

2. Psalm 91:1–2.

3. Psalm 23.

4. Job 13:15.

5. Job 19:25–26.

6. 1 Corinthians 15:20.

7. 1 Corinthians 15:53–54.

Chapter 3: Every Sparrow Falling, Every Grain of Sand

1. Simon Guillebaud, Newsletter November 2003.

2. Lord David Puttnam, from the Foreword to Julian Wilson, *Complete Surrender: A Biography of Eric Liddell* (Authentic Media; Revised edition, 2012).

3. Mike Bickle, *The Pleasures of Loving God* (Charisma House, 2000) 27–28.

4. *Open Heavens* Vol 1. CD produced by Wesley and Stacey Campbell, 2003.

5. Floyd McClung, from the Foreword to Pete Greig and Dave Roberts, *Red Moon Rising* (Kingsway, 2004) 13–14.

6. Greig & Roberts, *Red Moon Rising*, 60–62.

7. Ecclesiastes 3:11.

8. The full version of this prophetic word is published at www.worldtrumpetmission.org.

9. Isaiah 14:12, Luke 10:18.

10. Matthew 2:2.

11. Douglas Coupland, *Life after God* (Simon & Schuster, 1994) 359.

12. Matthew 24:35.

13. Isaiah 55:11 (ESV).

14. Ezekiel 4.

15. Ezekiel 4:16–17.

16. Jeremiah 23:9–40.

17. 1 Thessalonians 5:20–21.

18. Job 42:2.

19. Matthew 11:28.

20. Jean-Paul Sartre in an interview with Simone de Beauvoir, quoted in C. Stephen Evans, *Why Believe?: Reason and Mystery as Pointers to God* (Wm. B. Eerdmans Publishing, 1996) 50.

21. Galatians 4:4–5 (ESV).

22. Matthew 16:21–23.

23. Luke 22:42–44.

Chapter 4: The Hearts of the Fathers

1. Isaiah 49:15.

2. Bickle, *Pleasures of Loving God*, 147.

3. Carol Wimber, *John Wimber: The Way It Was* (Hodder, 1999).

4. Titus 1:4, 1 Timothy 1:2, Galatians 4:19.

5. 2 Corinthians 6:11, 13.

6. World Bank Data, 'Population ages 65 and above (% of total)'
   https://data.worldbank.org/indicator/SP.POP.65UP.TO.ZS
   ?locations=GB-US&view=chart.

7. John Humphrys, *Devil's Advocate* (Arrow, 2000) 3–6.

8. Douglas Coupland, *Generation X* (Abacus, 1996) 25–26.

9. Malachi 4:6.

10. Deuteronomy 6:6–9.

11. What Would Jesus Do?

12. Psalm 141:3.

13. Ephesians 4:32.

14. Psalm 78:1–7 (THE MESSAGE).

15. Psalm 22:30–31.

16. 1 Timothy 4:12.

17. 1 Timothy 4:14.

18. 2 Timothy 1:5 (THE MESSAGE).

19. Proverbs 1:1–4 (THE MESSAGE).

20. Scottish Syllabus for Sex Education 2004.

21. 'The State of our Nation', Maranatha Community, December 2004.

22. Department of Education, 'Children looked after in England (including
    adoption), year ending 31 March 2018', 15 November 2018 5
    https://assets.publishing.service.gov.uk/government/uploads/system
    /uploads/attachment_data/file/757922/Children_looked_after_in
    _England_2018_Text_revised.pdf.

23. POST – Parliamentary Office of Science and Technology, 'Parental Alcohol Misuse and Children', 9 February 2018 https://researchbriefings.parliament .uk/ResearchBriefing/Summary/POST-PN-0570.

24. http://www.fasdnetwork.org/what-is-fasd.html.

25. '3.3 The scale of child sexual abuse in England and Wales', Interim Report of the Independent Inquiry into Child Sexual Abuse, April 2018 https:// www.iicsa.org.uk/reports/interim/nature-effects-child-sexual-abuse/ scale-child-sexual-abuse-england-wales.

26. Paul Noblet, 'A fifth of young people are homeless – you just can't see them', *The Guardian,* 27 September 2017 https://www.theguardian.com/ housing-network/2017/sep/27/homelessness-young-people-centrepoint.

27. NHS Digital, 'Mental Health of Children and Young People in England, 2017 [PAS]', 22 November 2018 https:// digital.nhs.uk/data-and-information/publications/statistical/ mental-health-of-children-and-young-people-in-england/2017/2017.

28. Shehab Khan, 'Teenage suicides in England and Wales rise 67% since 2010', *Independent,* 4 September 2018 https://www.independent.co.uk/news/uk/ home-news/teenage-suicides-england-and-wales-2010-ons-a8522331.html.

29. Isaiah 54:1.

30. Ephesians 4:13–15 (THE MESSAGE).

Chapter 5: Simeons and Samuels, Hannahs and Annas

1. C. S. Lewis, *The Screwtape Letters* (Collins, Signature Classics Edition, 2012) 39–40.

2. 2 Chronicles 16:9.

3. Genesis 32:26.

4. 1 Samuel 1:9.

5. 1 Samuel 3:1.

6. Romans 8:26.

7. Hebrews 5:7.

8. E. M. Bounds, *A Treasury of Prayer* (Bethany House, 1961) 58.

9. 1 Samuel 1:17.

10. Luke 1:45.

Chapter 6: Slowing Down and Sweetening Up

1. Henri Nouwen, *Seeds of Hope* (DLT, 1989) 6.

2. Philippians 3:12.

3. The British Psychological Society, 'The sight of their own
   blood is important to some people who self-harm', 22
   March 2010 https://digest.bps.org.uk/2010/03/22/
   the-sight-of-their-own-blood-is-important-to-some-people-who-self-harm/.

4. 1 Samuel 16:21.

5. 1 Samuel 20:42.

6. Proverbs 27:6.

7. Mary Pytches, *Between Friends* (Hodder & Stoughton, 1992). Mary and her
   husband, David, founded New Wine in 1989.

8. Ephesians 4:15.

9. 2 Chronicles 20:7; Isaiah 41:8; James 2:23.

10. Genesis 18:17.

11. 2 Chronicles 20:7; Isaiah 41:8; James 2:23.

12. Genesis 18 & 19.

13. Exodus 33:11.

14. Matthew 6:22, 23.

15. Amos 3:7.

16. Matthew 23:37.

17. John 15:15.

18. John 15:13–14.

19. Bickle, *Pleasures of Loving God*, 2–3.

20. Romans 11:33.

21. 2 Corinthians 2:15.

22. 2 Corinthians 1:8–9.

Chapter 7: A Church for All Nations

1. Revelation 7:9.

2. Revelation 1:10–11.

3. 'Let the Sea Resound', video produced by the Sentinel Group (George Otis,
   2004).

4. Patrick Dixon, *Futurewise* (Profile Books, 2003).

5. Dixon, *Futurewise*, 149.

6. Luke 9:23–24 (ESV).

7. Revelation 7:9.

8. 2 Corinthians 2:14.

9. 'Youth With A Mission is a global movement of Christians from many cultures, age groups, and Christian traditions, dedicated to serving Jesus throughout the world.' Founded by Loren and Darlene Cunningham in 1960, YWAM's workers around the world 'unite in a common purpose to know God and to make Him known' https://www.ywam.org/about-us.

10. Brother Yun, *The Heavenly Man* (Monarch Books, 2002) 13.

11. Nomad, an online community founded in 2009: 'Stumbling through the post Christendom wilderness looking for signs of hope' https://www.nomadpodcast.co.uk.

12. 'How do different generations feel about brand loyalty?', Strength brand marketing https://strengagency.com/how-do-different-generations-feel-about-brand-loyalty/.

13. Bill Hybels, *Courageous Leadership* (Zondervan, 2002) 23. Despite the recent allegations of serious moral failings, Bill's words here remain true and compelling.

Chapter 8: All You Need Is Love

1. 1 Corinthians 13:1–3.

2. Thérèse de Lisieux, *Autobiography* (Doubleday, 1957) 62. The Ezekiel passage she refers to is Ezekiel 16:8–13.

3. Brother Lawrence, *The Practice of the Presence of God* (Hodder & Stoughton, 1981) 45.

4. Elisabeth Elliot (ed.), *The Journals of Jim Elliot* (Revell, 2002) 309.

5. Felix Bovet, *Count Zinzendorf: The Nobleman with a Heavenly Vision* trans. Rev T. Alexander Seed (Harvey Christian Publishers, 2014).

6. Psalm 63:1.

7. Matthew 17:1–8.

8. Repentance is the activity of reviewing one's actions and feeling contrition or regret for past wrongs, which is accompanied by commitment to change for the better.

9. Jeremiah 23:9–40.

10. Their story is told in Rolland and Heidi Baker, *There Is Always Enough* (Sovereign World, 2003).

11. Matthew 5:11–12 (THE MESSAGE).

12. Matthew 8:20.

13. Matthew 19:16ff.

14. 1 Corinthians 8:1.

15. Philippians 3:4–5.

16. 2 Corinthians 12:2–4.

17. 2 Corinthians 6:5.

18. Acts 28:16, 23.

19. John 2:1–10.

Chapter 9: A Reformation of Manners

1. International Justice Mission: https://www.ijm.org; A21 campaign: https://www.a21.org; Stop the Traffik: https://www.stopthetraffik.org.

2. Isaiah 58:6–7.

3. Michele Guinness, *Woman, the Full Story* (Zondervan, 2003) 98.

4. Josephine's letter to her sister Harriet, April 1883, quoted in Glen Petrie, *A Singular Iniquity* (Macmillan, 1971).

5. Joan C Johnson, *James and Mary Ellis: Background and Quaker Famine Relief in Letterfrack* (Historical Committee of the Religious Society of Friends in Ireland, 2000) 52.

6. Johnson, *James and Mary Ellis* 52.

7. See Esther 4:12–14.

8. Johnson, *James and Mary Ellis* 50.

9. Johnson, *James and Mary Ellis* 53.

10. Johnson, *James and Mary Ellis*.

11. Brycchan Carey, 'William Wilberforce (1759–1833): Biography' http://www.brycchancarey.com/abolition/wilberforce.htm Accessed 24 June 2019.

12. Guinness, *Woman* 97–98.

13. Luke 10:25ff.

14. Proverbs 14:31.

15. James 2:17, 1:22.

16. HIV.gov, 'Global Statistics', 20 November 2018 https://www.hiv.gov/hiv
-basics/overview/data-and-trends/global-statistics.

17. UNICEF, 'Child Labour', December 2017 https://data.unicef.org/topic
/child-protection/child-labour/.

18. UNICEF, 'Child Migration', December 2018 https://data.unicef.org/topic
/child-migration-and-displacement/migration/.

19. Unesco Social and Human Sciences, 'Street Children' http://www.unesco
.org/new/en/social-and-human-sciences/themes/fight-against-discrimination
/education-of-children-in-need/street-children/ Accessed 06 June 2019.

20. 'US President Donald Trump cast doubt on a report by his own government
warning of devastating effects from climate change. Asked outside the
White House about the findings that unchecked global warming would
wreak havoc on the US economy, he said: "I don't believe it."' 'Trump on
climate change report: "I don't believe it"', *BBC News,* 26 November 2018
https://www.bbc.co.uk/news/world-us-canada-46351940.

21. For more information visit the website www.arocha.org.

22. Aldates Community Transformation Initiatives.

23. Patrick Macdonald, *Reaching Children in Need* (Kingsway, 1997).

Chapter 10: God's Retirement Plan Is Out of This World

1. Hesketh Pearson, *The Smith of Smiths* (Faber & Faber, 2012) 268.

2. Dylan Thomas, *Collected Poems 1934–1952* (Dent, 1952).

3. C. S. Lewis, *The Business of Heaven* (Harper Collins, 1985) 318–19.

4. St Augustine, *City of God* Book XXII Ch 30 (Penguin Classics, 1985).

5. John Donne, *Sermons on the Psalms and Gospels with a selection of Prayers &
Meditations* (University of California Press, 2003) 241ff.

6. John Bunyan, *The works of that eminent servant of Christ, John Bunyan: minister
of the gospel and formerly Pastor of a Congregation at Bedford* (1831) 98.

7. Quoted in Laetitia Matilda Hawkins, *Anecdotes, Biographical Sketches and
Memoirs* vol. 1 (Longmans, 1824).

8. C. S. Lewis, *The Last Battle* (Puffin Books, 1975) 165.

9. Psalm 42:7.

10. C. S. Lewis, *The Four Loves* (Fount, 1986) 117–18.

11. Isaiah 51:6.

12. 1 Kings 8:27.

13. Psalm 103:11.

14. Isaiah 55:8–9.

15. 1 Kings 8:30.

16. Genesis 28:12–13.

17. Exodus 20:22.

18. Genesis 28:13–14.

19. 2 Chronicles 7:14.

20. Exodus 16:4.

21. Matthew 4:4.

22. Matthew 19:14.

23. Matthew 18:3–4.

24. Ezekiel 1:1.

25. Philip Pullman, *The Amber Spyglass* (Scholastic Press, 2001).

26. Philip Pullman, *The Book of Dust* (Penguin Random House, 2017).

27. Hebrews 12:18.

28. Isaiah 6:1–7.

29. 2 Chronicles 5:13–14.

30. Joshua 5:14.

31. 2 Corinthians 12:2.

32. Acts 26:19.

33. Acts 7:55–56.

34. Daniel 10:2; Revelation 1:12–16; 4:1.

35. Isaiah 65:1.

36. Acts 10:3.

37. Acts 10.

38. Philippians 3:20.

39. Dwight L Moody, frequently cited, e.g. https://allauthor.com/quotes/105568/.

40. John 17:3.

41. 1 Corinthians 15:42–43, 53.

42. From private correspondence to a circle of friends.

43. C. S. Lewis, *The Business of Heaven* (Harper Collins, 1985) 319.

Chapter 11: Freedom from Shame

1. Ravi Zacharias, *Cries of the Heart* (Thomas Nelson, 2010) 92–93.

2. Proverbs 19:26.

3. Genesis 3:8.

4. 2 Samuel 11:1–12:23.

5. James 1:15.

6. 2 Samuel 12:13.

7. *The Guardian*, 'Antony Pitts' resignation letter', 12 January 2005 https://www
.theguardian.com/media/2005/jan/12/radio.bbc.

8. 1 Samuel 15:22–23.

9. 1 Samuel 15:26, 28.

10. 1 Samuel 15:30.

11. C. S. Lewis, *Mere Christianity* (Fontana, 1955) 106.

12. Genesis 25–35.

13. Jean Vanier, *Community and Growth* (Paulist Press, 1989) 93.

14. John 10:10.

15. Charles Haddon Spurgeon, 'Forgiveness and Fear', Sermon 2882, delivered
on 26 March 1876, *The Complete Works of Charles Haddon Spurgeon* vol 50
(Delmarva Publications, 2013).

16. 1 John 1:9.

17. Karl Barth, *Church Dogmatics* IV (T&T Clark, 2004) 94.

18. Dag Hammarskjöld, *Markings* (Vintage Spiritual Classics, 2006).

19. Patrick Wintour, 'Hunt: postcolonial guilt hindering fight
against Christian persecution', *The Guardian*, 30 January
2019 https://www.theguardian.com/world/2019/jan/30/
hunt-postcolonial-guilt-hindering-fight-against-christian-persecution.

Chapter 12: Guilty Pleasures

1. See www.alpha.org for description and details.

2. James Madison, 'Why this Sexual Development Consultant is in high Demand',
The Times Magazine, 16 March 2019 27.

3. 1 Corinthians 6:13, 15–16.

4. Philip Larkin, 'Annus Mirabilis', *The Complete Poems* (Faber & Faber, 2014) 121.

5. Ian Macdonald, *Revolution in the Head* (Pimlico, 1998).

6. David Hilborn & Matt Bird, *God and the Generations* (Paternoster, 2002).

7. Hilborn & Bird, *God and the Generations*.

8. Isaiah 5:20.

9. 2 Samuel 13.

10. 1 Peter 5:8.

11. Theosophy: 'Any religious or philosophical system claiming to be based on or to express an intuitive insight into the divine nature', *Collins Dictionary* (1986). The Theosophical Society was founded in 1875 by Helena Blavatsky.

12. See Ray Yungen, *Alice Bailey: Mother of the New Age Movement and her plan to revitalize the Christian Church* (Lighthouse Trails Publishing, 2016).

13. Jeremiah 9:21.

14. Isaiah 43:25.

15. Isaiah 44:22.

16. Psalm 103:12.

17. Matthew 11:28–30 (THE MESSAGE).

18. Hebrews 6:19.

19. Isaiah 40:31.

Chapter 13: When Death Strikes Early

1. Lawrence Tuttiett, 'Father Let Me Dedicate', *Hymns Ancient & Modern* (1875) no 74.

2. Jeremiah 1:5.

3. Psalm 139:16.

4. Philippians 1:21–24.

5. 1 Corinthians 13:3.

6. Ephesians 4:13.

7. Timothy Keller, quoted in the *Bible In One Year* (12 March 2019) www.bibleinoneyear.org/bioy/commentary/3237.

8. Philippians 2:3.

9. Private correspondence with the author, 2003.

10. Joanna Jepson, in an interview with Madeleine Davies, 'If your face doesn't fit …', *Church Times*, 13 March 2015 https://www.churchtimes.co.uk/articles/2015/13-march/features/features/if-your-face-doesn-t-fit.

11. Private correspondence with the author, May 2019.

12. John 10:10.

13. Hebrews 11:16.

Chapter 14: Pain, the Gift Nobody Wants

1. Paul Brand with Philip Yancey, *Pain: The Gift Nobody Wants* (Harper Collins/STL, 1994).

2. Job 1:1.

3. Paul Bendor-Samuel, lecture given at the Oxford Centre for Mission Studies, 2018.

4. Proverbs 17:3.

5. 2 Corinthians 3:18.

6. 2 Corinthians 4:7.

7. 2 Corinthians 4:8–9.

8. Job 3:11.

9. Job 3:23.

10. Job 6:11.

11. Job 6:30.

12. Job 7:20.

13. Job 10:8.

14. 'The Most High is sovereign over all kingdoms on earth', Daniel 4:25.

15. Psalm 139:13–16.

16. Job 1:21; 2:10.

17. Exodus 33:15.

18. R Havard, M.D., Appendix note on the observed effects of pain, in C. S. Lewis, *The Problem of Pain* (Fontana, 1973) 144.

19. Lewis, *The Problem of Pain* 80–81.

20. Francis Schaeffer, *How Should we Then Live?* (Crossway Books, 1983).

21. 1 Peter 3:15.

22. E.g. Job 5:17.

23. Job 1:8.

24. Deuteronomy 28.

25. Galatians 6:7.

26. Psalm 73.

27. Richard Dawkins, *River Out of Eden* (Phoenix, 1995) 133.

28. Sharon Dirckx, *Why?: Looking At God, Evil & Suffering* (IVP, 2013) 131.

29. Paul Kurtz, 'Humanist Manifesto 2000' http://www.secularhumanism.org/index.php?section=main&page=manifesto.

30. Romans 8:22.

31. Job 37:8–9.

32. Job 1:6–7.

33. See Job 1:8–9.

34. See for example Eliphaz, Job 4; Zophar, Job 11.

35. Genesis 39.

36. Job 1:20.

37. Job 16:19–21.

38. Hebrews 7:25.

39. Job 7:11–15.

40. Job 13:15.

41. Job 42:7.

42. Song of Songs 2:14.

43. "Until You Do", track 10 on St Aldates Worship, *Until You Do (Live)*, Bespoke Records, 2019. Written by Esther-Jane White, Jamie Thomson. info@bespokerecords.com.

Chapter 15: The Voice of This Calling

1. Graham Tomlin, *The Provocative Church* (SPCK, 2013) 17.

2. Tomlin, *The Provocative Church* 18.

3. John Eldredge, *The Sacred Romance* (Nelson, 1997) 19.

4. Ephesians 2:6.

5. Ephesians 2:5.

6. Isaiah 50:10 (THE MESSAGE).

7. John 14:23.

8. 2 Corinthians 2:14–16.

9. T. S. Eliot, 'Little Gidding', *The Complete Poems and Plays* (Faber & Faber, 1969).

10. 1 Corinthians 9:22.

11. 'A D&C, also known as dilation and curettage, is a surgical procedure often performed after a first-trimester miscarriage. In a D&C, dilation refers to opening the cervix; curettage refers to removing the contents of the uterus.' American Pregnancy Association, 'D&C Procedure After A Miscarriage' 18 July 2017 https://americanpregnancy.org/pregnancy-complications/d-and-c-procedure-after-miscarriage/.

12. Psalm 139:13–16.

13. John 10:10.

14. John Foxe, *Foxe's Book of Martyrs* (OUP, 2009) 154.

15. See Charlie Cleverly, *The Passion that Shapes Nations* (Kingsway, 2005).

16. 1 Corinthians 15:33.

17. Ephesians 1:8–10.

18. Paulo Coelho, *The Alchemist* (Harper Collins, 1999) 22.

19. www.theministryofjesus-togo.org.

20. Ministry Newsletter 2005.

21. Luke 18:1–8.

22. Spiritual director: a person who accompanies another on their spiritual journey with God.

23. Genesis 3:9.

24. Exodus 33:11.

25. Matthew 24:6–7.

26. 2 Corinthians 12:1–4.

27. A prophetic word (of encouragement—see 1 Corinthians 14:3) given at a St Aldates service in January 2019.

For Further Reading

Baker, Rolland and Heidi, *There Is Always Enough*, Sovereign World, 2003

Bickle, Mike, *The Pleasures of Loving God*, Charisma House, 2000

Bounds, E. M., *A Treasury of Prayer*, Bethany House, 1961

Brand, Paul, with Philip Yancey, *Pain: The Gift Nobody Wants*, Harper Collins/ STL, 1994

Brother Lawrence, *The Practice of the Presence of God*, Hodder & Stoughton, 1981

Brother Yun, *The Heavenly Man*, Monarch Books, 2002

Brown, Brené, *Daring Greatly*, Penguin Random House UK, 2012

Cleverly, Charlie, *The Discipline of Intimacy*, David C Cook, 2019

Cleverly, Charlie, *Epiphanies of the Ordinary*, Hodder, 2013

Coupland, Douglas, *Life after God*, Simon & Schuster, 1994

Daniels, Robin, *The Virgin Eye*, Instant Apostle, 2016

de Lisieux, Thérèse, *Autobiography*, Doubleday, 1957

Dirckx, Sharon, *Why?: Looking At God, Evil & Suffering*, IVP, 2013

Emerson, Alain, *Luminous Dark*, Muddy Pearl, 2017

Gooder, Paula, *The Meaning Is in the Waiting*, Canterbury Press, 2008

Greig, Pete, *God on Mute*, Kingsway, 2007

Guinness, Michele, *Woman, the Full Story*, Zondervan, 2003

Lamott, Anne, *Traveling Mercies*, Anchor Books, 1999

Lewis, C. S., *The Business of Heaven*, Harper Collins, 1985

Lewis, C. S., *The Chronicles of Narnia*, Fontana Lions, 1980

Lewis, C. S., *The Four Loves*, Fount, 1986

Lewis, C. S., *A Grief Observed*, Faber & Faber, 2013

Lewis, C. S., *Mere Christianity*, Fontana, 1955

Lewis, C. S., *The Problem of Pain*, Fontana, 1973

Lewis, C. S., *The Screwtape Letters*, Collins, Signature Classics Edition, 2012

Mayne, Michael, *Learning to Dance*, DLT, 2001

Mayne, Michael, *This Sunrise of Wonder*, DLT, 2008

Nouwen, Henri, *Seeds of Hope*, DLT, 1989

Nouwen, Henri, with Michael J. Christensen and Rebecca J. Laird, *Spiritual Direction*, SPCK, 2011

Nouwen, Henri, *The Way of the Heart*, DLT, 1990

Oliver, Stephen, ed., *Inside Grief*, SPCK, 2013

Rolheiser, Ronald, *Sacred Fire*, Random House-Image, 2014

Samuel, Julia, *Grief Works*, Penguin Random House, 2018

St Augustine, *City of God*, Penguin Classics, 1985

Vanauken, Sheldon, *A Severe Mercy*, Harper & Row, 1977

Vanier, Jean, *Community and Growth*, Paulist Press, 1989

Zacharias, Ravi, *Cries of the Heart*, Thomas Nelson, 2010